THE HILLSIDE STRANGLER

THE THREE FACES OF AMERICA'S MOST SAVAGE RAPIST AND MURDERER AND THE SHOCKING REVELATIONS FROM THE SENSATIONAL LOS ANGELES TRIAL!

TED SCHWARZ

090352

Printed in the United States of America
Published by Quill Driver Books/Word Dancer Press, Inc.
1254 Commerce Way
Sanger, California 93657
559-876-2170 • 1-800-497-4909 • FAX 559-876-2180
QuillDriverBooks.com
Info@QuillDriverBooks.com

Quill Driver Books' titles may be purchased in quantity at special discounts for educational, fund-raising, business, or promotional use. Please contact Special Markets, Quill Driver Books/Word Dancer Press, Inc. at the above address or at 1-800-497-4909.

Quill Driver Books/Word Dancer Press, Inc. project cadre:
Susan Klassen, John David Marion, Cheree McCloud, Stephen Blake Mettee,
Brigitte Phillips, Linda Kay Weber

Third Edition, Second Printing

1-884956-37-8 • 978-1884956-37-9

To order another copy of this book, please call
1-800-497-4909

Library of Congress Cataloging-in-Publication Data

Schwarz, Ted, 1945-
   The Hillside Strangler : the three faces of America's most savage rapist and murderer and the shocking revelations from the sensational Los Angeles trial! / by Ted Schwarz.
       p. cm.
   ISBN 1-884956-37-8 (trade pbk.)
   1. Bianchi, Ken. 2. Murderers—United States—Biography. 3. Murder—United States. 4. Murder—California—Los Angeles. 5. Trials (Murder)—California—Los Angles. I. Title.

HV6248.B498S38 2004
364.152'3'092—dc22

                                                          2004005212

Other Books by Ted Schwarz

THE PETER LAWFORD STORY
   with Patricia Seaton Lawford

KEPT WOMEN
   with Leslie McRay

TRUST NO ONE
   with Tom Rybak

WALKING WITH THE DAMNED

Acknowledgements

Assistance in this project has been provided by a number of sources beyond the individuals quoted within the book. Dr. Pamela Reagor, of Newport Beach, California, provided indepth information on child abuse and the causes of emotional disturbance in adults who have been abused as children. Dr. John Watkins, of Missoula, Montana, has provided general information in the fields of multiple personality and child abuse. Dr. Ralph Allison, Davis, California, has served as a technical adviser in the fields of child abuse and multiple personality. Additional thanks is given to David Saenz of Tucson, Arizona, without whose assistance much of this project could not have been undertaken.

THE HILLSIDE STRANGLER

THE THREE FACES OF AMERICA'S MOST
SAVAGE RAPIST AND MURDERER AND
THE SHOCKING REVELATIONS FROM THE
SENSATIONAL LOS ANGELES TRIAL!

PART ONE

The Arrest

CHAPTER 1

It began as a training exercise. At 8:30 A.M. on Friday, January 12, 1979, Terry Mangan, the new chief of the Bellingham, Washington, Police Department, was alerted that two women students at Western Washington University were missing. Normally this meant that the lure of northern Washington state's ski country had overwhelmed any thought of attending Friday classes. Young men and women periodically took long weekends without telling their friends or coworkers where they were going. It was hoped that the current situation would be the same, though Chief Mangan and his men had the "gut" feeling that this case was different, that something was much more seriously wrong.

Karen Mandic and Diane Wilder, the missing Western Washington University students, were not typical of the routine weekend-disappearance reports. They were popular, conscientious students, not the type to run away from the responsibilities of job, school, and home, even for a three-day weekend. The fact that they were friendly with everyone, would have shared personal plans for a skiing vacation, and had disappeared when expected elsewhere were among the officers' justifications for taking immediate action.

Of course, Chief Mangan had neither suspects nor physical evidence indicating that a murder had been committed. Yet the scant knowledge available concerning the women's background made him feel certain it was worth committing the full facilities of the department. Even so, he hoped that in the end the investigation would prove to have been needless. Homicides by persons unknown were rare in the area, and he could consider the experience a training exercise.

What the chief did not know was that what was starting as a training exercise would lead to one of the most bizarre tales of murder and madness ever uncovered.

The violence which is common in so much of the United States is rare in Bellingham, Washington. The ocean's water endlessly laps the coastal shoreline; birth, life, and death fall in a natural cycle. When someone's moment upon the earth is tragically cut short, it is usually through a fishing accident on one of the hundreds of boats which ply the waters near the Canadian border.

There had been a time when Bellingham was divided by a strict social caste system. The lumber industry was the major source of revenue, with the families who owned the timberland forming the financial elite of the city. At the other extreme were the workers who labored in the woods and in the mill. Wages were low and the work was hard. Many died young. Others were crippled by ax blades or falling timber. Their families had little food and often inadequate shelter, yet the beauty of the land kept them from leaving the town. It was believed that one day life would get better. No one realized how much worse things could be.

It was shortly after the turn of the century that the nightmare began for Bellingham. The lumber mills closed quite literally overnight, relocating in Canada without notifying landowners or workers. In the morning, both rich and poor realized that the future they had seen for themselves was no longer a possibility. Many moved away. Those who stayed worked hard developing a new community in which the way a person committed himself to the city's betterment determined that individual's worth.

Typical of the community's spirit was the way in which Terry Mangan had been accepted as the new chief of police. In many small towns he would have been considered both an outsider and an oddball, regardless of the quality of his past work. The job would have gone to a longtime member of the department, a man who had been born and raised in the area and was well known to the citizenry. There would be political considerations, social concerns, and, only as a passing thought, a question about professional competence. Yet Bellingham was different. The people wanted the best professional for the job and they got him. However, he was as unusual as the rest of the city's history.

Terry Mangan was a man capable of compassion for both victims and criminals alike. He wanted to comfort the injured and understand those who did violence to their fellow man. He felt that when he could understand those who were committing crimes, there was a chance that he could help others in the future.

The people of Bellingham knew Mangan as a man of intellect and sensitivity. A color photograph hanging on the wall of his office showed him with his son, dressed in a child's version of his father's uniform. The photograph was typical of the man's deep love for his family, a love he extended to include the citizens of Bellingham.

Terry Mangan, who was forty when the case began, had entered police work gradually. He was the classic Irish Catholic child in a family of seven whose life revolved around the church. His destiny was to be a priest and he never seemed to consider any other career. He went from parochial school to the seminary and on to St. Albert's College, where he became Father Mangan with a master's degree in divinity.

Father Mangan spent his early years not only trying to understand others but also making a commitment to help. He taught religion and creative writing at Junipero High School in Monterey, California, eventually becoming dean of students. He also traveled to Selma, Alabama, to march with Dr. Martin Luther King, Jr. He was at ease with all races while maintaining a sensitivity to the special frustrations which eventually led to riots and violent unrest.

In 1966, the community of Seaside, California, began to undergo a change in its racial balance. The community had grown rapidly, changing from an all-white town to one that was almost 50 per cent black. The police force was small and most of the men had joined the department before racial integration had begun. They were having difficulty understanding the new social conditions. It was felt that the men needed training in sensitivity toward a group that had previously been foreign to them.

Father Mangan was intrigued with the potential of working as a counselor to the police. However, he went further than just providing sensitivity training. He began going to the police academy in order to become a reserve officer. He had a full uniform and started riding on patrol every night.

The police are often viewed as a closed society. Their uniforms, their right to use deadly force, their tendency to socialize exclusively with one another, all keep them from being seen as part of the world at large. They are the ultimate authority figures, often feared by adults in much the same way that children can be intimidated by their parents. They are either loved or hated, neither emotion being attached to the men and women who wear the uniforms. Instead, the reaction is to the stereotype of authority.

At first, Father Mangan shared this type of preconceived notion. Working as a reserve officer gave him the chance to see police officers as individuals. He watched the compassion and sensitivity they had for the public. He saw not only their pain when they were treated as stereotypes but also their compassion for the people they encountered on their jobs. Gradually, he found himself doing as much counseling work in uniform as he had been doing for the church, perhaps more.

While Father Mangan was learning about police work from inside the force, the church hierarchy was becoming concerned about the publicity the priest was getting. Carrying a gun was a violation of canon law for a priest. Mangan, only five feet eight inches tall, could never consider relying upon force. He found that rational conversation was often more effective than his gun, yet he also had come to understand that he would have little hesitation about deadly force when circumstances warranted. He was as comfortable with all aspects of police work as the church administrators were upset by the "pistol-packing priest" image conveyed by newspaper articles on Mangan. Father Mangan was given an order to either leave his police work or leave his church position.

Terry Mangan left the priesthood without bitterness. He remained as devout as he had ever been. He kept in touch with former friends and regularly attended mass. He knew he was continuing the counseling role which had so appealed to him as a priest. There was no sense of guilt or fear. He had not left just to get married, nor had he done anything he felt was counter to his vows. He had simply found a calling where he could spread love, help others, aid the community, and still consider himself a devout Catholic. The fact that he had to leave the priesthood to do it was of little concern.

Eventually Mangan began moving to better himself. He spent six years with the Seaside Police, then moved on to the role of safety director in another California community. During this period he also courted a woman named Charlotte Mauss, whom he married in June 1971, just prior to leaving Seaside.

In 1976, Terry Mangan became chief of the Bellingham force. He was too short for the job, an outsider in a role only a Bellingham man had held in the past, and an individual with one of the most unusual educations on the force. He also proved to be one of the most sophisticated and effective chiefs the department had ever known.

When Bellingham residents speak of the police before Terry Mangan took control, they recall a force of old-fashioned, head-banging officers with little sympathy for modern police methods.

Some of the men probably did fit this stereotype. However, Chief Mangan quickly saw that such general criticism was totally unwarranted. A number of the men were under-trained in current technology and some of the more advanced police methods. But limited training and experience has nothing to do with potential ability. He found that the men were generally intelligent and eager to upgrade themselves. The force might need some encouragement toward modernization, yet the raw material existed to make the department one that any community could respect.

Typical of the individuals on the Bellingham force was Robert Knudsen, who was fascinated by scientific investigation. Knudsen, regularly absorbed in books on fingerprint identification, laboratory analysis of trace evidence, photography of crime scenes, and other technical subjects, had attended special training schools in the past. Chief Mangan saw to it that Knudsen received as much additional specialized training as possible at the FBI Academy and elsewhere.

Similar situations existed among detectives and uniformed patrolmen. Mangan had the same caliber of men found on major city departments. They were just relatively under-trained, a situation the new chief began rectifying at once.

Chief Mangan prepared his men because of his conviction that a police officer should be trained to handle any situation, no matter how remote the chance it might occur. Though murders "by persons unknown" were rare in Bellingham, many violent killers would pass through the town, fleeing Seattle authorities and traveling north into Canada. Mangan wanted his men to be able to pursue the random, unknown killer and trained them accordingly, if only to instill greater pride.

Diane Wilder had always accepted the reality of death as a part of human existence. She had gone so far as to write a will, though at twenty-seven the need for such a document still seemed "centuries away." Instead of dwelling upon the finality of existence, she used her will as a celebration of life. She wrote, in part: "Do not expose me and my loved ones to a memorial service. Rather, remember sunshine and rain and green grass and trees, blue sky, salt water, alpine meadows alive with wildflowers and new growth, snowy mountains, autumn colors and life. These things I have loved. Return them to me quietly. I do not want my earthly remains to lie forever preserved within some perma-sealed urn, not contributing to life."

The fact that Diane had paused long enough to write such a document did not alter her seemingly endless vitality. Weekends were frequently spent hiking the mountains, weekdays giving to others and learning about different cultures. She had taught in the Seattle school system for several years, working with the deaf, the blind, and the retarded. She wanted to help those whose abilities were limited to experience the maximum of which they were capable.

In recent months Diane had become fascinated with the Middle East. Her interest began when she studied the classical art form of belly dancing. Then she quit her job to enroll in Western Washington University to expand her knowledge of Arab lands. She shared a home with Karen Mandic, a younger woman whose personal interests were similar enough to make them close friends despite the five years' difference in their ages.

Karen Mandic, twenty-two, was deeply imbued with the work ethic, which guided the members of most of the Bellingham families whose roots extended back before the turn of the century. She shared the attitude that she was only as good as the effort she made for others. Her father had a high enough income to put her through college, yet she insisted on working to earn her own money. She took a job as a clerk in the Fred Meyer's Department Store and enthusiastically labored with her boyfriend to grow a vegetable garden which would reduce the cost of groceries. She was warm and friendly toward everyone in town, yet she was cautious enough to avoid trusting strangers until she knew their intentions.

The night air was cold when Karen Mandic walked to her green Mercury Bobcat parked in the Fred Meyer's lot. It was just seven that Thursday night, the normal time for Karen's dinner break. She would not be eating as usual, though. She had been offered a job house-sitting in the wealthy Edgemoor section of Bellingham, a job which would pay her $100 for a total of two hours' time. Her employer was pleased with her good fortune and had willingly agreed to give her the extra time she needed that evening. She was one of the store's most conscientious employees, and he knew she would return promptly at 9 P.M. as she promised.

Karen drove home to pick up her roommate, then moved swiftly across town. The women were sharing equally in the insurance money being paid to have someone watch a home whose owners were traveling in Europe. The alarm system had failed, and Karen and Diane were to stay in the house during the short period when it would be turned off for repair. Many of the homes in the Edgemoor area were filled with expensive paintings, coin collections, quality jewelry, and other valuables. It was apparently worth a few hundred dollars to ensure that someone was present while the security system was being fixed. Both women felt themselves fortunate to be chosen for such an easy, high-paying job.

By eleven o'clock Thursday night, the manager of the Fred Meyer's store was worried. Karen had neither returned nor called to explain that she would be late. With any other employee he might not have given the matter a second thought. However, Karen was the type who would telephone from the highway to explain that she was caught in traffic and might be five minutes late. Two hours had passed since she had promised to return and that seemed cause for alarm.

Karen had a close friend who worked as a police officer for the local university. The manager decided to call him to see if he knew where she might have gone. The friend had been told about the house-sitting job, and Karen had given him the Bayside Road address of the residence. He had also been sworn to secrecy because Karen explained that she was not supposed to reveal the job until after the security-alarm system had been repaired. The friend had been bothered by the situation; the money paid seemed too much. Yet the Bayside address was a wealthy area, typical of the Edgemoor section, and it was likely the house was filled with valuables.

It was close to midnight when the security officer drove to both the Bayside address and Karen's house, looking for the two young women. There was no sign of them at either place. Frightened of what might have happened, he immediately called the Bellingham Police Department, explaining the situation to Officer Stephen Crabtree.

Officer Crabtree understood the implications of the security officer's story, and he requested permission from the two sergeants on duty to begin investigating.

When Karen had discussed the house-sitting job with her friend, she explained that she would be working as a temporary employee of the Coastal Security Agency, a highly reputable private security firm in the Bellingham area. The man who allegedly hired her was named Ken Bianchi. He had met Karen a few months after arriving in the city, when he worked as a security guard for Fred Meyer's store. He had been lured from Fred Meyer's to a job as supervisor for the uniformed division of Coastal Security, a tribute to his excellent past work record. He was also living with a local woman, Kelli Boyd, whose family had roots going well back into Bellingham's history.

The Bellingham police contacted the owner of Coastal Security, awakening him early Friday morning to question him about the house-sitting assignment. The owner was a former Bellingham police officer and well respected in the community. He explained that he knew nothing about any house-sitting job or alarm repair. He said that he should be familiar with the job, even if Bianchi had arranged it, adding that the police should also check with Bianchi, just in case there was a slipup. There could be legitimate reasons why he would not know of Bianchi's plans.

Mark Lawrence, the owner of Coastal Security, was concerned when the police officers left his home. He recognized that the Bellingham department would not have involved itself in a missing persons report after such a short time unless there seemed cause for alarm. He was also concerned that his agency's name had been used for what he felt certain was a fabrication. Ken Bianchi was too conscientious an individual to fail to report a housesitting job, unless there were unusual circumstances delaying his report. However, just to be certain, he called Bianchi at home. He was relieved to hear that not only was the story false, Bianchi did not even know the Mandic woman. As to his own activities Thursday night, Bianchi said he had been at a Sheriff's Reserve meeting.

Lawrence was still concerned with the use of his business's name when he hung up the telephone; but he had no qualms about Bianchi. The young man was proving himself beyond anyone's expectations. He had been given his first job with the agency on trust, because Kelli Boyd's family was on friendly terms with Lawrence. Bianchi had a small son and the love between the father and his child was obvious to everyone in the community who saw them together. In fact, when Ken willingly worked twelve-hour days, Lawrence knew the man was trying to earn extra money for Kelli and their baby, Sean. It was the type of attitude to which Mark Lawrence and his partner could relate and they were pleased with Ken's work.

During the summer Bianchi had left the security firm to work for the department store for a short period. The store job offered more pay and Mark recognized that if he were in Bianchi's position, he would have made the switch as well. However, when a number of the security agency's customers called to ask when they could use Ken again, the two men made an effort to find a way to rehire him. They decided to create a supervisory position, with better pay, in the uniformed division, and Bianchi returned to fill this post. Everyone was pleased.

Recently Bianchi had taken yet another step which benefited the security agency. He had joined the Sheriff's Reserve, an organization which provides law-enforcement training to county residents able to meet the stiff requirements. The men and women learned the skills of being a deputy sheriff and worked to support the department during emergencies and manpower shortages. They were not actually deputies and all worked at other jobs in the community. However, they were a respected resource of police assistance in the Bellingham area and Bianchi was the first security-agency employee who had joined the reserve. The action had greatly pleased Mark Lawrence. He felt that one day he and his partner might even make Bianchi a member of top management. Whatever was happening with the missing students, it certainly was not cause for concern about Bianchi.

Although the Bellingham Police were able to learn that Bianchi was scheduled to be at a Sheriff's Reserve meeting that Thursday night, the officers felt they had to be thorough in handling the missing-persons report and decided to check it out. Bianchi's was the only name that had arisen in relation to the two girls that night and, though the disappearance was probably meaningless, it was important to check everything. The men decided that if there was a problem, time was critical. They went to the home of the man in charge of the Sheriff's Reserve, awakening him to learn if Bianchi had attended the meeting that night. He had not.

It was clearly time to contact Bianchi. The officers disliked what they were doing. It was a boring, dull routine. They were building a case when there was no crime in evidence. No violence had been committed, as far as they knew. Yet it was only two-thirty in the morning on Friday and the first report had come in after eleven. Karen's friend was a police officer, but he worked for the college. Maybe he was overreacting. Maybe Karen and Diane had plans with other men. They wouldn't have had to tell him everything that was going on that night.

Regardless of the facts they might eventually uncover, for the moment routine procedures had to be followed. Thoroughness had to become a habit or they would overlook something if this did prove to be a serious crime. They could not afford to make mistakes. So what if Bianchi and the others were annoyed about being awakened? The community should take pride in the way the department was operating properly; the officers making no assumptions, checking every fact.

Ken Bianchi sounded tired but not angry when he was questioned. He told the officers that he had not gone to the Sheriff's Reserve meeting, though he offered no explanation. He said that he had chosen to drive around the county roads instead. He didn't feel like attending and had studied the first aid they were covering on Thursday when he had worked as an ambulance attendant in Rochester a few years earlier. Driving for a couple of hours had relaxed him.

There was nothing more to do except to keep all patrol cars alert for the missing Mercury and the two young women, until the police had evidence of some problem a little more serious than concerned friends calling about two women not returning from dinner.

At six o'clock in the morning the Bellingham police officers who had handled the original investigation of the missing women went off duty, knowing that a statewide teletype would go out giving police officers throughout Washington a description of both the car and the women. By the time the original investigating officers returned to duty, they hoped the story would be finished. The women would have been stopped and a logical explanation given for their leaving without bothering to tell their friends where they were going. There certainly was no reason to lose sleep by working overtime.

Terry Mangan arrived at his office at eight-thirty that Friday morning. The missing-persons report was waiting on his desk, but before he could look at it, he received a telephone call from a friend who was a captain in the Washington State Highway Patrol. During the night, the campus police officer who alerted the Bellingham authorities to the disappearance had contacted a mutual friend of Karen's. This was Bill Bryant, whose father was in the Highway Patrol and whose family was close to the Mandics. Bill also realized that the disappearance was out of character and had spent the night looking for the women.

Chief Mangan's success had come, in part, from his sensitivity to others. He had been a police officer in Los Angeles, where people regularly "disappeared" just to get away from family and friends for a few days. He had developed a cynicism toward missing-persons reports taken just a few hours after someone was first missed. However, he understood the differences between Bellingham and Los Angeles, the closeness of the people, and their knowledge of each other's habits.

After reviewing the reports to learn what steps had been taken, the detective supervisor, Sergeant Duane Schenck, decided to go to the women's house. "The report rang some sort of alarm bell in my head," said Mangan. There was definitely something more serious than two women going off for a weekend of fun in the snow.

Sergeant Schenck went to the house Diane and Karen shared. The first thing he noticed was Diane's cat. It was hungry and upset from not having been let outside to relieve itself.

Once again the uniqueness of Bellingham helped with the case. Chief Mangan quickly learned that Diane Wilder was totally devoted to her pet. She would take it with her whenever she was away from home for very long. The fact that the cat had had no attention for several hours was so out of character that the seriousness of the disappearance was no longer in question. No one knew what might have happened to the women but it was virtually certain now that Diane Wilder had not vanished willingly.

The police began searching the house, hoping to find some clue to the disappearance. They checked the area around the telephone, looking for notes which might have been made concerning the previous evening. After several minutes, they found a scrap of paper on which the Bayside address was written along with the notation, "7 p.m. to 9 p.m." The story of the house-sitting project had been confirmed.

Once again Coastal Security was checked. Mark Lawrence, concerned about what was happening, was looking into his records. He had remembered something being mentioned concerning a job in the Edgemoor area and was checking the cards for homes in that section. Each house with which the security agency was involved was listed on a separate information card. Keys to those homes were also held by the agency so that guards could enter after an alarm was sounded. There should have been one for the Bayside address but it was missing along with the keys.

The name of Ken Bianchi came up again. As supervisor of the uniformed division, he was responsible for the cards and the keys. The police discovered that he knew some cards were missing from the Edgemoor listings and that he had told some of the men under him that he would either find them or make new ones.

Bianchi had done something else which bothered the police. He had checked out one of the security-agency trucks for Thursday evening. He explained to the man who was supposed to have the vehicle that something was wrong with it and it would have to go into the shop. The man was to use his own car for work that night while Bianchi took the truck for repairs. However, a quick check of the repair shop revealed that Bianchi had not brought the truck in for servicing. More interesting was the fact that the truck had been in the shop recently enough that nothing should have been wrong with it. The situation was becoming more serious by the moment and there was still no sign of the women.

Terry Mangan was almost certain now that a double murder had taken place. There were no bodies, no signs of violence, yet the normal routine in the lives of the two women had been interrupted. The chief knew that people are consistent in their behavior. A person who becomes fed up with everyday stress and decides to take a vacation will still follow a pattern. A loved pet will not be abandoned. A conscientious employee will complete an already started work shift. A boyfriend who is normally aware in advance of a young woman's every plan will not suddenly be kept in the dark about an innocent skiing trip. The police had to plan a full-scale homicide investigation, a major financial and manpower commitment, even though there was still no concrete evidence of death.

Murders usually occur according to a certain logic. A lovers' quarrel becomes violent; the survivor of the quarrel becomes a prime suspect. Karen had a boy friend but he had an alibi.

A second logical suspect is the last person known to have been with the victim, although he or she is frequently not the killer. Often a secret or chance meeting results in the murder. Such random killings are hard to solve, though, so the last person known to have been with the victim is checked first, as a matter of routine.

By nine-thirty Chief Mangan was extremely worried about what might have happened. He was no stranger to violent death and innocent victims. Even his personal life had been indirectly touched with senseless violence. He was friendly with Sister Carmel Marie, O.P., a parochial school principal in Los Angeles, who had introduced him to the man who maintained the books for the diocese in the area. Chief Mangan chatted with the man briefly at the time, then had thought nothing further of him until he read that the man's daughter, Sonja Johnson, a fourteen-year-old, and her twelve-year-old friend, Dolores Cepeda, had disappeared from an Eagle Rock shopping center near Los Angeles. The girls were later found murdered, victims of the so-called Hillside Strangler, who had been randomly raping and killing throughout Southern California. Could such a thing, Mangan considered, have occurred again, in Bellingham?

Chief Mangan returned to his office and telephoned Stu Reynolds, the Highway Patrol captain who had first alerted him to the significance of the Mandic woman's disappearance. He asked that the Highway Patrol officers begin checking rural areas where a car could be abandoned or a murder victim could be dumped. He wanted them to look into gravel pits, travel back roads and dirt trails. "I think these girls are going to wind up dead," the chief told Reynolds. "It's a feeling I've got. I think we have to consider this a kidnapping and maybe a homicide."

The next step was to search the Bayside home where the girls had supposedly gone. Since the key was missing from the security firm and the owners were out of town, a locksmith had to be called for the entry.

Searching a possible crime scene is a very involved process. If the investigators move too quickly, they may trample small objects, shards of glass, bits of hair and similar, tiny items which could be essential clues. The search often has to be handled by dividing the scene into a grid and having each small section carefully studied with magnifying equipment, cameras, special vacuuming machinery, and other sophisticated tools. It is time-consuming, boring, and, for the most part, fruitless work. However, it can make the difference between stopping a killer and having a case go unsolved—until the murderer takes yet another life.

After the locksmith opened the front-door latch, three detectives entered the hallway, moving slowly and carefully throughout the house to see if the women were still there. They were tense as they walked, constantly alert for anything that might prove to be evidence later. Their first discovery was a still-wet footprint in the kitchen, which was studied and photographed. The humidity of Bellingham is such that the wet footprint had been made within the last few hours, probably by someone who was not authorized to be inside.

While one contingent of policemen continued to search the empty house, other investigators had found a friend and neighbor of the people whose house was now viewed as a possible murder scene. She had agreed to check the house each day, watering the plants and taking care of items that needed regular attention. She said that she had been called by a Ken Bianchi of the Coastal Security Agency. He had told her that she was not to go near the house on Thursday night. Some special work was being done and armed guards would be there. She might be mistaken for an intruder, a problem he wanted to prevent. He explained that the guards wouldn't know authorized friends and relatives of the owners, making the woman's presence a danger.

As more became known, the concern increased. Everything about the situation seemed to indicate foul play, yet there were no bodies and no sign of Karen Mandic's car.

Bill Bryant was carrying out his own investigation. He contacted Bianchi around 11 A.M., acting on his own, to see if Bianchi knew where Karen was. Bianchi knew Bryant and had contacted him earlier about getting Karen's telephone number for a job. Yet when Bryant called, Bianchi vehemently denied making the call. Bryant knew that Bianchi or someone identifying himself by that name had contacted him. Either Ken was lying or someone had used his name.

At noon, a little over twelve hours after the police had become involved, Terry Mangan turned to the news media for help. He contacted all the local radio stations and requested that they put out bulletins containing the descriptions of the women and the car, asking listeners to call in any information they might have. He already had alerted sheriffs' departments in two counties, in addition to the Highway Patrol. Four-wheel-drive vehicles owned by the police were being used off road as well.

The use of the broadcast media proved to be the most effective way to handle the search. At approximately 4:30 P.M., a woman listening to the radio realized that when she had left for work that morning, she had seen a car that fit the description of the missing Mercury. It was parked in a cul-de-sac near her home. The cul-de-sac was just off the main street but was so heavily wooded that passing traffic normally would have missed it. In fact, the location was just isolated enough that she refused to trust her memory. She returned to the location, checked, and confirmed what she thought she had seen. The car was there and, although curious, she respected the warning on the bulletin and did not approach it.

Detective Jim Geddes of the Bellingham Police Department was the man who was notified that the Mercury Bobcat had been spotted. He drove immediately to the spot, certain of what he would find even before he could check the back of the car. Inside, as feared, were the dead bodies of the missing women. The exercise in homicide investigation had turned into a serious search for a murderer.

The police felt they had to arrest Bianchi on suspicion of murder, and put together the details after they had him safely off the street. If they were wrong, Ken could be released in a day or two and would, they hoped, understand the logic behind their suspicion. If they were right, the citizens of Bellingham would be able to sleep safely that night.

The Bellingham Police were not about to take any chances arresting Ken Bianchi. As a trained security officer, he did not always carry a gun for his work but, if he had one, he knew how to use it. The officers also had to make the assumption that he had killed twice and would not hesitate to do so again. Therefore they felt that they had to surprise him in such a manner that neither they nor innocent bystanders ran the risk of being hurt.

The south side of Bellingham is a business district for the fishing industry and others. The wharves are there and hundreds of fishing boats use the area as a base. The area is a frequent target for thieves and thus a source of business for the various security agencies working in Bellingham. Coastal Security had a guard shack in the section, which the men and women handling security throughout the section could use as a base of operations. An arrest could be made there without much danger of anyone's being hurt should a gun battle ensue.

Mark Lawrence, shocked by the circumstances explained by the police, agreed that Bianchi had to be arrested. He was certain that Ken was not the killer and would be cleared. However, if he had been in the same position as the police, he would have accepted the probable-cause argument and gotten Bianchi into jail while the investigation intensified. He agreed to help set up a trap.

Bianchi was driving one of the three security-agency trucks, a vehicle of the type which had been seen on the night of the murders. He was contacted by radio, his location believed to be the central part of the city. No one checked to see if he was still there. Instead he was told to drive to the guard shack on the south side of town to await a telephone call, a normal contact arrangement which gave Bianchi no reason for concern. Had he been in the central city, he would have had a ten-minute drive and the police would have had ample time to place men in position for the arrest. They wanted him to be met with overwhelming force so he would not resist.

As it happened, however, Bianchi was not in the central city, but was actually in the Edgemoor area again, much closer to the guard shack than anticipated. He drove his truck to the rendezvous, arriving before the police had time to get into position.

Detective Terry Wight and a police sergeant made the arrest. Bianchi was unarmed and made no effort to get away. He leaned against the wall as directed, allowing himself to be handcuffed and taken to the station.

The police should have been pleased with the way the arrest took place. They should have been happy that there was no resistance and that Bianchi had been so cooperative. The problem was his attitude. It was as though he was certain of his innocence. He acted like a man who realized that, given time, his complete lack of guilt would be shown to the world. He had killed no one. He could not even remember meeting Karen Mandic. He was an innocent man, wronged by circumstances which would soon change. He went along willingly, knowing he would quickly be released.

The Coastal Security truck was immediately impounded and searched. Inside was the card for the Bayside house and a key to the door. There was also a woman's scarf, an object made all the more suspicious by the fact that Diane Wilder loved scarves and collected dozens of them. The owner of the scarf could not be immediately identified but the coincidence was too great. It was another circumstantial link which told the police they were arresting the right man.

Kelli Boyd was called to the police station shortly after the arrest of the man with whom she lived. She was shocked by the telephone message and immediately called her stepmother and father to come and baby-sit for Sean. There was no reason to suspect Ken of any crime. He was a gentle lover, an adoring father, and a man who had never given her a reason to think he might be violent.

Detectives were waiting to talk with Kelli when she arrived. They questioned her about the previous night, asking detailed questions about Ken's activities. She answered truthfully, horrified that the man she loved might even be considered to be involved in a brutal double murder. That Friday night both she and Bianchi gave the police permission to completely search the house. They both seemed to feel that Ken would be absolved if they cooperated.

While detectives at the station questioned Kelli, other officers were searching the Mercury Bobcat and the house where the murders were presumed to have taken place. The key to the car hatchback was missing and a locksmith had to be called again. He drilled the lock so the bodies could be removed.

The Bellingham Police conducted what is now considered to be a perfect crime-scene investigation. Every fact-gathering method was used.

First the authorities sealed the grounds around the car. This included a large area both above and below the paved section of the cul-de-sac in case any evidence had been left a distance from the vehicle.

The Fire Department was contacted and a truck with a large platform was brought in. The platform was fitted with spotlights, then raised high above the crime scene. Videotape equipment was brought in and the lighting was used to record everything that was taking place. Still cameras were also brought to the scene. Both the general location and the specific details on the car and the grounds were recorded. The car was also carefully checked for fingerprints. It was obvious that the hatchback, steering wheel, and other parts had been wiped clean.

Footprints in the mud were located, then casts were made. Fresh, green heather attached to the rear license plate was removed since heather did not grow in the cul-de-sac. Everything was measured, recorded, bagged, and prepared for laboratory analysis. No object was too small or unimportant to be checked. There was no way to tell when a cigarette butt, a piece of metal, a button, a hair, or some other seemingly harmless object might be a key link with the crime.

A loose pubic hair was discovered and carefully preserved for crime-lab analysis. It would have been lost if there had been any mishandling of the evidence, a serious concern since the hair eventually proved to be a key link with the killer.

The check of the Mercury Bobcat by Officer Bob Knudsen and Investigator Rick Nolte revealed a small dent in the bottom of the gas tank. It seemed to be a fresh dent and its presence could be important. It was carefully measured and the area all around it examined for mud spots, dents, or any other damage which might relate to the scene.

A clean sheet, devoid of any foreign matter, was laid out for wrapping the body of each victim before transporting to Jones Mortuary. The bodies of the two women were superficially checked for the cause of death. They had been strangled and marks on their bodies indicated that they had probably been bound and subjected to other violence. What was of greatest concern to the investigators, even before the autopsies could be performed, was the angle of the strangulations. The marks showed that the murderer had been behind and slightly above the victims—the kind of marks which might have been made if the women were strangled while walking down steps with the murderer behind them.

Knowledge of the strangulation marks helped the investigators. They carefully checked every inch of space in the Edgemoor house where someone could comfortably assume the angle to the women indicated by the obvious strangulation marks. This included the staircase, so each step was explored, inch by inch, using tweezers and a magnifying glass. Hairs, loose fibers, tiny bits of wire, pieces of tobacco, and anything else that was noticed was all carefully bagged for later examination.

The search of the house began at approximately 1 P.M. Friday and was as thorough as that at the scene where the car had been found. The vacuum cleaner belonging to the family was carefully emptied and its contents preserved for laboratory analysis, and a new vacuuming was done of the entire house. There was more fingerprinting. Metal detectors were used, and eventually divers would check the bay for a weapon which might have been thrown away.

The officers searched the grounds of the house carefully and found a clump of heather and a rock that had obviously been scored by the gas tank. Further investigation indicated that the Bobcat had probably passed over the rock both on the way into the driveway and when it was moved to the hillside. The weight of the two women did not lower the car body enough for the gas tank to be dented. However, the weight of the two women and a third person, the murderer, would have lowered it enough to make the dent. Since there was only a single dent, another piece of evidence for the case was solidly confirmed.

The scientific investigation was paralleled by routine police work: officers knocked on neighbors' doors, asking questions. Witnesses to any activities of the previous night had to be found. Could someone link Bianchi or anyone else to the house at the same time the women were there? Had someone heard screaming? Gunshots? Anything which would add details concerning what might have happened?

The work was slow but productive. One person in the area had been driving and been cut off by what was obviously a Coastal Security truck. The police had learned that three such trucks were in use that night and the whereabouts of two of them could be positively determined during the two hours when the murders seemed to have taken place. The third truck was the one taken by Bianchi.

Kelli Boyd provided the clothing Bianchi had worn Thursday night, cooperating fully with the officers. Semen stains had been found on the women's clothing and more semen stains were on Bianchi's underwear. There was also some menstrual blood on Bianchi's underwear; the autopsy disclosed that Diane Wilder had had her period when she was murdered. The web was growing tighter around Bianchi, who continued to deny any knowledge of the occurrence. He was cooperative with the police, somewhat indignant about being arrested, and confused each time he was confronted with the growing body of evidence linking him with the death scene.

A business card Bianchi carried was found in Karen's room. Karen's telephone number was found in the home Bianchi shared with Kelli. The evidence was still circumstantial, but already it was enough to convince most juries that Bianchi was the murderer.

Other searches had to be conducted. Dumping sites were checked to see if the victims' possessions could be found. Unfortunately the volume of refuse dumped at such locations was enormous. It was assumed that the purses and other items were there but, if they were, they were hidden under tons of waste.

The dock area where Bianchi had been arrested was also searched. Diane Wilder's coat was located. The water was checked for items which might have been thrown into the depths, although this search proved fruitless.

As often as possible, the searches were timed to coincide with routine press conferences. There was a chance that reporters and other observers might inadvertently destroy evidence if they crowded around the searchers. By sending out the men during the time that press conferences were being held, the police continued searching without interference.

*   *   *

And yet, something was wrong. The police were increasingly certain that no one but Bianchi could have killed the women. But with it all, the people who knew Bianchi felt such a crime was impossible. He was too gentle, too conscientious, too involved with Kelli and their son. Even his employer, a skilled investigator in his own right, wanted to hire the best scientific people in the country to find the real killer and clear Bianchi's name. It seemed that only a madman could have the kind of Jekyll-and-Hyde personality necessary to have such respect in the community and also be able to brutally murder.

Terry Mangan and the other officers kept probing. They talked with Kelli about her past with Ken, before they had lived together in Bellingham. They learned of Bianchi's background in Los Angeles and, prior to that, in Rochester, New York, the city where he was raised. They knew they would have to request information from those cities as well.

As they prepared to make the effort to seek the background details on Bianchi, Chief Mangan remembered a former acquaintance whose daughter had been killed. He knew that the child's killing had also involved strangulation and that the person responsible had not been caught. It was a curiosity in light of the present case, though he in no way assumed that Bianchi was involved.

At approximately 2:30 A.M. Saturday, an exhausted Terry Mangan and Captain Telmer Kveven of his department sat drinking milk shakes and reviewing the situation. As they talked; Mangan remembered not only the death of the parochial school student but also the death of Cindy Lee Hudspeth. Hudspeth was another victim of the Los Angeles killer and her body had been found on February 17, Terry Mangan's birthday. It was only then, as Mangan began remembering yet another of the Los Angeles deaths, that he began debating whether or not the case of the Hillside Strangler could be connected with the current murders in Bellingham. No conclusions were reached, but at 8 A.M. Dan Fitzgerald of the Bellingham Police called the Rochester, Los Angeles, and Glendale Police Departments as well as the Los Angeles Sheriff's Office.

The timing of Bianchi's arrival in Washington coincided exactly with the last of the Los Angeles murders. No one was sure whether a major discovery had been made or if there were just a number of coincidences. All that was certain was that detectives had to be dispatched from Los Angeles to interrogate Bianchi.

CHAPTER 2

The language of police work is exact, unemotional, a shorthand code used for everything from the shoplifting of a grocery-store candy bar to the most brutal of deaths. For the Bellingham Police, the arrest of Ken Bianchi became Event No. 79B-00770, and this number was dutifully applied to each item of clothing the suspect possessed. The clothing would be evidence in the trial. Tag #8, bearing Impound No. D7067, for example, was attached to his Sam Brown belt and gun. These possessions, seemingly unrelated to the trial evidence, would probably be returned before the trial.

The people of Bellingham were not so dispassionate about the police filing system. Two members of the community were dead and no one was certain whether or not the murderer had been caught. After all, Ken Bianchi had happily settled down with Kelli Boyd, a local woman. He was an outsider and they wanted desperately to believe that a nonresident had taken the lives of "their girls," yet everyone who knew Ken was certain he was incapable of violence.

Reporters for the *Bellingham Herald* canvassed the neighborhood where the murders had taken place. Dan Shaw, one of the reporters, documented the people's fear. He quoted one parent saying, "I have a high school girl. Some of us have formed a car pool to take the kids to school. It's still dark when the kids leave in the morning, and there's something about darkness. . . ."

Chief Mangan moved to reassure the public. He told the newspaper, "We feel we have a good suspect in custody, and that it [the crime] was done by a single person. Therefore, there is no cause for alarm in the community about this situation."

Few criminals, no matter how careful they may be, are capable of committing the perfect crime and avoiding arrest. A thorough crime-scene search usually results in microscopic trace evidence which can be as devastating as an eyewitness. The detectives' careful bagging of every hair and fiber seemed painstaking to the point of absurdity. However, the care taken had been worth the effort. When Diane Wilder's body was carefully removed from the car at the dump site, a pubic hair dropped onto the sterile sheet placed under her. Two more pubic hairs were found on the staircase leading to the basement of the Catlow house. Carpet fibers were found on the bodies of both girls, as well as the soles of their shoes, and these fibers matched the carpeting in the Catlow home. When sent to the FBI Crime Lab for analysis under some of the most sophisticated instruments invented, it would be possible to link the hairs and the fibers to the person who was probably the killer. If it was Ken Bianchi, the case against him would tighten conclusively.

The police work would take time, however. Lab analysis would require several days and they did not want Bianchi released until the case was completed. If he had killed twice, as they now suspected, he would not hesitate to either kill again or flee the city. They could not yet charge him with murder, so they decided to find a valid, alternative excuse to hold him. The search of the house he shared with Kelli gave them that evidence.

The search warrant obtained by Detective Terry Wight and signed by District Court Judge Ed Ross was quite specific. The home had been checked with the permission of both Bianchi and Boyd. A number of unusual items had been spotted and the warrant allowed their seizure. Among other items were "Four Bell System Touch Tone Telephones" and "One Homelite Chainsaw and Box," along with "One Princess Bell System Telephone." The items were all hidden in the basement and were not the personal possessions of Bianchi. They were going to be used against him in order to bring a charge of theft. The items had been reported missing from sites where Bianchi had been assigned as a security guard.

On January 16, a story by Megan Floyd headlined the *Bellingham Herald*. It told of Bianchi being held for theft in lieu of $150,000 bail, a sum far in excess of the value of the allegedly stolen items. The story was a delaying tactic while the murder evidence was analyzed by the FBI lab. When the story appeared, the public was slightly relieved that the deaths of Karen and Diane had apparently been solved.

Ken Bianchi could not believe what was happening to him. He had no memory of the murders, or so he told the investigating officers. He knew, though, that evidence was being uncovered which was creating an inextricable link with the deaths. He was provided with reports of charges being brought against him and he retained a lawyer, Dean Brett, who began to prepare his defense. Yet to Bianchi, everything was wrong.

"The letters he wrote to me during this time drained my emotions," said Kelli Boyd. "I no longer knew what to believe. I read in the paper things that made Ken sound guilty. But Ken wrote to me to forget about the press. He said that I should think what it takes to end a life. He told me he couldn't imagine how anyone could do it. I knew he was no saint and he admitted he gets angry like everybody else, but he kept talking about how hard it would be to take a life. He said that only a maniac could have killed like that and he prayed that God would forgive whoever he might be.

"Ken told me of the people who were offering to be character witnesses for him. Our friends, people I respected. They weren't fools and Ken was right, I knew he couldn't take a life.

"Ken told of his love for Sean. I knew that the chance he might never again see his son would keep him from taking a life. Ken even mentioned the Sheriff's Reserve and the fact that he had decided to leave because every time he asked himself if he could shoot somebody in the line of duty, the answer always came up negative. He spent two years trying to save lives as an ambulance technician. He said he could never live with himself if he took a life after all that. He reminded me how horrified he was of even the idea of hitting an animal with the car and I knew he carefully watched out for them when we drove in the country together."

There was too much good about Ken Bianchi for Kelli to lose faith in the chance that this was all a frightening, tragic mistake. She was terrified by his depression in jail and wondered if he could survive until what was undoubtedly a miscarriage of justice could be rectified.

"I remember the letter he wrote telling me how poorly he was doing. He told me of his loneliness, calling it a 'lingering beast' that was always with him. He said he smoked cigarettes, listened to the radio, and played cards whenever there was an opening in one of the games.

"Ken was in a large holding area most of the time. He said the room was twenty-four feet by fifty feet with two long tables, a seatless toilet, sink, and shower. The place was cold, damp, dirty, and poorly lighted. It was meant for short-term use and the county never had quite enough money for improvements. I had heard a lot about the problems of jail, but what Ken described was even worse. It was a time of helplessness and anguish for me unlike any I've ever known."

The pain of confinement and the separation from loved ones made Ken Bianchi a sympathetic figure to those who believed in him. One young woman had fallen in love with him when he worked for the security agency just prior to his arrest. According to Bianchi's employer, Bianchi had gotten her a job with the agency, though she never returned to work after her first four-hour shift. This young woman even went so far as to try to establish an alibi for Ken for the night of the murders. However, her statements never checked out, and the police dismissed her efforts on Ken's behalf.

Bianchi later stated that there was no romantic involvement on his part, though he found the young woman extremely attractive and liked the idea that she could be so taken by him. He seemed to feel that if his relationship with Kelli ever deteriorated after the real killer was found and he was released, the woman might be worth dating.

Meanwhile, he found her letters of support extremely comforting.

Bianchi also heard from others. Many people sent religious tracts. The majority, if aware of his background and the circumstances, empathized with his frustration at knowing his own innocence.

Dean Brett, Bianchi's attorney, was confused by all that was going on. He was viewing the evidence in the case as the police were uncovering it. The deaths of the two women were being carefully reconstructed and the crime itself was horrifying. The girls were apparently bound, gagged, and separately assaulted before each was strangled to death. He could see the logic in charging the man who was last known to be with them. Yet the genuine love Bianchi showed for Kelli and Sean made his client's guilt highly unlikely. He believed Bianchi's protestations of innocence and was desperately trying to determine who might have been lying in wait for the women after they went to the house.

PART TWO

When Los Angeles Lived in Fear

CHAPTER 3

There is no pain in Hollywood. The most troubled lives discover a happy ending in two breathtaking hours of Technicolor film and Dolby modified stereophonic sound. The only difference between rich and poor is the size of their swimming pools. It is a city whose image is that of the miraculous, its magnetic appeal annually luring thousands of young adults from large and small communities throughout the country.

Some of Hollywood's new arrivals are beautiful young women and handsome young men for whom the trip seems the next logical step in careers already marked with triumph. These are the ones who performed to vast acclaim in their high school drama club productions. The yearbooks showed that they were the ones most likely to succeed and their relatives financed the trip they all knew would result in each youth's being presented with riches, fame—and a movie contract—upon arrival.

Others travel to Hollywood in desperation. They hitchhike or bus across country, reciting a litany of stories about divorce, broken homes, or just the hassle of fighting blizzards and rush-hour traffic while traveling to and from dead-end jobs. For them, Hollywood is like a Lourdes for the emotionally disabled.

The reality of America's glamour capital is discovered when you walk along Hollywood Boulevard, one of the main streets of the community. It is twelve miles long, a fraction of the 18.69 square miles which comprised the community in 1978. A population of 139,308 lives in the surrounding area, with many times that number visiting for a day, a week, or what tragically proves to be a lifetime. The street stretches from an apartment and single family residence area through a business district where restaurants and family movie theaters vie for tourist dollars with such enterprises as *Le Sex Shoppe*, a store selling pornographic literature, movies, and sex aids.

Most people traveling Hollywood Boulevard on vacation feel that the most shocking sight they could encounter would be a movie star enjoying a laid-back, euphoric, thousand-dollar high from cocaine while resting in a redwood hot tub. Instead they spot a vomit-stained junkie sprawled in an alley. Prostitutes are everywhere, though the heaviest concentrations congregate along the parallel streets of Hollywood and Sunset Boulevards, on the edge of the motion-picture-studio production areas. CBS Television has a facility on Sunset; the Sunset-Gower Studio parking entrance also faces the street. A total of 1914 arrests were made for prostitution in these general areas, a figure experts feel represents but a small fraction of this activity. An unknown number of women along Hollywood Boulevard indulge in casual sex without charge, though that figure is believed by police to outstrip the prostitutes by at least ten to one.

Hollywood and Vine has a Howard Johnson's Restaurant which, in 1978, was a frequent resting point for prostitutes meeting with their pimps. They could enjoy a quiet hamburger and a cup of coffee while relaxing between "johns." It was a neutral territory where they could blend with tourist families, teens from Hollywood High or nearby Highland, and other straight individuals. No one would be picked up there and no business was conducted other than turning over the early-evening profits to the pimps.

Teen-aged runaways flock to Hollywood by the thousands from all over the United States. The exact numbers are unknown because survival depends upon blending with those who came before them. Many spend their time near Hollywood High, mingling with the students as they stand on street corners, smoking marijuana, drinking, or just talking. Only 191 juveniles were arrested as runaways in the Hollywood area during 1978, a fraction of the true total. Most adopt dress styles that make them appear older. Even when they don't blend in, the police do not feel that juveniles should be a priority for them. If they stopped and questioned all the people in the Hollywood street scene, there would be charges of juvenile harassment. There is no way to tell the difference between the runaway from Cleveland and the daughter of a millionaire movie star without stopping and checking identification.

Ken Bianchi might have been considered similar to the runaways when he first arrived in Hollywood at age twenty-six. He, too, pursued the desperate Hollywood fantasy of happiness when he first walked the streets of that community. He had come too far, suffered too much, to think that instant happiness could not be at least a possibility. The Hollywood street scene was like an adolescent's conception of heaven. Flash a roll of bills and you could take home a woman, a man, or a man dressed as a woman. Whatever you wanted to do, just express your desire, pay your price, and someone will help you enjoy it. It was as though all the things Ken had been told were taboo while he was growing up in Rochester had suddenly been taken off the restricted list and laid before his feet. More important, neither parent nor priest was on hand to make him feel guilty if he decided to sample some of the more tempting delights.

Ken Bianchi had mixed feelings when he arrived in California. His cousin, Angelo Buono, had agreed to open his home to Ken. Buono's home was connected with his Glendale upholstery shop and was different from anything Ken had ever experienced. The house was remodeled, and the inside doors had been removed. There was no kitchen as such because Angelo and his son, an older youth who still lived at home, went out for their meals.

Bianchi was not particularly comfortable with the new living arrangements. Angelo was a sarcastic individual whose cruel sense of humor Ken found painful at first. He was also unused to so casual a life-style. There were not even regularly timed meals.

Whenever they stopped working in the shop, Angelo would go to a restaurant and often ate liver, his favorite main dish.

The unusual home life made Ken miss Rochester, and he realized he needed his own place where he could maintain his own schedule. He was still glad he had left New York. He was enjoying the sun, the water, and a city where his car would not rust from the treachery of winter snows and rock salt.

Some of the opportunities Ken found with his cousin were exciting at first. Angelo almost seemed to be going through a second adolescence. Although he was almost forty in late 1975, when Ken arrived, he liked to go to restaurants and bars where the Hollywood street people hung around. According to Ken, he had gotten to know some of the prostitutes, especially the younger girls, and he introduced Ken to them. Ken, closer to their age, was also physically attracted and he did have sex with hookers a few times. The problem was that he did not truly enjoy the sex. He wanted an ongoing relationship where sex was part of true lovemaking, not only a means of relieving the tension in his groin.

Even when Ken did have a date with a "straight" girl he could seriously consider dating for a longer term, he wanted to try some of the different experiences available to him for the first time—especially drugs.

The drug scene seemed exciting until the night Ken and a date went to a friend's house. The friend emptied the bottom drawer of his dresser, removing some marijuana he had hidden there. Ken had been drinking beer when he and his girl were offered a joint. He smoked a quarter of it, not really feeling anything from it. The others at the party became quite sick, though, throwing up in the bathroom before Ken left.

Ken and the girl drove down the street after the party. He was just halfway down the block, approaching a cross street, when he suddenly saw a giant explosion in front of him. The explosion seemed to be vibrantly colored, scaring him as he slammed on the brakes. He stopped the car, leaped out the door, then realized that nothing had happened. There was no explosion, no fire, just silence. The hallucinogenic properties of the pot had apparently triggered the experience. He decided that though he might occasionally take one or two puffs on a joint at a party in future, never again would he seriously consider smoking dope or taking drugs.

As Ken was able to taste a few of the Hollywood offerings, he realized that he did not like the unstructured and relatively wild life. He wanted his own place, with doors, a kitchen, and set hours for sleeping and eating. He wanted friends other than people who turned tricks, hung out in bars, or sat in restaurants night after night, trying to decide their next hustle and its potential victim. But that took money, and to get money he needed a job.

There was only one career which strongly interested Bianchi—police work. He had admired police officers since he was a child and he attempted to join the Los Angeles department. However, openings were few and he knew he would have to look elsewhere or stay with Angelo.

There had been job offers in Rochester, good job offers. One was with the Eastman Kodak Company. Another had been with the Post Office. But each of those involved the influence of family or friends. He was ready to consider career possibilities and to make his own way.

Each day Ken Bianchi went looking for work. He would scan the newspapers, answer advertisements, make cold calls to businesses which interested him, and generally pound the pavement like thousands of other California newcomers. Sometimes he would stay at his cousin's upholstery shop, working at whatever semiskilled task his cousin had for him. Other times he would go to the shop before and after job hunting, sweeping the floors and helping to clean up the place. The latter was not really a job but more a way of earning at least part of the price of being carried by his cousin while he tried to become selfsupporting.

Gradually Bianchi became frustrated. He would only go out every two or three days, spending the rest of the time with his cousin, painting, making deliveries of reupholstered cars, and doing whatever else he could. The two men were different enough so that they gradually got on each other's nerves. Angelo seemed to want Ken out and Ken realized that he could not enjoy living there any longer. However, Ken also had no place to go and knew that as long as Angelo realized that, Angelo would not evict him, at least for the moment. There was an underlying tension much of the time.

Finally Ken, miserable, almost broke, went to the bank to get his last few dollars from the savings account. There was a young woman working as teller and Ken talked with her a bit about his personal problems. She mentioned that her brother worked for a title company that needed new personnel. Ken managed to borrow a car, drove to the company, and was hired that same day.

Suddenly the world was perfect. Within two days of being employed, Ken found an apartment, then used his first paycheck to buy a used car from his cousin Anthony, Angelo's son. He was finally beginning to get everything he wanted, though the double obligation of apartment rent and car payment with just one paycheck represented the type of irresponsible attitude toward money which would later plague his personal life. Ken lacked the patience to wait for his purchases. The apartment rental had been essential, but Ken had no cash reserves for food, clothing, and other necessities. Buying the car had been premature. However, he was happy for the first time since he had arrived in Los Angeles and he did not care about whether or not he might be over-extending his finances.

Ken began his job working in customer service for California Land Title. He had a place to live, money he was earning on his own and a job with a future if he stayed. For the first time since he left high school, Ken Bianchi had a strong feeling of self-respect.

In one sense, this was the first time Ken had been on his own. He had been miserably unhappy since his father died of a heart attack when Ken was just thirteen. The high school years had been troubled as he and his mother tried to adjust to life without his father. He had had relatively few friends, though his interest in athletics and his handsome features enabled him to have his share of girls.

The high school girls Ken dated were divided into two categories. There were those you dated, inevitably virgins whose "honor" you might try to take but with whom you never made it "all the way," and the ones the boys at Gates-Chile High School called "roundheels." They would go to bed with anyone at any time and were used for the type of advanced fondling which helps adolescent boys understand their emerging manhood.

It was only when Ken met Laura that he experienced the intense physical and emotional desires of a serious first love. Ken never really seemed to know Laura, nor she him. Both had mothers who were strong influences in their lives. Both had a tendency to want to call their mothers whenever they had an argument which a more mature couple would have settled between themselves. And both seemed to have different immediate goals. Ken wanted to work, to earn money so they could have children, a house, and a future. Laura may have wanted that, but she also wanted a little excitement while she was young.

The marriage took place in 1971, shortly after Ken's high school graduation. Neither Ken nor Laura was ready for that type of commitment, nor were they ready to truly discuss their personal feelings and needs. The couple argued frequently and Ken hoped that if he could learn to suppress his emotions, saying nothing about his true feelings, everything would work out. What he failed to realize was that Laura apparently used his lack of communication as an excuse to lead her own, separate life. She allegedly had affairs during the eight months they were together, one of which, apparently was with a man for whom Ken worked.

Ken was desperate to hold the marriage together. He wrote Laura poetry and sent her flowers. He wooed and courted her, yet she dismissed his efforts as being too romantic. She took his actions as a sign of immaturity—and decided to end the relationship.

"I knew they had no business being married," said one friend who knew the couple during their marriage. "Every time they had a fight, Laura was on the telephone to her mother. She wanted approval like a little kid. It was like she was playing house, playing with sex, playing with being a grown-up, then reassuring herself that Mommy was still there to help her cross the street when things got rough.

"Ken wasn't much better. I had the feeling his mother wouldn't baby him during that period, so maybe it was a little harder for him. He had to be his own support but he didn't really know what to do. It was like they both married to get away from home, then didn't know what they should do once they did get away. I don't think they were any different than any other kids who think they know what they're doing when they get married right out of high school. They just broke up sooner. The others I've known usually lasted about two years before the divorce."

None of Ken's friends seemed to be able to point out to Ken how rapidly his marriage was disintegrating. "He seemed to live in a fantasy world about the marriage," said a girl who knew the couple then. "It was like he thought he could avoid talking about his problems, go about his business and everything would magically be okay."

But life wasn't all right. Eight months after the marriage, Ken Bianchi came home to an empty apartment. All the furniture and personal belongings were gone. Laura had taken everything, then filed for an annulment. There had been no warning of which Ken was aware and the emotional shock was overwhelming. He felt betrayed, angrier than he had ever been, yet totally crushed as well.

Marriage was supposed to be "forever." Marriage was supposed to mean a shared home, babies, and emotional security. The couple had a sex life together but Ken had to face the nightmare that it was a relationship without love, apparently filled with deception. Yet there was nothing he could do except endure a situation over which he felt he had no control.

"He used to talk about being dumped on," said one friend. "It was like he sometimes felt the whole world was against him. I think he was angry that his father died, like it was a special punishment. And Laura really screwed him over even if he was wrong in the way he handled the marriage, too. Everyone was dumping on him, in his eyes. He never did anything wrong. He never saw his own tendency to withdraw from others, which probably hurt Laura a bit. In his eyes, everything was black and white and Laura had dumped on him with the annulment."

Ken was unable to settle down after his annulment. He attended Monroe Community College in Rochester, taking courses in police science, political science, and other subjects. His grades were generally high C's, nowhere near the quality he thought they should be. He had trouble concentrating and finally decided to drop out of school.

A military career was also a consideration. He went to Buffalo, New York, to take the Air Force qualifying test. He found that he could enter the electronics field if he was interested. That fact pleased him but a military career was not what he was after.

There were other jobs. He worked as a bouncer in a bar, quitting after he had to become violent with a drunken customer. The man wanted to tear up the place so Ken hit him hard enough to discourage a fight. He couldn't handle the idea that he had to hurt someone else, and he chose to quit rather than continue with work of that nature.

The best job he obtained during the next few months was with an ambulance service. He took advanced first aid training and learned how to transport people who had been severely injured. He delighted in knowing that he was saving lives and helping the injured. If they had had a paramedic program or if he had been able to join the police force, he might have considered staying in New York. However, neither job was possible for him at that time and he did not want to make a career of the ambulance work.

There were women in Ken's life during this time as well. Bianchi met them at work, through friends and in bars. None of them became special in his mind and at least one actually frightened him by her possessive jealousy. This was Eve, who apparently felt she had been led on when she learned she was not his "one and only."

"She and I were going out," Bianchi later explained. "Nothing hot and heavy. Just going out, and she discovered . . . she ran into another girl I was going out with and . . . there was nothing wrong with it in my book, but apparently she really took offense to it.

"There was a knock on my door one night, and I opened my door and here comes this ball of fire, Eve. I had an antique mug collection and I had antiques all over my apartment. I was living alone in the town of Greece, just outside Rochester. And she went through my apartment like a tornado. Whatever she could grab her hands onto she did, and just winged everything at me. I lost all kinds of mugs. And she finally picked up a small wrench and she winged it at me and that hit me in the head.

"Then what happened, I just jumped for her and grabbed her and threw her down. And the police came because of the disturbance and they asked me if I wanted to press charges on her because there had been a couple eyewitnesses that had come into the hallway. She just tore my apartment apart. Crazy."

Finally Ken decided that he had to leave Rochester. His only meaningful relationship had ended in annulment and he felt the girls he was dating wanted a commitment from him that he was not yet ready to make. He desperately wanted marriage and a family, but only with the right person. He wanted a career, yet the jobs he held or had been offered also gave him no pleasure. Leaving would mean a new chance, new job potential, and an end to the hassles of snow, cold, and people who always seemed to be dumping on him.

The only reason for staying in New York was his mother, with whom he had become extremely close, especially after his father died when he was thirteen. Yet she was remarried, had her own life, and encouraged him to do what was best for his own emotional needs.

Ken's older cousin, Angelo Buono, ran a successful car upholstery business in Los Angeles. Angelo's parents were divorced and the families had drifted apart. However, they were all raised with an ethic requiring each person to come to the aid of the rest of the family in times of trouble. Ken knew that he could stay with his cousin, at least until he could find a job and become self-sustaining.

Night after night Ken and his mother talked about his leaving his home city. The separation would be painful. She did not really want to see him go, yet she knew he must. He was young, hurt, and trying to find his way. He could not seem to find the happiness he sought in Rochester, so she gave him her blessings, hoping that this move would bring him genuine love and happiness.

Ken Bianchi got in his car and began driving west to join the thousands of other men and women drawn to Hollywood and the other glamour areas of Los Angeles. When he arrived, he cruised the streets, fascinated by the endless parade of hookers, pimps, drug dealers, souvenir vendors, tourists, and others. Even his cousin Angelo was a delightful character when he first met him. Ken felt that Angelo was regularly involved with young women engaged in prostitution, and this made him the ideal companion, at least for the moment. And when he tired of the unconventional, there were far more single women his own age in Los Angeles than there were in Rochester.

Kelli Boyd avoided the Hollywood scene altogether. She lived on Franklin Avenue, in an area where families are raised with traditional values. It is mostly white, middle-class, and quiet, a typical residential area even though the Hollywood street scene is quite nearby. People led quiet lives, the type of neighborhood you could find in any city in the country.

Bellingham, Washington, had been Kelli's childhood home— a coastal city in the northern part of the state, just over the border from Vancouver, British Columbia. She had once vowed she would spend all her life on that sloping terrain, lulled by the cry of the birds continuously swooping down on the docks to check the day's fish catch. The endless, rhythmic lapping of the waves gave the city a sense of eternal tranquility as peaceful as the womb.

Kelli was four years younger than Ken Bianchi but their lives had followed a similar pattern. His father died when he was thirteen; her parents were divorced when she was only slightly older. She was married briefly right after high school and she subsequently had problems finding new relationships with which she was comfortable. Some of her family had moved to Los Angeles and in May 1976 she decided to join them. It would mean a radical change in life-style and she was glad for the opportunity.

Kelli first went to work for Pier I Imports, selling gifts and household items. Then she decided to take a secretarial position at California Laud Title Company, a job which offered better pay and a chance to advance. Her sister was working for the same company, though in a different branch office, and she enjoyed the work.

In November, Kelli was working in the Universal City office of Cal-Land and her sister was working in the downtown Los Angeles branch. A new employee had been hired and Kelli's sister thought they might like each other. That employee was Ken Bianchi.

Kelli liked Ken from the start. He was tall, with dark hair and a mustache. His arms were well muscled, yet he was a gentle, friendly young man, eager to help anyone in trouble. He checked the mechanical condition of the car Kelli's sister, Linda, was driving before she took a long trip, for example, but he never asked for any kind of compensation. However, it was not until the end of the year, after Bianchi was transferred to Universal City, that the two of them dated.

There had been another girl in Ken's life, or so he told Kelli before their first date on New Year's Eve. The girl had never been particularly serious about Ken, as Kelli found out from her later. However, Ken seemed to want Kelli to think it was more of a romance than it was so she would not pressure him. The girl was an excuse to not see Kelli again if their date did not work. Ken's slight misrepresentation was a way of protecting himself against possible rejection.

The couple went to two different parties given by friends of Kelli's. There was drinking by everyone and a few of the guests were using marijuana fairly heavily. Ken socialized but shied away from those who were getting drunk or high. He preferred talking quietly with Kelli, discussing his dream of a home of his own and a family.

Compared to the other men at the party, Ken seemed tremendously attractive to Kelli. Most of the others had no goals, no dreams, no thoughts beyond themselves and the sensual pleasures of smoking and drinking. They were seeking a thrill for the moment, not a long-term relationship, which Ken so obviously desired. It seemed silly to feel a sense of commitment on a first date, yet that is exactly the sensation Kelli and Ken had for each other. Somehow the night had no business coming to an end. They had led two separate lives before the parties yet now they felt themselves becoming intertwined in ways they sensed would last.

Ken was tired when he and Kelli reached the house where she was living. Kelli asked him if he wanted to stay, not certain why she did, yet knowing that somehow she did not want to see him go. He said yes, though he was equally uneasy.

The following morning was as frightening as the moments they spent deciding upon whether or not to stay together the night before. Ken was concerned that Kelli was nothing more than a pickup, a woman who enjoyed sex with every man who dated her. He didn't realize that not only was Kelli's action radically new for her, she was also frightened he would think she was cheap. Each kept trying to seek reassurance from the other that the night and the relationship had been unique, special.

They spent the next few days getting to know each other. Though the intensity of that first night did not persist, each still feared how the other might be viewing the situation. Only gradually did they come to see that they had one of those unusual relationships in which everything seems to fit together.

Ken and Kelli had both known the pain of a shattered home life. They had both experienced the mistake of marrying too young and for all the wrong reasons. They both were basically quiet individuals who wanted a home and family. They became lovers, but more importantly, they became close friends, intimates in those myriad ways known to couples who eventually share a lifetime together. The Hollywood magic was real. They moved into his tiny, motel-like apartment on Garfield Avenue in Glendale, knowing they would never separate again.

The Garfield apartment, though in the city, had a wooded back yard that gave the impression of a country home if you only looked out the bedroom window and had a good imagination. Kelli and Ken had the imagination. On weekends, when they did not have to be at work, they would awaken in each other's arms, listening to the birds singing on the windowsill. At that moment they could fantasize about having their home, located in the country, away from the pressures and cares of the world. Those were times of joy, of gentle touching, caressing, lovemaking that was slow yet powerful. It was an idyllic relationship and Kelli thought it would last forever.

Weekdays were exhausting for Ken and Kelli. They both worked at Cal-Land but their jobs required different time involvements. In the evening, Ken liked to watch television and Kelli would read a book. Sometimes she would watch television with him, but usually she would just read. He had no interest in books and both of them enjoyed the closeness they could feel sitting together while pursuing their separate interests.

Ken only liked two types of programs regularly. One type depicted happy home lives; the other was the police procedural with continuing heroes. If he wasn't viewing *Eight Is Enough* or *Family*, he would be delighting in the adventures of the California Highway Patrol in the show called *CHIPs*. He always admired the police, and *CHIPs* fit his image of the motorcycle-riding, handsome officers he would have liked to join.

There was uneasiness with the joy. Ken never seemed able to overcome his concern that Kelli might hurt him as Laura had. He appeared insecure to Kelli, so convinced that he might not have strong enough appeal to keep her happy that he was jealous of her friends. He wanted to be the only male in her life, something that was impossible. He was concerned about their coworkers and the male friends of her brother and sister. He would have preferred that she spend her life around the apartment when she was not at work, even though he knew he would be miserable if he tried to live that way.

When there were no programs on television he specifically wanted to see, Ken enjoyed going over to his cousin Angelo's to play cards. Kelli was invited along, but she chose not to go. She felt uneasy with Angelo, a man she sensed did not like or respect women. Part of this may have been the large age difference between the two; part may have been Angelo's upbringing in a culture where men were friends with each other, the women staying in the kitchen. Whatever the case, Ken realized that neither Kelli nor Angelo was particularly pleased with the other's company. He always offered to have her accompany him to Angelo' and she always declined.

"I wanted to show Ken that a relationship could be built on trust, not jealousy," said Kelli. "If Ken wanted to play cards until two or three in the morning, I wasn't going to say anything about it. I knew I was the woman he wanted in life and I thought that I could show him that jealousy was unnecessary. I figured that if I said nothing about his going out at night, he would stop complaining when I wanted to be with friends at times that he couldn't come along."

In August 1977, Kelli and Ken moved to an apartment at 1150 North Tamarind in Hollywood. Their suite was a one-bedroom unit at the end of the building on the third floor. The apartment was newer than the other, better maintained, and considerably larger.

The Tamarind lacked the rural feeling of the smaller apartment in Glendale. However, because it was larger and the walls were slightly thicker, Ken and Kelly actually had more privacy. The people who lived in the Tamarind tended to withdraw into their suites rather than to interact with other tenants. It was not the type of place where parties were constantly given, everyone's door was open, and people ran in and out of each other's suites. There was a nodding acquaintance with neighbors, but little more.

The more Ken and Kelli lived together, the more she questioned his maturity. Ken would borrow Kelli's car, drive it all over the city, then return it without filling the gas tank. When he went out at night, he would often forget to turn off the lights. There were numerous mornings when her car would not start as a result of his carelessness and she resented that fact.

Finances were another problem. Ken bought a Cadillac to impress Kelli, then couldn't afford the payments. Instead of telling her and turning it back in, he simply ignored the bills until the car was repossessed. He was not trying to live off her income, but this sense of priorities seemed all wrong to Kelli. They had a mutual account for their shared living expenses, yet Kelli kept finding herself providing more of the money. Ken was invariably broke from not planning ahead.

Ken was irresponsible in other ways. His job was boring at times, something he seemed unable to accept. He would call in sick, then go over to Angelo's to play cards.

Kelli was the more conscientious of the two. She had a sense of personal responsibility and obligation to others. She felt that it was wrong not to meet commitments if it was at all possible, and she kept refusing Ken's proposals of marriage as a way of trying to force him to act with equal maturity.

The financial problems resulted in numerous arguments. Ken seldom became angry and, when he did, he would usually shake his finger at Kelli while trying to make his points. Then he would walk out, never really having expressed extreme emotions.

In May 1977, Ken and Kelli went to Las Vegas with friends. They wanted to have some fun and spend some time together. The immaturity that had caused so many arguments seemed not to matter at that moment. They were like honeymooners and, unknown to either of them, Kelli became pregnant.

Gretchen, a friend of Kelli's, visited her in Los Angeles that August. The two women had been close friends in Bellingham for several years and they decided that traveling together would be a good way to relax and catch up on the time apart. They decided to go camping, alternating time on the road with occasional stays at motels. Ken seemed understanding, apparently realizing, at least that once, that his jealousy was unnecessary. The two women gathered their equipment and began driving east, eventually reaching Denver, where they stopped at a Ramada Inn.

Kelli and Gretchen went to a bar one evening to drink and listen to music. Two men came over to see them, and the women enjoyed their company, but had no interest in dating them. The men had other ideas, though, something neither woman would know until too late.

Gretchen had to leave the bar for a few minutes and one of the men accompanied her, leaving Kelli alone with the other one. He was tall, heavy, and muscular. He was also rather boring, spending the evening doing more drinking than talking. After a while, his massive hulk seemed to turn to rubber and he slumped against the table.

He's drunk, thought Kelli as the man looked at her through half-closed eyes. He told her that he was going to pass out soon and needed to get back to his room and he begged Kelli to escort him lest he be arrested for drunkenness. Gretchen was late returning and Kelli didn't know what to do. She finally decided that the man was right about his condition and, since he had bought her drinks, helping him back was the least she could do in return.

The trip to the motel room seemed endless. Kelli was trying to support the man's weight as he sagged against her. He seemed to be moving in and out of consciousness and Kelli could not wait until he collapsed inside his room so she could get back to the bar, where Gretchen would be looking for her.

The moment the man stepped inside his room, everything changed. He had consumed a large quantity of liquor but his large frame kept him from becoming anywhere near as drunk as he seemed at first. He pushed Kelli aside, locked the door, and took her in his arms. She struggled, arguing with him to leave her alone, but he made it clear he was going to have sex with her. She could cooperate and leave or she could be beaten into submission. He would enjoy it either way.

Kelli hoped that Gretchen would return to the bar, remember the room number the man had mentioned to both of them earlier, and come looking for her friend. She also realized that the man would not hesitate to be extremely violent. Just the way he was holding her was painful. She said she would cooperate, undressing as slowly as she could in the vain hope that, at any moment, Gretchen would come to the door.

The Hollywood apartment Kelli shared with Ken had become home to her and she was never more pleased to be back than after the nightmare of the Denver rape. Ken was a gentle, loving man, incapable of the brutality with which she had been treated by that stranger in Denver. They happily went to bed together, Kelli lost in Ken's protective arms. The nightmare was over and she saw no reason to mention what was past. She had not reported the incident to the police because she was so anxious to return. It was done, finished forever, a bad dream she knew she would eventually forget. What she did not realize was that she had contracted venereal disease as a result of the incident.

Ken caught the VD from Kelli and the two of them had to be treated by a doctor. It was then that Kelli's pregnancy was also discovered.

Once again Ken Bianchi's world seemed shattered. He wanted to believe Kelli's story about what happened but felt betrayed that she had not told him sooner. He was suspicious of the fact that she had neither bruise marks on her body nor a police report to confirm her statements. He wondered if he was going to be faced with the same pattern of infidelity he had innocently endured with Laura. The thought haunted him, even though he realized that his relationship with Kelli was deeper and more intense than he had ever known with his wife.

By contrast, the idea that he was going to have a baby—a family—was overwhelmingly exciting. Perhaps now Kelli would agree to be his wife. Perhaps he would finally have the type of life in Hollywood that had so painfully eluded him in Rochester. He worried about what had happened in Denver, and yet Kelli was the mother of his child.

The Hollywood street scene was not a place to visit for Yolanda Washington; it was her home, her office, the focal point of her existence. She made her living by bringing love and affection to any man who had the price. She was known to the vice-squad officers in the area, one of many young women who plied their trade on the streets.

Yolanda had a small son whose father did not support him. She adored her baby and was determined to be a good mother to him. As her friends later told investigators, she decided that she should work at whatever job would both pay well and give her extra time with her child. The fact that this meant selling her body and, according to friends, periodically dealing in drugs, did not matter. The opportunity to spend most of her time with her boy, helping him to grow into a better man than his father had been, was what mattered. Prostitution meant as much as $300 a night. A few hours' work gave her more money than some professional women earned in legitimate business. The exact earnings were uncertain, but estimates from friends and vice-squad officers indicate that she probably netted between $500 and $1000 in an average week.

Yolanda didn't care how the outside world saw her. She was accepted in Hollywood and enjoyed the full benefits of her work. She had a few nice clothes, some jewelry—such as her turquoise ring with the overlapping leaf holding the stone in place—and plenty of food for the baby.

No one knew that Yolanda Washington's world would come to an abrupt end on the night of October 17, 1977. She was working the streets of Sunset and Vista, watching for the cruising men to slow and stop. She would turn a few tricks and go home to her baby.

The negotiations would have been quick. Everyone who used Los Angeles street girls knew the rules. The minimum fee was $25, even for a fast blow job. If the guy wanted something kinky, the charge rose to match. It was all there for a price and she liked to see the way the money came rolling in. She'd never be the big-time call girl who worked from a hotel and had a steady stream of clients giving her as much per night as she now earned in a month. But she made a good living and the johns never complained. Even that night—if she had to do it in the car—would not be all bad. It was no worse than for the girls whose first time was at a drive-in movie.

And then Yolanda Washington disappeared. It was 11 P.M. as best as anyone could tell. She went off with a john in a black car or a blue car, a red one, a green one, European, Japanese, American, big, little . . . Faulty memories of an unimportant event. People remembered her. People remembered her being picked up. But where and when was unknown.

The homicide detectives dispatched from the Hollywood division of the Los Angeles Police Department were no strangers to murder. The coroner's office receives an average of forty-eight bodies a day, one every thirty minutes, around the clock. Some are natural deaths occurring in unexpected circumstances. A man races for a bus, suddenly stops, clutching his heart, then topples over, dead from a heart attack. Or an elderly woman is paralyzed by a stroke while in her bathtub. Her body slips below the surface of the water and she drowns. There can be any number of possibilities, none of them involving foul play, but all of them must be checked through autopsy. A tiny pinprick, freshly made in an artery, could turn the runner's heart attack into a suspected homicide. Bruise marks on the body of the old woman might indicate that a greedy nephew decided to hasten her demise and thus his inheritance. Usually such exotic crimes are not involved with this type of death, but autopsies must be performed.

There are other deaths which must be investigated. Suicides, traffic accidents, and other forms of violence are all explored to see if crimes have been committed.

Actual premeditated murder happens less frequently, but nothing can ever be assumed. Every case must be checked and special field investigators are sent to the scene where a body is discovered. The detectives specializing in homicide are spotted throughout the city in satellite stations as well as in Parker Center, the downtown headquarters. They travel each time violence is suspected. The Yolanda Washington slaying was no exception.

Uniformed patrol officers are almost always the first officials to arrive at the scene of a murder. Their job is to prevent the destruction of the crime scene. They have to isolate the body and as much of the surrounding area as possible if it seems to relate to the violence. Curiosity seekers have to be kept back, though each person is questioned to see if he or she has any idea what happened or who the victim might be. Little other work is done until the detectives arrive to take charge of searching the area.

The detectives found the nude body of Yolanda Washington on a hillside along Forest Lawn Drive south of the Ventura Freeway, near Forest Lawn Cemetery. Yolanda was known to work along Ventura Boulevard, the detectives would later discover, and it would have been easy to pick her up, then drive out the freeway which cuts through the area.

The detectives stood at the top of the hill and surveyed the ground leading to the body. Marks damaging the vegetation indicated that the corpse had been tossed from a car on the freeway, and had then rolled down the hill.

A tossed corpse is always a nuisance for detectives. It's much easier to solve the murder if you know where it took place. Evidence of a struggle, spent cartridges from a gun, a knife tossed casually away, or some other weapon left behind might be a conclusive link. There can be bits of clothing, hair samples, cigarette butts, and numerous other items at the scene which can conclusively link a victim with a killer. The longer it takes to learn where a crime was actually committed, the harder it is to solve the case.

The first police officer arriving at the scene of a crime will walk to the body along a fixed, narrow line, watching the terrain as he moves so he does not destroy any cigarette butt, beer-can pull top, or other minute pieces of evidence. This officer then alerts all the other officers and detectives as to which path was taken so they can follow his footsteps. The minimum area disturbance possible is made to protect the ground.

The detectives walked down this narrow path to the body. The scientific investigation team and the coroner's investigator would be handling the technical details of identifying all marks, determining the cause of death and other factors, but the detectives were all experienced and could frequently tell the cause of death from the external signs.

This time it was fairly obvious: the woman had been strangled with intense force. There were other marks as well, but they looked as if they had been made when she was tossed down the hillside. No matter what else may have happened to the woman, strangulation was a contributing factor.

The location of the body was the first problem. The second was that there was no purse or clothing which could lead to identification. A ring appeared to have been taken from her finger, a fact that was noted in case she turned out to be a robbery victim.

Actual physical evidence at the scene was nonexistent. A detailed autopsy would prove productive, but none of the items secured on the ground related to the murder. Cigarette butts, evidence of beer cans, bottles, broken pencils, and other items dropped over the years were just that—details from the past. They had no relationship to the killing. Yet everything had to be taken, logged, analyzed. Nothing was insignificant because no one knew what the case might eventually prove to be. Until they had more details concerning the death, details which would probably not be known until after a killer was captured, everything had to be assumed to be significant.

The next procedures were clear. The coroner would autopsy the body and the detective, his partner, and the other men assigned to the area would have to start knocking on doors to try and learn the identity of the woman. They would find the homes nearest the area and start there. With luck, she would be a local person or someone known to one of the residents. There might also be a missing-persons report on her in a day or two. If not, they would be that much further from determining the identity of the killer.

The coroner's investigator was checking for the approximate time of death as the detective watched. The ground temperature was taken, then a special probe was inserted into the victim in order to learn the temperature of the liver. By knowing the temperature of the ground, the lowest temperature during the night, and the temperature of the liver, an approximate time of death could be determined. The detective noted that the investigator carefully checked the skin surface before inserting the probe. The puncture mark from the thermometer might obliterate a hole, even a pinprick could be a clue.

Once the body had been checked and photographed, the area to be searched was divided into a grid. The investigators worked on their hands and knees at times, checking the grass, looking for cigarette butts, buttons, anything.

The house-to-house search was routine and fruitless. Had anyone heard or seen anything unusual? Did anyone see a car stop long enough for the body to be tossed onto the hillside?

The detectives carefully noted each homeowner's reaction, an approach the other officers were also following. Nervousness or other indications that the person might be hiding something were reasons to check back later. Some people are nervous whenever they are questioned by any authority figure. Others might be nervous because of personal involvement, or the concern that a friend or family member might be involved.

The victim's fingerprints were taken to be checked against police files. If she had ever been arrested, worked for a high-security agency, or otherwise had her prints recorded in the past, they could be cross-checked and her identity established.

The autopsy was revealing. The strangulation marks indicated that cloth had been used. There was a chance the victim had been killed by her own blouse. The angle was such that she could have been killed on the floor of a car or any similar location where the murderer was above her.

Sexual relations had occurred before death; according to the semen samples, at least two men had been involved. One man lacked the ability to secrete the full chemical range of semen, a fact which would not hinder his sex life or his ability to have a family, but it did cause an obvious difference in the chemical analysis. It was a clue, a real clue, even though there probably were several hundred thousand such nonsecreters in all of Los Angeles and a few million throughout the country. Still, it was more information than the police had had before.

The question was whether or not the men who had relations with Yolanda had also killed her. The marks indicated that only one person was likely to have strangled her, and there was no evidence of that individual's sex.

The detectives did not have long to wait in order to identify Yolanda Washington. She had an arrest record showing her to be one of the Hollywood Boulevard prostitutes.

A good detective knows that he or she can never try to prove assumptions when attempting to solve a case. Frequently, as with Yolanda, the evidence seems obvious. She was murdered turning tricks. Perhaps she went with someone a little strange, a man who got turned on by violence and went too far. Or there might have been an argument over pay. It was possible that the woman worked for a pimp who was being attacked by a rival. The second pimp could have murdered Yolanda as a means of leaving more territory for his own women. The answers would come but the knowledge that she was a prostitute narrowed the areas where the detectives would start looking. The Hollywood street scene was the place to begin.

Newspaper editors follow a policy of discrimination by necessity when determining how much space to give a story. Is the item so shocking or of such broad interest that it warrants front-page headlines? Should it receive fairly large play on an inside page? Or is the story one which, while it should be reported to the people, is of limited interest or concern to anyone? The amount of space provided determines not only how many newspapers will be sold but also the importance the public gives each story.

The Los Angeles news media analyzed Yolanda Washington's death the same way as the police. She was part of a subculture, her death having little meaning to those who regularly bought newspapers. All that made her important was the fact that a murder had taken place. Yet even that did not matter very much because the criminal was probably no one who could ever prove a threat to decent people. The value and moral judgment may have been un-fair but it resulted in the news media's almost ignoring the story.

*   *   *

Ken Bianchi and Kelli Boyd never saw the story of Yolanda Washington's murder and they probably would not have cared if they had. They were having their own problems. Kelli hated be-ing pregnant and the nausea prevented her from having fun when she felt well enough to leave home in the evening.

Around the time of the Washington murder, Ken and Kelli went to see the Walt Disney movie *Pete the Dragon,* an activity which should have been fun for them both. Ken delighted in ani-mated fantasy and had been anxious to see it. Kelli was not par-ticularly thrilled with the film but the childlike joy that Ken got from it delighted her. As she watched him viewing the movie, her feelings of love for him intensified. Unfortunately she became too sick to stay with him and spent the remainder of the movie in the bathroom or outside in the car. She wanted him to stay through to the end and she hated the fact that she could not be with him.

The happy times were mingled with tension and periodic separations. She was pregnant, planning to have a baby who needed the security of a home, food, and clothing. Ken worked hard when he worked and he was never without a job, yet his casual attitude toward his responsibilities worried Kelli. She wanted a husband of greater maturity, yet she loved the gentle, quiet manner and sensitive vulnerability of the strong, good-looking man she lived with.

The jealousy was another stress point. She never denied Ken a chance to go out for an evening on his own and never ques-tioned where he might go. She trusted his statement that he was with Angelo, hoping that he would see her sense of security with him and show her the same respect. Yet the fact that the prob-lem continued to exist also added to her concern about their re-lationship.

Then, when the tension seemed almost unbearable, Ken would bring her flowers and write poetry for her. He spoke of his love, the most tender passions of his heart revealed in the poems. The flowers he bought or picked delighted her. At times she would even move in with friends in order to get an emotional break from him. However, if he could just grow to the level where his maturity in handling money equaled the romantic tenderness of his heart, Kelli felt she would have an ideal man.

*　　*　　*

Judith Ann Miller was ready for the big time. Fifteen years old, bored with school, frustrated with her home life, she knew what she wanted from the world. She longed for good friends, the laid-back, mellow feeling that pot and pills could provide, and a chance to be someone, maybe a movie star or a fashion model. She wasn't certain just where she was headed but she knew from living in Los Angeles that Hollywood Boulevard was where the action was. Maybe she would be discovered by a big-time producer or a handsome movie star. She could see her name in lights, shining down on her former classmates at the high school she had held in disdain.

Hollywood provided friends for Judy Miller. If you got into a group, you stayed with them. They became your connection, your supplier, your extended family. Some of the people she knew were pimps and whores, others were drug dealers or stoned-out users. Still others were like herself, kids who were trying to grow up too fast or adults who had followed her path, discovering too late that their fantasy of the world didn't work. What mattered was the acceptance, the love, the chance to be special, if only to the street people and outcasts of straight existence.

The moral standards of many of the Hollywood street people are different from those of most outsiders. Yolanda was a part-time prostitute with definite goals. Other young women either enjoyed sex with a variety of men or thought that such sharing was the proper way to live. The latter would accept money or gifts when they were offered. At other times, they simply relieved the needs of their male friends.

Judy belonged in the category of girls who never worked full time at prostitution but accepted sex as part of the street life. She probably didn't remember when she had lost her virginity but she quickly learned that sex was no big deal. Turning an occasional trick was a way to make some money. If a friend couldn't pay, she would give it away, the detectives were later told. That's what friends were for. The nice thing about Hollywood was that you seldom got hassled and your friends were always waiting when you got back, sharing their love and helping you forget your problems.

Hollywood Boulevard and Wilcox was the street where Judy Miller was last seen alive. It was Monday, October 31, 1977, and no one questioned her activities. Some say she was turning tricks. Others say they don't know what she was doing. All that is certain is her last known location, though there is a question as to where she was picked up.

The next time Judy Miller was seen was in the area of Terrace and La Crescenta, outside the city. Her body had been tossed, apparently by two individuals, and it landed somewhat stiffly, never to move again.

This time the detectives were from the Los Angeles Sheriff's Office. That department, headquartered in an older building fairly near the Police Department's Parker Center, had a strongly competitive attitude toward the police. The homicide detectives considered themselves the best in the country and most other people in the legal system tended to agree.

The Sheriff's Department looked upon the homicide force as the elite among their detectives. Every man was carefully screened, first having proved himself superior enough as a uniformed officer to move into the detective division, perhaps handling robbery or some other specialty. Then, if the man was outstanding, he would be in a position to move up to homicide. This was different from the L.A. Police Department, where a uniformed patrolman could go to the homicide division as his first detective assignment. The police felt that all their men were at least the equal of the Sheriff's homicide unit, but criminal attorneys often joked that if their clients had to commit murder, they hoped it would be within the city itself, where only the police would be involved.

The Sheriff's detectives worked similarly to the men handling the police homicide calls. The first man at the scene of Judy

Miller's dumping recognized immediately that they did not have the location of the murder unless she had been killed right on the road.

"We knew immediately that two people were probably involved," said one Sheriff's homicide detective. "The position of the body was one we often see when two people carry a dead victim. There is a natural way to carry someone under these circumstances, one person taking the arms and the other the legs, using the knees like handles. If one person carried the body, that person would have to carefully arrange it and that almost never happens. Besides, there was evidence on the ground that two people had been there. Somebody might have gone later and found the body without reporting it, but that doesn't make much sense. We assumed we had two killers from the start or at least a killer and somebody who helped. We also assumed that one killer was a man because we suspected she had been raped. We just didn't know if it was two men or a man and a woman."

The techniques used to identify the victim were the same as those used with Yolanda Washington. Once again a corpse could be traced back to Hollywood, though the detectives were unaware of the similarities in the two cases. They also assumed that a pimp war or an angry john could have been the cause of the strangulation.

The one concern the detectives had was the marks on Judy's body. The autopsy revealed bits of adhesive on her face, indicating that a gag had been used. The wrists and ankles were also marked, so it was obvious she had been bound. The killer might have deliberately kidnapped her or she might have turned a trick with a man who tied her up first. The latter situation seemed likely. Bondage, the detectives learned, was a fairly common sex game of both straight couples and men using prostitutes. Alex Comfort, Nancy Friday, and other writers about sex for lovers have frequently discussed the tying of one partner by the other to prolong foreplay during sex. Prostitutes interviewed by vice-squad members and other police made it clear that tying up a customer at his request or being bound before sex was not at all an unusual request.

The problem with the sex game is that it could turn deadly when one of the partners was a sadist. At such times, the restraint was used not to heighten sexual arousal but to prevent resistance to what amounted to mild torture. If this was the case, marks other than strangulation should have been left on the body, and these could not be found in the autopsy.

Once again the lack of a crime scene presented a problem. There were countless questions and the only answer was a dead body. Who the murderers might be, where they lived, and why they chose Judy were all unknowns.

* * *

Jim Mitchell was typical of the career-minded broadcaster who seeks to make his mark in a major city such as Los Angeles, Chicago, and New York. He was an investigative and general-assignment reporter for KFWB Radio, the kind of job that is either the high point of a broadcasting career or a stepping-stone to the big time. There is tremendous freedom on the job as long as you produce regular stories which can dominate the news. You can work as many hours as you like: only the results matter. This was ideal for someone like Mitchell who had a tendency to live his work, eventually to the detriment of his home life. He could become obsessive about a story, taking it personally and becoming determined to find a solution to whatever problem he perceived might exist.

Mitchell's physical appearance matches the intensity of his workday. He is of medium height, perhaps five feet eight or nine, lean, with honey-blond hair and fingernails bitten to the quick. He lights cigarette after cigarette, not quite chain-smoking, yet never really relaxing to enjoy the cigarette. He speaks rapidly when off the air, as though he is filled with thoughts and emotions he can express so seldom that he uses his few chances to erupt in a torrent of verbiage.

Mitchell had always been considered one of the most aggressive newsmen in the Los Angeles area. He won several awards with the radio station and continued to be given extensive air time after switching to CBS Television. It was the Hillside Strangler case which gave him his greatest notoriety and caused strong public awareness during the early discoveries of the bodies. His actions won both the praise and the damnation of law-enforcement officers involved with the case.

Mitchell had been a reporter for ten years when the bodies first appeared. Murder was not a new experience for him; he had seen a number of killings, suicides, and accidental deaths during his career.

Judy Miller's death was the first of the Hillside Strangler series that Mitchell covered. "I had never, in all my experience, found a rape and murder victim like that," said Mitchell several months after the murderer had been caught. "I had never heard of such a thing. That is, simply, she was lying in this little parkway between the curb and sidewalk.

"She was completely nude," Mitchell continued, "and she was sprawled out on the grass almost as if she were about to engage in an act of sex with a man. The knees were up in the air, her legs were spread apart, the hands were at about a forty-five degree angle from her sides, almost in a position of supplication. They weren't out straight in crucifix fashion, palms up, and my first reaction when I saw her was it was probably an OD, because when I drove up there I didn't know what had happened. Then when I realized that she had been strangled, I said, now wait a minute, something has gone wrong here. And I had a conversation a short time later with one of the police detectives and I asked him.

"I said, 'I have never seen anything like this before in my life.' He said that he had never heard of it either and I said, 'Do you think it could be some psycho?' And he said, it could be. So at that point I did the story but I made no reference to the possibility of a psycho."

"We tried to help the press as little as possible," said a Sheriffs Department investigator. "Our first responsibility is to build a case and get the killer off the street so the public is protected. An erroneous conclusion on a reporter's part was encouraged. It meant that if the real killer ever confessed, he or she would mention details that had not been read.

"The reporters who saw deep significance in body placement simply weren't as experienced or well trained as we were. We knew immediately that the body position meant two people even though it looked grotesque with her nude and all. It's like, the coroner found two different narks on her wrists. We knew she had probably been both handcuffed and tied, but we weren't going to give that detail out. Most people would use one method of restraint or the other; the double use was an extra clue.

"The almost microscopic particles of adhesive on her face helped, too. It was logical to assume both that she had been gagged and that the gag involved tape. We saw most of these things right at the crime scene and learned the rest through autopsy. But kill an erroneous conclusion by a reporter? Never!"

Mitchell and some of the other reporters felt certain that the body's position indicated a deviant sexual motive behind the killing, even though the more experienced homicide detectives would have explained that this inference was not justified by the evidence.

The reporter noted the way the legs seemed to have been positioned so that someone spotting the body would have his attention drawn directly to the pubic hair. Mitchell, for example, seemed to have the impression that the killer deliberately manipulated the body in a way that was sexually meaningful.

Investigation into broadcasts during this period has not revealed specific examples of news reports mentioning the careful corpse placement. However, the general public felt the message was being conveyed that the killer was so sick he had to carefully bend and angle his victims' naked bodies after death. People began assuming that if there was a sexual ritual after death, there had to have been one before it.

Murder was the furthest thought from the minds of Ken and Kelli. They were close again, enjoying one of the good times. They, like the rest of Los Angeles, had little interest in Judy Miller's death. The Saturday night before Halloween, for example, they had decided to go to a nightclub called Circus Maximus. This club was frequented primarily by gay men and lesbians, though many straight couples were attracted by the loud music and exotic atmosphere. Many of Ken and Kelli's friends enjoyed the night life there. They persuaded the couple to join them for occasional visits.

That Saturday night, Ken and Kelli donned matching costumes for an evening at Circus Maximus. They stayed quite late, dancing, listening to the music, drinking, and enjoying the "floor show."

On Sunday, the day of Judy's murder, they relaxed from the excitement of the previous night. Monday, when they were back at work, the violence of the Hollywood street scene was not a topic of conversation.

Jim Mitchell may have been the first person to begin making a connection among the murder victims. Certainly it was early in the case when he began noticing unusual links that made him realize there was more to the deaths than Hollywood whores being strangled in a pimp war.

Pimp wars were fairly obvious. The girls were merchandise, a means of earning a living. Killing them was counterproductive. You might threaten them, break a few bones, cut them a bit where it wouldn't show, in order to move them from a section of the city. Murder was just not good form. Besides, all the victims were found on hillsides, nude and strangled—hardly the style of an occasional pimp war.

The third corpse was discovered on Sunday, November 6, 1977. The victim's name was Lissa Teresa Kastin and unlike the first two victims, she was a "good girl." She was neither a prostitute nor a drug user. She was also found in Glendale, a new jurisdiction.

Kastin was a dancer, totally committed to bringing classic, structured form to the wildly spontaneous disco beats. She had formed a group known as the LA Knockers, an all-woman act which danced in clubs. Despite the name, the group was quite serious and increasingly successful. Lissa herself had studied ballet for many years and all the women worked to entertain while utilizing line, form, and structured movement for best effect.

Lissa was temporarily out of the group at the time of her death. Because of a weight problem coupled with hypoglycemia, she was earning her living as a waitress and working part time for her father's real-estate and construction business. She had planned to study in San Francisco, continuing her education in dance, voice, and foreign languages while returning to professional dancing. Her plans were never fulfilled.

The report of Lissa Kastin's disappearance came earlier than some because she was such a conscientious employee. Her boss at the restaurant contacted the family when she did not appear for work. Her father checked her apartment, then got in touch with the police. However, as he drove to his daughter's residence, he heard a news broadcast on KFWB indicating that an unknown body had been found in Glendale. The description matched that of his daughter but he chose to ignore the possible implications.

The manager of the complex where Lissa Kastin lived used his passkey to let her father into the studio she rented. The room gave no indication that his daughter had been home. The double bed was made. Her possessions were undisturbed and a suitcase was open, two thirds packed in anticipation of a planned trip to San Francisco. All that was missing was her car, which was not parked on the grounds.

Lissa Kastin's father used the apartment manager's telephone to call the Glendale Police Department. He explained about the news report he had heard and the fact that his daughter was missing. He provided enough physical details, including the fact that each earlobe had been pierced three times, so that he was asked to come to the station.

Glendale Police homicide detective Dave O'Conner handled the questioning of Lissa Kastin's father. He obtained enough information about her appearance to convince him that there was a good chance that the unidentified body was this man's daughter. O'Connor took him to the morgue, where a closed-circuit television system was used for the identification. The camera was focused close on the head of the corpse so the father could view Lissa on the television screen. It was a less traumatic way to make an identification.

There was no question about the identification, even though Lissa's father wanted to deny the reality of what he saw. He called his ex-wife, Lissa's mother, asking her to come over. However, the intensity of his shock convinced the detectives that a further confirmation by the mother would change nothing. They had identified the previously unknown corpse.

As the unsolved killings increased, Mitchell began studying similarities. "I hadn't at first paid too much attention to the Glendale murder," said Mitchell. "I knew that it was similar in some general respects, but at that time I didn't know what the specifics were. I think I may have reported something to the effect of the murder was similar to that of a woman found in La Crescenta but, still, that really didn't quite do it. We didn't have a Strangler at that point."

Mitchell was bothered by the circumstances of the discoveries of the bodies. "There may be similar cases . . . where women have been raped and strangled and then their nude bodies found . . . The position of the body also disturbed me a great deal because it was plainly apparent that she didn't fall into that position. She wasn't simply pushed out of the car. And in retrospect there is another aspect of it that was intriguing. At the time I don't think I was that much aware of it. It occurred later on when we had more cases to deal with, but the selection of the site for dumping this body was superb.

"It was in a location where the body could be dropped, or placed, as it appeared to be, without the individual being accidentally observed. It was a cul-de-sac, it was on a hillside. There were no houses above the street and the houses on the lower side of the street, the houses were low enough that someone looking out of a living room window wouldn't have been very likely to have noticed the activity up on the street."

Mitchell continued, "I began to develop a great sense of appreciation for the incredible expertise that was displayed by this killer and sometimes I was just absolutely amazed at, and so were a lot of the police, how efficient they were. Incredibly efficient . . ."

The detectives who met together after the Kastin death had all been alerted by the coroner's office to look for links among the three victims. Since the jurisdictions involved three different city and county departments, representatives of those departments were forced to admit that standard investigative procedures were not working. None of the departments—Los Angeles Police, Glendale Police, nor Los Angeles Sheriff—had located the place where the murders had been committed. More information was essential and it was hoped that when the men talked with each other some overlooked clue would be mentioned and everything would fall into place. It did not. There was inadequate evidence to determine anything further.

The problems within the city were compounded by a sudden increase in corpses. Throughout November 1977 it seemed as though the strangled bodies of women were turning up everywhere. Jill Barcomb, eighteen, last seen at Sunset Boulevard and Poinsettia, was found nude and strangled on November 10 at Franklin Cyn Drive and Mulholland. Once convicted for prostitution in New York, she had last lived in Hollywood. Kathleen Robinson, seventeen, last seen at Pico and Ocean Boulevards, her clothed, strangled body was found on November 17. She was also considered part of the Hollywood street scene. Kristina Weckler, twenty, an art student who lived in Glendale and studied in Pasadena, was last seen along the 810 block of Garfield in Glendale; her nude, strangled body was found November 20 at Ranons Way and Nawona. Sonia Johnson, fourteen, and Dollie Cepeda, twelve, last seen at York and Avenue 46 near the Eagle Rock Shopping Center; their bodies were found at Landa and Stadium Way on November 20. Both had been parochial-school students and friends. Jane King, twenty-eight, an actress and Scientology student who modeled part time, was last seen in the area of Franklin and Tamarind; her body was discovered November 23 in the Los Feliz extension area near the westbound Golden State Freeway. Lauren Wagner, eighteen, a business school student studying to become a secretary, was last seen in the 9500 block of Lemona. Her nude, strangled body was found at 1200 Cliff Drive.

The links were intriguing. The victims were almost all nude, all strangled. Sexual relations were involved in each case, and they had all been bound or handcuffed prior to death. They had all been found on hillsides and at least two people had been involved with dumping the bodies. In most of the cases, intercourse involved two men and one of them was a nonsecreter.

By November 1977, each new corpse was reported in the press as another victim of the mysterious "Hillside Strangler." There is now no way of knowing whether the expression was coined by the police or the press. A mass murderer had obviously reached Los Angeles; terror was about to grip the city.

CHAPTER 4

By the end of November, with ten women dead, the police were facing panic within the city. Absenteeism from Hollywood High and schools in the surrounding area had increased. Many women were driving with lead pipes and baseball bats under the front seats of their cars. Even some of the police officers were establishing check-in times and codes for their family members to use.

"My daughter was in high school and she had to call when she left school, giving her destination. She had to call upon arriving and call when she went somewhere else. My wife worked and I had her to do the same thing. We had two messages to leave. One would be if everything was normal and the second was a code that the person was in trouble. Every time I was out, one of the guys would take it. We lived in the Glendale area and my wife often shopped where the two little girls disappeared. Maybe I can take care of myself as a cop, but I felt helpless worrying about my family."

The politicians were delighted to use the Hillside Strangler fear for personal gain. Those in office pressed the police in an effort to have the case solved so they could take credit for being a factor in ending the nightmare. Potential candidates began decrying the ineffectual city governments and implied that if they had been elected during the previous voting, the Hillside Strangler would miraculously have been caught. Everyone in government knew that they would have no effect, one way or the other. They were just capitalizing on an inflammatory situation and the public was so hysterical that the speeches seemed to make sense.

The police knew that they had to make capturing the Hillside Strangler a priority. They decided to create a combined task force from among members of the Los Angeles Police, the Glendale Police, and the Los Angeles sheriff's office. This would not change the method of police work but would concentrate manpower and make interviewing the thousands of suspects and supposed witnesses much easier. The Los Angeles Police Department and Sheriff's office had enough manpower so that the officers they contributed to the task force could work on the case full time; other officers could be shifted to cover their regular case loads. The Glendale Police, however, had a smaller operation; the homicide detectives also handle robbery and they had to continue their work as much as possible. The reduction of manpower meant that criminal activity was reevaluated and certain crimes were not investigated as thoroughly as before. Prostitution, for example, was almost completely ignored as long as those involved were consenting adults and no violence occurred.

Many detectives were frustrated when word reached them that a Hillside Strangler Task Force was being formed. It was the end of November and the politicians were having a grand time putting pressure on the police to break the case. The publicity being generated could make or destroy careers, so everyone wanted to do whatever was necessary to avoid criticism. The task force appeared to be one answer. It sounded good, it looked good, and the detectives knew that in the long run they would just receive more flak if the case continued unsolved.

To the people of Los Angeles, raised on comic strips like Dick Tracy and the fantasy world of television cop shows, the task force became something almost mystical. The average citizen assumed that it had unlimited equipment, magical powers, and space-age technology which could hone in on the murderer. The task-force publicity conjured an image of thousands of specialized computers, laser weapons and other electronic gadgetry being used by an elite investigative team whose members could each single-handedly outwit and outfight James Bond.

The detectives knew that the task force would never approach the public's expectations. Human minds programmed computers, invented sophisticated lasers, and solved murders. The detectives were dealing with an irrational killer. There was a randomness to the selection, the only similarity being that the victims all appeared to be in their late teens. There might be some geographical connection, but the girls were not linked in any way that seemed identifiable, except in the mind of the killer. A computer is designed for the logical storage and retrieval of information. It can make factual links, but it cannot duplicate the sophisticated thought processes of the human mind. A detective's own brain was the most efficient way to determine what motivations might cause an irrational individual to kill over and over again.

However, the task force would mean a concentration of manpower and the sharing of information. They would also have a computer for the storage of information. They could cross-reference clues with a giant chart which eventually circled the room they used. They would be able to have a clearinghouse for information and this would move things faster.

Lieutenant Stan Bachman of the Los Angeles County Sheriff's Office Homicide Unit described the task force. He said, "We had all our people who were assigned to the task force. We removed them from the other work force and gave them a room of their own with their own telephones and their own nerve center, so to speak. Every piece of information that came in regarding the cases, or any inquiries regarding whatever, went to the same spot and to the same two or maybe three people who were assigned to answer the phones. And they kept a log on everything so that you could go back and trace it. If someone called in today and says, 'Well, I saw a yellow Chevrolet, such and such, with such people in it,' you could go back and see if that piece of information had already come in from someone else, or how many times, or whatever.

"We had a visual chart that ended up going almost around the room. It was on paper and we had a young lady who is in the computer field who is quite adept at 'pert charting.'

"We started the first day of the first body. We had the victim and then we just had lines drawn and each major incident that would occur, like body found, autopsy, second body found, whatever. . . . All the bodies involved, all the girls, all the victims, and how they would relate. So you could start at this end and just read it all the way around. All it does is that it saves you from reading the stacks of supplementary reports that all investigators put in. It is all condensed onto these graphic charts and it is just easier to read.

"You can see the connection because you have lines. Let's say that victim one and victim twelve lived in the same apartment building. It would show it on that graphic chart. It would have a line going between the two and then it would have a symbol on there saying 'resided in the same apartment building.'

"You keep looking at it and you can see the connections that you had. Whereas if you just kept reading these hundreds of reports that come in, you might miss this."

There was no magic, no twenty-first-century electronic miracle. Just men and women pooling information, avoiding duplication of effort, and searching for the common links among the victims, their life-styles or anything else which might pinpoint the killer. It was as efficient a means of handling the investigation as anyone could realistically create under the circumstances. Yet the public did not understand this. The city was running scared and the police were the ones who were supposed to restore calm by arresting the monster who was killing over and over again.

One detective knew that his understanding of the task force would not help him work with the public. He had relatives who had canceled a planned visit from their home in northern California. His wife occasionally came home in tears because friends seemed to consider his inability to solve the case instantly a personal affront. The city had had far worse criminals walking loose in the past but none had generated such a climate of fear and frustration.

The homicide detectives tried to be coldly analytical, dispassionate, despite the fear and anger they were experiencing. Most of them were embarrassed by their own emotions and would not admit their concerns about their loved ones. They liked to convey the impression that they were in control, slowly narrowing the grid until they could squeeze the Strangler into a trap. In reality, they were almost as close to panic as the public because they realized how helpless they seemed to be. The more dead ends they followed, the more corpses littered the landscape, the more the killers seemed impossible to capture. They knew they would get them eventually but at what price along the way?

The two little girls seemed to be the odd links in all this. Sonja was the daughter of Tony Johnson, an accountant who worked with a private Catholic school whose head was a friend of Terry Mangan. In fact, one of the nuns who taught at the school called Mangan in Bellingham, hoping he could help find the killer. It was an action taken in the desperation of grief. There was nothing the Bellingham chief could do from so far away, and, even in Los Angeles, he would have been at as much of a loss as the investigators.

The detectives realized that on the night of the murder that the girls did not look their ages. They were slightly wild, never doing anything bad but in a hurry to look older. The way they were dressed would have made them seem to be at least eighteen or nineteen in the artificial light of the shopping center.

Jane King was at the other extreme in age. She was the oldest victim, at twenty-eight, and again there was concern that this represented some new pattern. However, once again the pictures of the body and interviews with friends revealed that she looked much younger than her years when she was murdered.

The victims had been dumped in a random pattern. The Los Angeles Police Department's Hollywood Division handled the first, the Sheriff's Department handled the second, the next went to the Glendale Police, then the West Los Angeles Police Division, the Wilshire Division, the Northeast Division, and the last three cases went to the Rampart Division. Hollywood and Glendale appeared to be the most common areas. There was one on Garfield, another at Tamarind and Franklin, a third at Sunset and Poinsettia, a fourth at Sunset and Vista, and so on.

The locations could be narrowed considerably if only the apparent pickup points were considered, yet even this information provided limited value. The strangulations were fairly consistent and the police now felt that the semen stains indicated two men. But how old were the men? Were they tall or short? What did they use to lure the women without a struggle? The few answers actually led to more questions.

There had been a witness to Lauren Wagner's disappearance who provided unnerving details. Lauren was a quiet, serious, hardworking young woman whose life revolved primarily around school and her steady boyfriend. She had returned from visiting the boy around 10 P.M. and was seen talking with two men. The girl was so calm that the neighbor thought nothing of the incident. She was certain Lauren was in no danger and that she went willingly with the men. The witness had the impression that the men were probably police officers, and the reaction of the victim seemed to corroborate her statement.

Life in Los Angeles seemed to be an endless round of emotional extremes for Kelli Boyd. Every time she found happiness, something seemed to shatter her dreams. Ken was so close to being Mr. Right, yet his jealousy and financial irresponsibility caused her frequent anguish. Every pleasure seemed to have a price, a fact that became quite apparent to her when she bought two kittens.

Kelli was an animal lover. She liked the selfless love a pet shares with its owner, the joy of coming home to an animal which accepted you as a friend no matter what anyone else might have said or done that day. Since she and Ken were in the Tamarind Apartments, as permanently settled as they could foresee themselves being for the next several months, she suggested they get a pet. A kitten seemed ideal for her since it could be left alone all day and would have a litter box in which to relieve itself.

Ken was upset about the idea. He had an allergy to animal fur and the doctor had told him he should never own a cat or dog. At the same time, he realized how much a kitten meant to Kelli. He saw the animal as a way of providing her with companionship when she was home alone, so he decided to try. They could always give the kitten away if things became too rough. For the moment it seemed worth the risk, just to give Kelli that happiness.

For the next several days, Kelli studied the classified advertisements in the *Los Angeles Times* and *Los Angeles Herald Examiner.* She finally found someone offering kittens without charge, and they drove to Pasadena that weekend to examine the kitten.

The kittens, tiny brown shorthairs, were irresistible to Kelli. Ken had said that one kitten would be the limit; however, Kelli was like a small child pleading with her father. She told him how miserable the kittens would be if separated, what good company they would be for each other when the two of them were away from home. She showed such intense feelings that Ken had to agree to her request.

Kelli was delighted. She held the kittens in the car, letting them climb about her legs and shoulders. They stopped only long enough to buy cat litter, a box, food, and tiny flea collars.

In a few days, Ken was coughing and having trouble breathing. Kelli felt they should give away the kittens, but Ken decided to first get a checkup at the clinic.

Ken was depressed when he returned from the clinic. He said that he had been X-rayed and that there was a chance he did not have an allergic reaction. It was suspected that he had a "mass," or a tumor, and the doctors wanted to take a biopsy.

The terror made Kelli think only of the good the couple had shared and the horrible possibility that their joy might be over. She took the day off work when he went for his biopsy, wanting to go with him. He felt it would be best if he went alone, though, so she spent the day cleaning their apartment, buying flowers to make the home more colorful, and placing a card on the dinner table. She tried to let the work keep her mind off the illness. The biopsy would certainly show that the tumor was benign, having no trace of cancer.

Kelli thought the biopsy would be over quickly. Ken had said it was a quick in-and-out procedure. He had gone alone, assuring her that not only did he want to face the news by himself first, he also had been told by his doctor that he would have no problem driving back. Yet the hours passed slowly. By three in the afternoon she was quite frightened. Suppose they had to operate immediately? Suppose he had been given something that made him sleepy and he had had an accident. Suppose . . .

It was around eight in the evening when a depressed Ken Bianchi came home. He told Kelli that the biopsy had gone quickly but that he had then gone to Angelo's home to play cards. He said that the news was bad, that he had been unable to face Kelli with what had been found. The biopsy had shown he had a malignant tumor. There was a chance that Ken would die from cancer.

He spoke calmly, saying words like "chemotherapy" and "radiation therapy." He talked of his hair falling out and the types of treatments he might undergo. He explained that everything would be handled on an outpatient basis and he wanted to take the treatments alone. He would be able to drive or Kelli could drive him and wait in the car. He needed her support but that could come at home. She didn't need to be exposed to viewing the treatments as they were given.

Kelli had worked briefly as a secretary in a hospital while she lived in Bellingham, but she had almost no medical training. Ken had had extensive first aid and general medical training when he worked for the ambulance company in Rochester. She accepted his word about what would be happening and how much of an involvement would be necessary on her part.

That night the couple held each other, watching television, talking, trying to be as close as possible. Ken was calm, accepting. Kelli tried to hold back the tears but her emotions kept taking control and she would periodically break down. She wanted to be the strong one. She knew she would have to take care of Ken and the baby. But for the moment she needed whatever strength was in him. She held him close all through the night.

Ken began missing work after the therapy started. He told Kelli of nausea and frequently spent time at the apartment. He never missed enough work to get fired, though he convinced her that his employer should not know the truth. Cancer is not contagious, yet many people think it is. He feared being fired unfairly before he really became too sick to work. He stretched his sick leave to the limit, though, and Kelli worried about any cutoff of income which might occur as a result.

One day in mid-December when Ken was home from work, police detectives knocked at the door of the apartment. He and

Kelli were aware that yet another murder had taken place and he was not surprised to be talking with them. Kelli had spoken of her growing fear, especially with the baby inside of her. Ken had assured her that the pattern of the murders seemed to indicate that a pregnant woman would not be attacked. However, they did not really know and Ken made certain that Kelli always carried her Shriek Alarm.

This latest murder had possibly taken place at the Tamarind Apartments where Ken lived, and he was aware of that fact. As far as he and Kelli knew, he had not been around that night. Sound carried easily through the halls; most of the people in the building were aware of the sounds of a struggle. And Ken was the type to go out and get involved, to learn the cause of an unusual noise and come to the aid of someone who might be in trouble.

The press carried only the sketchiest details about this latest death, the strangulation murder of Kimberly Diane Martin. The police were withholding as much information as they could because they hoped that for once they were ahead of themselves.

The story the police pieced together was that the victim was a seventeen-year-old who earned her living as a prostitute. She was tough, experienced, and concerned with the potential dangers of the street. She knew she could work for a pimp who would do some screening of the johns and secure payment in advance. But the pimps could be as dangerous as the johns. She decided that as long as the streets were rough and the Hillside Strangler on the loose, she would begin utilizing an outcall service.

An outcall prostitution service often worked through a supposedly legitimate front such as a massage parlor or a nude-modeling studio. The massage parlor had the prostitutes giving genuine massages, though making certain they handled a man's private parts enough to sexually arouse him. Then they offered him relief for fees which rose according to the technique desired. A quick blow job cost very little. The price escalated with the degree of physical involvement required prior to orgasm; the terms were always settled in advance. The men could not leave without paying and the girls were protected.

Similarly, the modeling-agency girls posed for Polaroid pictures taken with agency-supplied cameras. Customers could have nude pictures taken or set down the camera and become more intimately involved with the "models," all for a price. Money bought whatever brought you pleasure.

Many of the modeling agencies and the massage parlors offered "home delivery." Sometimes the prostitutes would be sent from the agency building, other times they worked from home. Many carried the beeper paging devices used by doctors.

On December 11, 1977, Kimberly had taken a job with the Climax Nude Modeling Service, a company whose name made it very clear that photography was not the only service they provided. Two days later, all her fears concerning the dangers of the streets would become a reality.

The call came in at 8:30 P.M., according to the records the detectives obtained from the service. A man living in Hollywood said that his wife was out of town for the first time in two years. He thought that having a pretty blond model wearing black stockings and a dress would be just the entertainment he needed. He asked the price and found forty dollars for a "nude-modeling service" quite fair. A girl was promised in fifteen minutes.

The staff of the Climax did a good job of screening calls. They had learned to tell the serious customers from the frauds, the teenagers out for a lark, and the "sickies." They felt this call was legitimate, never realizing that it was being made from a pay telephone at an area library. They decided to send a girl over when, by chance, Kimberly checked in to see if she could go to work. The time was eight forty-five, and when she heard the statements the caller had made, she decided that it was legitimate. She would go to the address in the Tamarind Apartments where her modeling skills were in demand.

The detectives assumed that the murderers had a link with the Tamarind Apartments. Either one or both lived there now or in the past, or the person was friendly with someone in the apartment complex. It was possible for a stranger to the building to have used it since a check of the tenant list near the door would reveal vacant suites. The fact that the suite had been entered forcibly and the killers wore gloves also did not prove anything. A tenant using a vacant suite would have done the same.

Each male was questioned, the detectives trying to determine alibis for the night, reactions to the pressure of interrogation, and any other clues which might provide an answer. Most of the tenants had no verifiable alibi for the night. Several were extremely nervous because they had heard a commotion and done nothing. The detectives were obviously angered by this and that added to the nervous reaction.

The killers were waiting inside the vacant apartment when Kimberly arrived. The girl probably entered all the way before becoming suspicious. Then it was too late.

The detectives had studied what little evidence of violence they could find in the apartment and also talked with friends of Kimberly. It was assumed that she had fought savagely but eventually been overpowered. The men probably smashed her head against the wall in order to get her to quietly accompany them to a car. No one was certain how badly she was hurt in the Tamarind Apartments, but the autopsy report showed a skull fracture and blood dripping from her ear. Evidence indicated that the victim had been bound, gagged, and strangled. Yet this time everything could have been over if the men and women who lived in the Tamarind had done something about the suspicious noises they were hearing.

The detectives investigating the Tamarind Apartments incident hated everyone they were talking to that day; every man in that building was a potential killer. Yet they apparently hid their anger as they questioned Ken Bianchi, and the interrogation was easier than many of the others. Ken was not surprised when he answered the door of his apartment. After the first few tenants had been interviewed, word traveled fast concerning what was happening. He was intrigued by the idea of being interrogated because it would be a new experience and break the monotony of being at home, worrying about his illness.

He had not been there that night so he had not been a witness to anything. He was calm, understanding about the need to talk with everyone, and sympathetic about the hell the police were experiencing. He told them of his involvement in August with the ride-along program, which enabled civilians to go in the patrol cars and of his efforts to join the force. He was as sickened as they were by what was happening.

The detectives felt better about Bianchi than the others. He was not the type of person to stand by and do nothing when someone was in trouble. The interview had been yet another waste of time, though essential for proper police work. Every possibility had to be checked—eventually more than ten thousand leads would be followed.

Ken Bianchi was intrigued with the experience. He told Kelli what had happened and she found it humorous. Numerous other people they knew from the area had been questioned and Kelli jokingly asked if Ken really was the strangler. The question hurt him deeply, as it would other men in the city.

No one is born a police officer. An attempt is made to psychologically screen men who apply for work in the police department and this is effective in the majority of cases. However, in Los Angeles as in every other city, an occasional misfit succeeds in joining the force. The person might be a thief, a man or woman who seeks bribes, even a killer.

As the investigation into the Hillside Strangler case continued, it became obvious that there was a chance that a police officer had been involved. None of the victims seemed to have struggled when first picked up by the killers. They seem to have gone willingly with the assailants, at least at first. This was especially true of the two young girls who were apparently picked up at a bus stop near a shopping center. Had they struggled or screamed, it seemed likely that someone's attention would have been called to the incident. Since they probably would not have gone willingly with anyone other than someone known to them or someone they felt was a safe authority figure, the chance of the criminal being a police officer could not be overlooked.

The detectives were forced to begin doing internal investigations as quietly as possible. They started with beat officers who drove in areas where the crimes occurred. Logbooks were checked to ascertain the location of each man on the nights of the murders, whether or not his involvement with some other activity could be documented. When the officer was either in the area but not on specific call or at home with no alibi, further investigation, including surveillance, might follow. At least one officer was interviewed before being cleared. It was an essential, extremely unpleasant job.

Another problem the detectives faced was the effort of the press to solve the case. It was better to let a reporter think that incorrect information was actually factual than to give him evidence which might prevent the capture of the real killer.

Jim Mitchell, for example, was convinced that he had found the solution to the strangulation method. He later stated that what he withheld "for a year and a half was the specific details on how the women were strangled." He said, "The method of strangulation involved, apparently, a very thin wire. And from the marks which existed on the wrists and the ankles and around the neck, the operating assumption at least was that these women were being palm-tied, and their feet and wrists tied behind them with the same strand of wire drawn around their necks, so that left to their own devices, they would eventually strangle. And then they were being untied. Of course, assuming that they were being physically attacked at the time, they probably strangled that much faster."

The police talked with Mitchell about his information. "When they knew I knew it, they asked me to withhold it because, and they admitted it to me at the time, that it was the only poly-clue they had. When they say poly-clue, generally what they mean is a piece of information they want to withhold so they can weed out good and bad suspects." But Mitchell was wrong. The elaborate bondage/ strangulation ritual Mitchell developed as a theory had no relationship with the coroner's evidence. The actual marks did not indicate that such a ritual had taken place.

The task force kept studying, but it was no use. They needed that crime scene. Without it, they seemed to be working without any real hope.

The first signs of genuine panic appeared in the Hollywood area. By the first part of December, the publicity about the murders finally penetrated the numbed emotions of many of the street people. The prostitutes were aware of the "nicer" girls such as Kristina, but assumed that either someone made a mistake or that the other girls were also in "the life." Whatever the case, prostitutes began going out only with a friend, one woman making the deal with the john, the second woman taking down his license number, description of his car, and anything else that would identify him. They also began reporting every suspicious man on the streets.

Vice-squad detectives, not officially assigned to investigate the Hillside Strangler activity, became conduits for reports to the station. One detective was approached by a battered prostitute who had spent the night in the hospital. Her "date" had been a man who drove a rolling hotel room and she was convinced he was the killer. He had a van-type truck which he had customized for his special taste in sexual relations. The van was equipped, among other things, with a specially bolted bed that allowed for sex in his own unique manner. As soon as he drove to a deserted location, he and the prostitute stopped the van, went around the back, and got inside. He ordered her to take off her clothing, then put her hands behind her back.

So far, nothing was out of the ordinary. A number of johns liked to tie you up, then paddle your rear, the prostitute explained. The harder the spanking, the greater their arousal. It hurt a bit but that was why they were paid so much. It was no big deal to her, even when he tied her feet, then gagged her mouth more tightly than she felt was necessary. It was only when he used an additional rope to tie her securely to the bed that she began to worry.

"You whores are all alike," he allegedly told the prostitute. "Rotten bitches teasing a man, then throwing him out like a piece of shit. You need to be taught a lesson. You need an avenger to show you how bad you filthy bitches really are."

The man took out a straight razor. The prostitute was suddenly terrified. She knew she was about to die. She was going to be tortured, strangled, and tossed onto the hillside. Her face would be the one in the paper the next day. Her battered body would be stripped for autopsy like all the others. She had let herself be placed in a situation where she was helpless, and there was nothing she could do but pray the pain of death would be over quickly.

To the prostitute's later surprise, the cutting went rapidly. He sliced at her back, breaking the skin and drawing blood in a way that seemed to indicate he had done it before. The pain was that of a hundred tiny paper cuts—sharp, intense, yet in no way life-threatening.

Perhaps he was playing with her. Perhaps he would go deeper and deeper before he killed her. Perhaps . . .

Suddenly it was over. The razor was put away and he climbed on her back, entering her from behind. He climaxed, then freed her and paid her a substantial sum of money. After dressing he took her back to Hollywood and left her on the street.

The prostitute was hysterical. She remained convinced that she had had an encounter with the Hillside Strangler, yet had somehow been spared. Frantically she gave the detective the description and the detective passed on the report for further investigation.

"He wasn't the Strangler," said a more experienced vice-squad detective who recognized the situation when he heard the report. "The guy's a psycho, but he was well known in the area. Did it to one of the girls every few weeks and even had a couple of regulars who agreed to that insanity on a frequent basis because he paid so much. We checked his background and he just couldn't have done it. A real nut case, but he wasn't the nut we needed."

What the police did not realize was that the man who carved prostitutes, although he was the most bizarre individual who would be reported, was going to be the first of several thousand leads. Hysteria would soon grip the city and all the law-enforcement agencies could do was keep investigating until they got lucky. The question was, how many people would die before the leads resulted in an arrest?

Perhaps it can be said that in California, more than anywhere else in the country, death is viewed as an enemy to be fought with all the passion normally reserved for a nation at war. Even the potential for death, the natural aging process, is seen as a cataclysm.

Yet by the end of November 1977, the people who lived in Los Angeles, Glendale, and the other communities which comprise Los Angeles County, were being forced to face the specter of death daily.

Ken Bianchi and Kelli Boyd shared this awareness of their own mortality. Every day it seemed as though they were forced to face the fact that Kelli, as a woman, could be a target for unexpected violence. They thought that perhaps the killers would avoid their area, then Ken was shocked into realizing their vulnerability when he was questioned at the Tamarind Apartments. Kelli and the women with whom she worked never traveled alone or without their Shriek Alarms and, in a few cases, weapons such as carving knives or small-caliber automatics. Trying to relax in front of television meant seeing regular updates on the case during news reports.

In December Ken participated once again in the ride-along program with the Los Angeles Police, and talk of the Strangler dominated the conversations in the patrol cars.

Everyone seemed to be running scared. Kelli curtailed her evening activities as much as possible if she would have to go out alone.

Some of the people who worked with Ken and Kelli went further. A few of the women joined countless other Los Angeles females in studying self-defense. Special rape-prevention classes were being held at many local colleges, and the students, in their enthusiasm, often became unexpectedly violent. An instructor's nose was broken by one student who failed to refrain from delivering the full force of the blow she was learning. A man came doubled over to the emergency room when his girlfriend, practicing what she learned at the YWCA, kicked him in the groin with unusual gusto. He later told the nurse it was because he was breaking up with the girl at the time. The girlfriend told the nurse it was an accident, then giggled as the nurse listed the various injuries he had sustained.

Kelli was secure with Ken and their friends. Other women felt that every possible protective device should be obtained.

Weapons, both legal and otherwise, began appearing in pockets, purses, and even an occasional bra holster. Small handguns, such as the tiny .25-caliber automatic, disappeared from dealer shelves. Button and switchblade knives became part of the "uniform" worn when going to work or on a date.

Women purchased guard dogs, then became even more paranoid about attack when an unsympathetic landlord refused to let them keep them. One apartment renter announced to the police that her landlord was the Strangler because he wouldn't let her keep her new German shepherd. However, investigators found other reasons for the landlord's hostility. Dog feces and urine had stained the outside entrance, the hall, and the elevator. Air freshener, incense, and other products had been used in vain. The woman had the only dog in the building, making the identity of the offending animal and its owner evident to every resident.

Women tried to walk only in pairs when at all possible. Home burglar alarms were sold in growing numbers. Customers and waitresses of all-night diners were escorted to their cars, then watched until they drove safely down the street.

The newspaper reporters realized that they were involved with one of the biggest stories to hit the city in many years. None of them wanted to play detective, yet they all hoped they'd stumble on a clue that would enable them to break the case. Each reporter answering the telephone hoped that the caller would be the killer or an eyewitness to one of the crimes. Unfortunately, the supposed witnesses never proved very effective.

Even the Glendale Police Department went so far as to make one arrest based on erroneous eyewitness information during that period. The witnesses had worked with police on the preparation of a composite drawing of a man who had been seen in Lissa Kastin's car. The composite was run in the newspapers along with the description of his features. According to a Steve Comus story in the November 25, 1977, Los Angeles *Herald Examiner:*

"The man was described as Caucasian or Latin with olive complexion and acne on his face, about 27 or 28 years old, about 6-feet-2 or 6-feet-3 and weighing 150 to 160 pounds. The man also had a thick mustache and had a small black mark high on his left cheek which police think may be a mole."

For the next several days, reporters answered their telephones anxiously. They were hoping for a confessor, someone who would be so overwhelmed by the notoriety that he would feel compelled to turn himself in.

"I was living this television fantasy," admitted one columnist. "I'd known guys to get calls from criminals who were afraid of the police and wanted to turn themselves in to a reporter. I did some writing about the Strangler and figured the guy was a real psycho. I also thought I had a pretty good reputation for being accepting of people in some pretty weird circumstances. I got to admit, I got so caught up in my own fantasies that I even left numbers where I could be reached twenty-four hours a day. The only strange man who called the whole time was calling about a late payment on my car. I felt like kind of an ass."

An arrest did result from the drawing, but not as a result of anyone's contacting the papers. The man was Bennett Merett, a clothing-store clerk who lived in Hesperia: he was arrested with women's clothing in his car.

The reporters, though—disappointed that they had not been involved more directly with the arrest, still hoped with the rest of the public that the murderer had been caught. However, the police involved with the case kept cautioning that the man was not a prime suspect. He was arrested for questioning because of the circumstances of the possession of clothing and the witness reports. However, after a thorough background check and a police lineup, he was cleared. Television news ratings went up during the time he was held, and a few more newspapers than usual were sold, but the Hillside Stranglings remained a mystery.

Reporters were also not immune from the hysteria of the case. For example, there was the night that Jim Mitchell came home much earlier than anticipated. He was expected to be working until one or two in the morning and his wife was visiting a friend. She had hired a babysitter to look after their three children, but when Jim returned home around 10:30 P.M., he saw no reason to keep the sitter. He told his oldest child to watch the younger ones until he returned, then drove the sitter to her home five miles away.

No sooner were Mitchell and the sitter around the corner and out of sight than Jim's wife returned. The older child had fallen back to sleep, so there was no way for the woman to know what had happened. All she knew was that the sitter was gone, vanished.

Mitchell did not return home right away. After dropping off the sitter, he stopped by a late-night store to buy ice cream and other items. Meanwhile, his wife decided that the sitter had been carried off by the Hillside Strangler and, even worse, that her husband might be the guilty party. She knew how obsessed he had become with the case. She knew that he was regularly going to every crime scene each time a new body was discovered. She had never considered him violent and it would be totally out of character. Yet the Strangler was a crazy man and who knew?

Mitchell returned home and eased his wife's fears. She was angry with him for the scare but he did convince her of his innocence. Not much later, however, their marriage fell apart and the couple separated.

The Mitchell story is not unique. The long hours and intense fears caused the marriages of a number of police officers and media representatives to fall apart. Others stayed together only through counseling. The entire community was suffering from the tension of the unknown, of the monster who seemed to walk in their midst, unseen, unstoppable.

The detectives kept reading their reports. No one bothered counting overtime hours. They were constantly on the streets, knocking on doors, talking to people, exploring leads until they were ready to drop. Then they would take some coffee or a brief nap and relax by reading the new reports of Strangler suspects coming regularly through the task force office.

For example, one woman telephoned to say that her husband was the Strangler. She had been awakened at two in the morning with a handkerchief stuffed in her mouth and his hands on her shoulders, shaking her violently. The couple had been married only a few months and she was terrified that she had become involved with a killer. However, before anyone could handle the check of what the officers felt would prove to be a very weak lead, the woman called back again.

"It's all right. My husband's not the Strangler. He played a tape recording he made before he put the handkerchief in my mouth. I . . . I . . . I snore. I didn't know it and he said he'd put up with it for months. He said it's like being in the middle of a rock band's amplifier and—and—I think he's right. He wasn't trying to hurt me. He just couldn't stand it anymore. I've got an appointment with a nose doctor and . . . I—I'm sorry."

Another call was from a terrified prostitute. She had seen a man cruising the streets in Hollywood. He was just out of jail and looking for action. What terrified her was the fact that he had been jailed for picking up prostitutes, then beating them with a baseball bat. He never came near to killing any of them but she thought he had just gotten meaner. However, the Strangler did not beat the women, and this suspect was interrogated and released.

Perhaps the most unusual and persistent reports came from people who had suspicions about the police officers they had met. The stories were all similar and all frightening for a dedicated officer. One woman said:

"I was driving along Wilshire when I saw flashing lights in my mirror. It looked fairly normal, like any other cop car, and I didn't think I had done anything wrong. I pulled right to let him go by but the guy just pulled alongside me. He was wearing a uniform and signaled me to stop.

"I had sort of an uneasy feeling. I don't know. A friend of mine is psychic and she's always getting these premonitions about things. Usually she's wrong but this time I think I knew what she meant. It was like everything was okay and it wasn't. He had the badge, the gun, the blue uniform. I don't know. Maybe he didn't seem professional enough.

"The guy got out of his car holding a flashlight and a clipboard. He started chewing me out about my license. It's a new car and my tags were kind of hidden and all. But he made a big deal of it. Like I was the criminal of the year or something. Real nut case. Started screaming about how he could throw me in jail for improper driving. He could put me away for six months. A ticket's a courtesy. He could haul me into jail, have me fingerprinted, make me post bail. I mean, Jesus, a lousy traffic offense and I think I was in the right anyway. Real screwball, but I figured—L.A. cops? Everybody knows the town's nuts. Why not the cops?

"Then I got to thinking. The papers said the Strangler didn't seem to have met any resistance. Everybody went along with the guy so far as they knew. I mean, this guy didn't touch me or anything, but, Jesus, I mean, maybe I just got lucky."

The stories varied in the definition of the offense for which the women were "charged" and the lecture they received. Careful questioning revealed that the police uniforms were often odd or that the car lights and some of the other equipment were a little different from what the force actually used. The men reported were of various heights and builds. One man was practically a midget and another was so fat he would never have been allowed on the force.

The detectives and other officers from all departments were told to be on the alert for regular cruisers, checking them out as they had the time. Something was happening in the city, something that should not have been going on, and nobody was certain quite what it was or what it meant. Was the Strangler a police officer or was it something else?

The answers came slowly and they shocked the department. There were men, no one knew how many, who would buy state Highway Patrol cars at auctions. These were black-and-white cars similar to standard LAPD cruisers. They had been stripped of all equipment and the hard driving, rough braking, and extreme handling had left the vehicles no longer practical for continued patrol. However, they still had value and were therefore sold "as is" at auction.

Some of the buyers were teenagers who wanted an inexpensive, high-performance car. Endless tinkering with the well-worn engines often restored them to the speed and performance level that once made them so desirable for the police.

Other buyers, a minority, yet still a large number, were buffs. Some were frustrated would-be police officers—men who were too short, too fat, lacking in intelligence, or otherwise unable to join the department. Others were men who had never applied but who wanted to be seen as virile authority figures. Still others fantasized themselves as secret avengers, patrolling dangerous city streets, striking terror in the hearts of evildoers, saving damsels in distress.

The would-be police officers obtained extra equipment any way they could. Police radios were made by adapting regular scanners to police frequencies or even by stealing walkie-talkies. Lights were makeshift or purchased as scrap when a genuine cruiser had to be destroyed after a particularly bad accident. Uniforms were obtained from costume shops, and guns could be purchased both legitimately and from criminals who sold such items in the less savory night spots around the city.

Some of the fake cops even went so far as to have forms printed, and this was how a number of them were discovered. The forms could be traced and the men who ordered them usually left a name and a telephone number. Others were arrested at the scene by legitimate police. In a few instances, the fake officers were so deluded that they truly believed they worked for the Los Angeles Police Department and were shocked when they were handcuffed and taken to jail. In all, several dozen were discovered, according to legitimate officers.

Word of the fake police reached the public and added to the panic. In desperation, the Los Angeles Police announced that anyone stopped by a police officer had the option to keep moving. Instead of stopping when he or she saw the flashing red light, the person could slowly proceed to a place of reasonable safety: a well-lighted, well-traveled street, the person's home, or a police station. The driver was cautioned to slow down and make it obvious that he or she would stop eventually. The person just did not have to stop immediately in a dark, secluded, unsafe section.

The detectives realized that no one could be immune from suspicion. One call that was received at the end of December involved a famous Hollywood producer. This man enjoyed the sexual favors of teenagers barely old enough for him to avoid prosecution for statutory rape. He liked to slowly cruise the streets, staring at girls, deciding which ones to approach. He tried to have a steady diet of new young women and repeated his ritual frequently when he wasn't working on a motion picture. He found jobs for many of the girls, paid some of them money, and took special pleasure in those who would do it just to say they had had sex with someone famous.

One day the producer borrowed a friend's car, not knowing that his friend had been convicted of rape and happened to carry phony police identification in the glove compartment. The producer was spotted by someone who did not know him, and his behavior behind the wheel, watching girls, was obviously out of the ordinary. When the producer picked up a young girl the observer called the police, providing the license number and a description of the car.

A computer check of the license showed that it was registered in the name of a man with a felony record for rape. Instantly the police were certain they had their Strangler. Patrolmen in the area where the car had been sighted were alerted and eventually converged on the producer and the extremely frightened teenager in his car.

Once again the police were frustrated by the odd habits of the citizens of the Hollywood area. The girl knew what she was doing and the producer had alibis for the times of the murders.

A man on the fringes of the movie business was checked after being turned in by a "starlet" who had never had a role. He had spent ten years in Hollywood, acting in a few commercials, appearing in minor speaking parts in movies and on television. He supported himself doing restaurant work, selling aspirin tablets to runaways who thought they were buying amphetamines from a big-time dealer. He also took money from unsuspecting new actresses who thought he could introduce them to producers. He was a hustler whose face was familiar on television even though he never worked more than a few weeks a year in the motion-picture industry.

The starlet complained that the man invited her to his apartment to audition for a movie. He told her that he was doing preliminary screen-testing for Cecil B. De Mille, a name familiar enough to the girl that she was impressed. Unfortunately, she did not know that De Mille was dead and that legitimate auditions aren't conducted that way.

"He had these mirrors and lights and things, and this camera on a tripod," the girl complained. "He said the movie was going to be an upbeat, adult version of *Gone with the Wind*, only it would have the Russians invading Atlanta. I was going to be Scarlett O'Hara and I would be auditioning the part where I was ravaged by the Russian general. He had what looked like a script and everything, but he said I should just improvise with him.

"Then he had me on this bed and he was dressed in leather and wearing this army hat. He started hitting me with a whip while the camera was on. I was supposed to be aroused by the agony but the bastard really hurt. When I started to complain, he handcuffed me to the bed, held his hand over my mouth, and told me to shut up, that he was the Hillside Strangler.

"I nearly freaked out. I tried to scream and hit at him but he was too strong. Finally he said he just said it so I would show a good fear reaction for the movie producer.

"I thought it was pretty dumb of him to think I would believe his story. I figured he really was the Hillside Strangler and I was lucky to get away with my life. I figured this time he lost his nerve and I busted ass getting out of there.

"I told my roommate about him and she told me to turn him in. She figured maybe this guy didn't know De Mille and he was using the producer's name to pick up girls. That's when I figured he was telling the truth about being the Hillside Strangler and I turned him in."

Lieutenant Dan Cook of the Los Angeles Police Department's press-relations office appeared on television to discuss the murders and what was being done to stop them. Pictures of some of the crime scenes were also shown. Strangler hot line numbers were provided, and several callers responded.

The television broadcast was seen by a woman in Long Beach who described the "killer" down to his white hair. She was uncertain about his height but the facial features were flawless. However, when the officers studied the resulting composite sketch, their earlier hope turned to disbelief and disgust. The woman had provided a perfect likeness of Lieutenant Cook.

The panic was building and the business community began to suffer as well. Business fell off at the Eagle Rock Shopping Center when the press reported that it had been the last place the two children had been seen before their murder. People were afraid to go there after dark and some wondered if a salesman in one of the stores was actually a criminal. Though the pickup spot was probably random, the public wanted the killer to work from a particular location, never venturing from that spot, waiting silently, like a cat stalking a bird, for the moment when the victim would approach.

A monster killer working from one location could be avoided. He could be spotted from afar and you could turn and run away. The idea that this murderer might be just a man, normal flesh and blood, traveling the streets and striking without warning, was terrifying. A larger-than-life killer could be handled. Not knowing was the most horrifying feeling of all. The idea that anyone's father, anyone's son, anyone's lover, might be the Hillside Strangler filled the entire county with dread.

The police were becoming desperate. They had no crime scene, no serious suspects. The task-force concept enabled them to see more people, ask more questions, obtain more information. It would not improve the quality of that information, however. They interviewed everyone who lived in the apartments where the victims had lived. They interviewed everyone who had worked with the women, gone out with the women. They began finding that they could prove that Tom knew three of the victims and worked with a fourth. Jim lived near two of them and hung around the same club as a third. Larry had an acquaintance with two and probably was aware of the other two just by virtue of where he traveled every day. Yet no one could be placed with enough of the girls to justify an arrest. There were too many good suspects and not enough conclusive information to do anything about any of them.

Finally the police became frustrated. When they couldn't find a suspect to arrest, they played up the arrest of the occasional "confessor," the man who either had something to gain or was mentally disturbed enough to want to achieve glamour through going to jail. Whenever a confessor could provide enough information for the newspapers to consider him a serious suspect, the story would be published. For a few days, the citizens of Los Angeles breathed easier. But it was all a ruse, as the growing number of corpses quickly proved.

CHAPTER 5

Typical of the newspaper action during the height of the panic was a story which appeared in the Los Angeles *Herald Examiner* dated December 16, 1977, two months after the first strangling. It stated: "Why can't the Los Angeles Police Department, which is considered one of the best in the nation, solve the Hillside Strangler murder case?

"Bolstered by a 58-member task force of crack investigators and experts in solving strangulation cases working around the clock under conditions of strict, closed-door secrecy, the department still is unable to come up with the break it needs to solve the case.

"Can one killer pose such a problem for the same police force that cracked cases like the Manson murders, the Alphabet Bomber, the Westside Rapist and the Skid Row Slasher—each of which was solved in just two months?"

The article continued with quotes from women and city officials critical of the police and/or expressing fear for their safety. Other stories spoke of the police frustration and the efforts to beef up the task force. But always the implication was that somehow the case should have been solved. Somehow the leads the police were being given by the public should miraculously lead to an arrest, even though those leads were wrong, incomplete or insufficient. The story was a good copy, a way to get the public tuned to the evening news, and it was played up as much as possible.

Then, early in February, a letter arrived at the mayor's office. It read, in part: "Dear Mr. Mayor—PLEASE!!

"Lisson to me. I am very sick but I do not want to go back to that place I hate that place. My mother told me to kill those bad and evil ladys its not my fault. My mother makes my head hurt that why I kill her but I can't get her out of my head she keeps comin' back I hate her."

The letter had actually been sent several days earlier. It was six pages long and the mayor's office staff had accidentally delayed reading it. However, when it was released to the press by the police, the letter made headlines.

The task-force detectives were annoyed by the release of the letter. They had seen it when it first came in, discussed it among themselves, and applied the information known from previous confessions involving other crimes.

Most psychopaths followed a pattern. Their actions may result from an irrational way of viewing the world, but there is usually a consistency to the acts they commit. A confessor always talks about the crimes, often justifying them in rather demented ways. This particular letter, however, provided no new information. The writer did not discuss the murders in a way that would indicate he had even as much familiarity with them as someone who read the newspapers, listened to the radio, or watched the news on television. The detectives knew there was no way the writer could be the killer and they were angry that the mayor's office and the press-relations section of the Police Department had decided to release the contents.

The detectives were also concerned about learning the letter writer's identity. Was this man a crazy confessor or was he responsible for other crimes? The Hillside Strangler cases were not the only unsolved murders in the Los Angeles County area. If a girl was strangled and her killer not known, her name was likely to be added to the list by the papers.

One such case had occurred back in September, and some of the reporters were trying to link her with the Strangler. The victim had been Laura Collins, a twenty-six-year-old black woman who was last seen on Sunday, September 4, in the area of the Ventura Freeway and Lankershim. She was found five days later by Forest Lawn Drive and the Ventura Freeway. She had been strangled but was not nude. This was the same area where Yolanda Washington was discovered and the newspapers eventually linked the cases. Later the police press information kits carried her name with the other cases, primarily because the killer was not known. However, there was no linkage discovered as the cases progressed and it is now felt that Yolanda Washington, who disappeared on October 17, was the first Strangler victim.

The hostility between the detectives and the press would have grown had the detectives known that some reporters had met the letter writer at the scene of some of the stranglings. The man was a former mental patient in his late twenties or early thirties who had been released just a few weeks earlier. Deeply troubled and hating himself, he had walked up to almost anyone who would listen, talking about himself and how he could write to the mayor. He had been interviewed in depth several times, then checked out by a few of the members of the press.

The facts were that the former mental patient probably was a murderer. He had apparently killed his mother, a woman suffering from asthma and emphysema. She was able to breathe with difficulty but without assistance during the day. At night she had to use an oxygen tank, a mask clamped over her mouth while she slept.

One night, when the man was a boy of around ten or eleven, he allegedly removed the tubing and stopped the flow of oxygen. The next morning the woman was dead, though whether or not this was just the result of the tubing being removed or some other cause is unknown. The child was not charged with a crime but his guilt feelings resulted in a complete mental breakdown, and he was institutionalized for many years.

The former mental patient apparently saw the hospital as a prison and wanted to be returned as a fitting punishment for his actions. He was not considered dangerous to anyone else, though there was a possibility that his unresolved feelings of guilt could lead him to become suicidal. Yet none of the reporters who heard the story made any effort to get him help or to report the situation to the police. The newspaper stories published at this time also do not mention the identity of the man. The idea that he could actually be the Hillside Strangler was allowed to continue, further terrifying the public.

The situation was compounded when Police Department officials announced the arrest of a suspect, actor Ned York. As one Los Angeles Sheriff's Office homicide detective later commented, "Ned York was a tragic case. We never thought he had anything to do with the case from the moment he came in. We figured the guy for a psycho and wanted to ignore the thing. But the LAPD felt that since York confessed, they should make a big deal about his arrest, and take some of the heat off. It was a dumb move and the guy was just shown to be sick like we knew all along."

York, a thirty-seven-year-old actor, had only one link with the murders: one of his friends knew Kristina Weckler. There were no other connections.

The actor had had a series of emotional traumas in recent months. He had worked both as a criminal and as a police officer in the television show *Starsky and Hutch*. He was also involved with an evangelical Baptist group, planning to appear in productions the group was performing. His wife had recently left him and he was suffering from complete physical and emotional exhaustion.

No one ever learned why Ned York felt that the way to obtain emotional help was through confessing to the Hillside Strangler murders. He was a sick man at a low point in his life. Normally such an action would have gone unreported and York could have had the help he needed in private. Instead, his arrest was given such attention by the police that headlines were achieved around the country. Even the tabloid *National Enquirer* carried the story. His career was severely and needlessly damaged by the hysteria of the city.

Ken Bianchi was scared during the Christmas and New Year holidays. He had come to Los Angeles to find peace, happiness, and a new beginning. He found Kelli Boyd, a woman he truly loved, a good job, and the chance for a family. But now everything was going wrong. He had cancer, and Kelli, faced with the double stress of the pregnancy and his condition, was constantly tense and irritable.

Part of it was the fighting over money, which had gotten worse since he began missing work. Kelli was concerned about saving money for the baby they were expecting. She was upset when he spent so much time at home, missing work. Yet they always had the money they needed for whatever they wanted. They lived from paycheck to paycheck, but they never were really in debt. Ken knew he had not always been responsible about money in the past, but he was working to find ways to make more than before.

One of his jobs involved taking advantage of the way people had always come to him. He was the type of man to whom people readily turned for advice about their problems. He was a good listener and apparently had a mature overview of what was wrong and how they could correct it. Maybe he didn't do the best job with his relationship with Kelli, but he certainly could help others.

Ken decided that instead of giving advice for free, he would open a counseling service. He wouldn't charge much, especially not after having done the same work without charge for friends. He would request a few dollars to answer questions as an alternative to high-priced doctors. He shared his office with legitimate doctors in a building on Lankershim. However, despite good intentions and a location that could have resulted in referrals, no one came to him. He even sent out advertising flyers but the effort was just a waste of printing costs.

Ken also did occasional work for his cousin Angelo, odd jobs such as delivering a car, but he did not spend a great deal of time at Angelo's anymore. He had mixed feelings about Angelo and he knew that Kelli didn't like him.

At one point the arguments about money became physical. Ken was angry, shaking his finger at Kelli, shouting and seeming to try to overwhelm her with the intensity of what he was saying. She was stymied by his unwillingness to let her talk and angry that he would argue when she was feeling badly from the pregnancy. In frustration, she began striking him.

Ken, shocked by the physical attack, unthinkingly defended himself by hitting her. He had meant the blow to be a light one but the adrenaline of the anger caused him to knock her against the wall. She fell to the floor, amazed, yet embarrassed by the knowledge that she had started the fight by hitting him first.

He rushed to her side, the anguish obvious in his face. He was horrified that he had lost control of himself in that way. He wept, fearful that he might have hurt her or the baby inside. He helped her to her feet and was relieved that the situation had not been any worse than it was.

Kelli was overwrought during this period, not knowing where to go or what to do. She was angry with Ken for starting the counseling service. She had seen the diplomas he displayed, diplomas in psychology apparently earned before they met. Yet a diploma did not make a good psychologist and she thought Ken was too immature about himself to truly be able to advise anyone else. She saw the work as fraudulent since she did not feel he could be effective as a counselor no matter what degrees the diploma said he had.

The cancer condition kept bothering her, too. Something about the illness, the treatment, and the way Ken was acting didn't make sense. He was irate when she suggested talking with the doctor, yet he was able to bring home receipts that seemed valid. Kelli had no idea what the receipts should say, nor what information was on them since the hospital used codes and medical terms she did not know. She finally decided that she must be reacting to the emotional stress of the pregnancy. She didn't know how cancer should progress or what the treatments should be doing to Ken. She realized she was being selfish, that she should be thankful he was in such good shape at the moment.

The worst of all the problems was the feeling of being trapped. Kelli knew she would be loyal to Ken if he was sick. She would care for him to the end. She would not turn away from him even though she increasingly found herself taking a day or two to stay with friends or relatives in order to avoid the arguments. They were both on edge and the emotional problems from the pregnancy didn't help.

A lot of the stress was the Hillside Strangler and the entire Los Angeles scene. Everybody was tense. Their friends were always talking about this wild maniac who was walking the streets. Ken tried to forget about the psychopath. He knew that Kelli was vulnerable, like the other women in the area, and he wanted her protected as much as possible. It was just that when they were all together with friends and could have relaxed a bit, the Strangler remained the topic of conversation.

Maybe it would have been different if Ken and Kelli had been raised in New York or some other city, but both of them were from relatively small towns where crimes of violence were not common. They were scared of what was happening and never could fully experience peace. Kelli was right. Perhaps they should move away.

There were numerous separations during this period. Kelli would move out and stay with her brother. Then Ken would follow, covering her car with flowers, leaving her love notes and poetry, wooing her back. One or the other seemed to be constantly changing address as they argued and went back together. Kelli lived on East Palmer and Adelante. There was also an apartment on Verdugo, and Ken later took a suite on Corona. It was as though they were doomed to drift from place to place; being together was always better than being separated, yet there were so many problems to work out, so many arguments.

At the end of January 1978, Kelli quit her job because the baby was due in a few weeks. She and Ken had studied the Lamaze method of natural birth and were planning to work together during the delivery. As her time approached, the tension between the two of them increased. They were living apart and Ken was frightened that he would not be at hand when the baby was born.

Despite their closeness, Kelli remained angry with the way Ken failed to use the best judgment when it came to his planning. During Christmas, for example, she had wanted presents only for the baby. There were so many things they would need and Ken spent his money on presents Kelli felt were needless. He bought her a yogurt maker and an electric shaver, for example, which she hated; she traded it in for baby clothing and blankets.

Despite the anger, they felt a deepening love for each other as the birth approached. The morning sickness, the nausea, the restlessness at night—none of it mattered now. They had made a child, a tangible result of their relationship. A healthy child, a happy child, hopefully part of a much larger family to come, was what really mattered to them both.

Toward the end of February Ken and Kelli's son, Sean, was born. That last week had been hectic for both of them. Kelli had been having false labor pains for a week. She was in pain, frustrated by the illusion of giving birth, which was being shattered repeatedly as each day passed without the birth. She was also separated from Ken during this time and desperately wanted his comforting, even though she would not make the first move to tell him so.

Ken longed to be with Kelli, and he still feared that he would be rejected at the last moment. However, at the same time he knew that the Lamaze training would enable him to be with her during delivery, to help emotionally with the birth. Even with the tension of the past few weeks, life would be beautiful again, the frustrations and anxieties overshadowed by the joy of sharing the birth.

Once again Ken was rejected, though this time it was not by Kelli. An unforeseen complication of birthing arose. Kelli had a spinal block; Sean was stuck in the birth canal. The hospital staff had to make such an effort to save the life of mother and son that Ken had to be excluded from the delivery. He understood, but still it was emotionally difficult for him.

There was a story in the paper about another Hillside Strangling during this tense period. On February 17 a woman named Cindy Lee Hudspeth was found strangled and nude in the trunk of her car. She had last been seen on East Garfield in Glendale, near where Ken and Kelli used to go when they would visit his cousin. The victim might have been Kelli, considering the location, and Ken did not mention the crime to her. Now was a time for joy, not anxiety.

Ken was allowed into the recovery room to talk with Kelli, then he went out and began calling both families, sharing the wonderment of being a parent for the first time. He returned the next day with a soft orange-and-yellow elephant wrapped with a big orange ribbon. Probably the baby thought nothing of the gift, but Kelli realized how loving, gentle, and caring Ken could be.

Somehow she knew they would have to try living together again. They shared too great a closeness to let past problems spoil their future together.

There were complications for baby Sean at first. A mild case of jaundice necessitated that he remain in the hospital for observation. Kelli came several times a day, breastfeeding the baby so that he would have the best chance of growing up healthy. Her infant son looked exactly like baby pictures of Ken that his mother had sent. She was determined to help Sean grow up to be as wonderful, as tall, strong, and handsome as his father.

While Ken Bianchi and much of the rest of Los Angeles were aware of the murder of Cindy Hudspeth, neither he nor anyone else realized that the Hillside Stranglings were now over. One dozen young women lay dead and area citizens continued to live in constant fear of the man who would make the number thirteen. The public clamored for an arrest and the police were more than willing to oblige when possible.

The story of the Hillside Strangler became important news throughout the world. Reporters from Australia, England, France, Italy, Germany, Japan, and countless other countries contacted the police departments and citizens involved with the case. Papers in every city of the nation carried wire-service stories or first-hand reports of what was happening. Thus it was not surprising that the first break in the case, or so it was thought at the time, came not from California but from Massachusetts.

George Shamshak, a twenty-seven-year-old inmate in a Massachusetts penitentiary, had not been having an easy time of survival. He was hated by a number of his fellow prisoners for reasons which have only been partially discovered. He claimed that he had stopped the rape of an inmate by three other prisoners. If this was true, the fact that he spoke against them would be reason for threats against his life. And rumor in the penitentiary was that Shamshak regularly "ratted" to the guards, an action which frequently marked a man for death. Whatever the case, he felt that the healthiest way to survive was to get out of the prison as quickly as possible.

On October 24,1977, Shamshak escaped from the minimum security prison in Leominster, Massachusetts. Shamshak enjoyed 107 days of freedom before being recaptured in Cambridge, Massachusetts, in February. At that time he began talking about his involvement with California's Hillside Strangling case, agreeing to make a deal. It was a way of buying time rather than being returned to the prison from which he escaped. And Shamshak seemed to know enough details to warrant bringing him to Los Angeles for further questioning.

"We never took him seriously as a suspect in the Hillside Stranglings," said one Los Angeles Sheriff's Homicide detective. "The cases we could conclusively link had to have been done by the same two people. We knew Shamshak was in prison into October and we were finding bodies before that. There was a chance he had killed somebody down here after his escape, but it wasn't one of the girls in the Hillside Strangling case."

The press headlined the Shamshak story, though this time it wasn't because of anything done by the police or reporters. Shamshak himself knew how to generate publicity and he did it quite effectively. He telephoned the Los Angeles *Herald Examiner,* offering to provide the paper with the exclusive sight to tape recordings of at least one of the killings. The cost for this privilege would be $10,000, a discount price compared with the up to $50,000 he had already been offered by other media. The fact that he claimed to have been offered more money but wanted the paper to have the rights to the material made little sense. However, even if he was lying about the money he had been offered, there was a chance he actually did have the tapes he claimed.

Just prior to his telephone call. Shamshak said that he had worked with an accomplice in the Hillside Strangler killings. The accomplice was a Beverly Hills handyman named Peter Mark Jones. Jones had been arrested by police at the end of March and released April 3 after four days of questioning. There was no doubt in the minds of the police that Jones, who had known Shamshak in Massachusetts, was being used as a pawn. Jones was apparently the only Los Angeles area man Shamshak knew well and he implicated Jones only when Shamshak realized that evidence indicated two people had done the killings.

Shamshak said that the murders were committed in a van. He claimed that he had been blackmailed ("a willing dupe—a pawn—somebody held something over my head," he told the *Herald Examiner)* into helping. He said that he had been tape-recording music and that the tape happened to also record the killing of one of the victims. He implicated himself in three murders, saying that one of the three victims had helped kill the other two girls before she also met her death.

The more Shamshak talked, the more anyone who understood the circumstances of the killings would have been skeptical. He credited Jones and other unnamed individuals with the murders when the consistency of the methods made it obvious that no more than two killers acted in every case.

The police interviews with Shamshak proved meaningless. He could identify only two victims and they were the ones whose pictures had prominently appeared in newspapers to which the convict had had access. When Shamshak told how Jones had killed the victims, he said that one victim was strangled but the other two died of stab wounds, in one case, and a blow to the head in the other. The information did not match the known evidence.

The sad part of the case was the implication of Peter Jones. Those who knew Jones where he worked at the Beverly Hills Clinic Building on South Lasky Drive felt he was a gentle, hard-working man. He was a loner, but even that fact did not make clearing his name very difficult. He was arrested only to ensure that he could be investigated without fear that he might run. It was a precautionary move which was normal procedure, not a means of harassment.

Reporters in the Los Angeles area were unwilling to dismiss Shamshak so readily. One radio reporter became convinced that there must have been some factual basis for Shamshak's confession. He attempted to link the Massachusetts convict with another unsolved murder in which the victim was found with her head bashed in. She was not part of the Hillside Strangler series. He was convinced that Shamshak had been the killer, yet a substantial investigation by homicide detectives indicated that Shamshak could not have committed that murder, either.

In the end, Shamshak earned a chance to stay away from Massachusetts for a while. Peter Jones, the innocent man he had implicated, felt as though his life had been ruined. The trauma of the situation was not lessened by the fact that the police convinced themselves that he had been the innocent victim of a liar. He felt that he could no longer stay in Los Angeles and quietly left the city. He had become yet another victim of the Hillside Strangler case.

Meanwhile, task-force detectives were still investigating the possibility that a law-enforcement officer could be the Strangler. The investigation of police officers was not a casual matter. The investigators looked into only the logical possibilities. Was a man known to be too friendly with women while on duty, or did he perhaps have complaints in his file from women who said he touched them or made passes at them? Was a man regularly on patrol in the areas where the women were killed? Vice-squad detectives and uniformed officers working the Hollywood area knew some of the girls.

Security guards had already been checked. For example, a man named Fat Mike was a likely suspect because he ran a crash pad where young teens and prostitutes often stayed the night. He had been involved with three of the women and looked like a good suspect until he was cleared of the other crimes. The same situation existed with a number of police officers who had to be checked.

Most police officers could be eliminated through a quick examination of the patrol log. Each time a man responded to a call, the log showed the location of the call, the emergency that had arisen, and how long the officer was involved. Whenever the calls placed the officer so far from the murder scene that involvement in the stranglings was impossible, the suspect was dismissed from concern.

A few officers could not account for their time. They could be conclusively linked with the time and area where some of the girls were killed. However, they were off duty the other nights and their whereabouts could not be checked. Such individuals had to be questioned more closely, along with their neighbors, friends, and families. Few officers were confronted, but such an action was a great source of embarrassment for everyone involved. Fortunately the majority of patrolmen interviewed understood the frustrations of the task force and the need to be thorough. Only a handful were irate at what they felt was the preposterousness of the action.

Newspaper, radio, and television reporters were checked. Photographs of crowds gathered at the crime scene were studied on the off chance that the murderer took enough pride in his work to return to watch. Yet nothing checked out. Day after day the leads poured in: "My uncle did it." "My husband's been acting strangely." "The guy who runs the convenience store grabbed my ass in check-out so I know . . ." "He got my dress off at the drive-in but when I wouldn't allow him to take off any thing else, he went all to pieces. That kind of guy must be . . ." "Tommy . . ." "Frank . . ." "Eustice . . ." "Mario . . . "Jose . . ." All the leads were inconclusive at best.

There were good suspects and there were better suspects, yet never were there grounds for arrest.

By March 1978, Kelli Boyd and Ken Bianchi had stopped worrying about the Hillside Strangler, the Hollywood street scene, or anything else relating to Southern California. Their relationship was falling apart. They loved each other. They loved the baby. Yet nothing was going as it should. Ken had cancer, according to the medical reports he mentioned to Kelli. He was going for chemotherapy treatments during which Kelli would sit in the car while Ken entered the hospital. He said the treatments were too horrible for her to watch and he didn't want her upsetting herself by talking with the doctor. She had enough concern with the baby. Kelli disagreed but wasn't about to further strain their relationship by arguing.

Ken was irresponsible about work and about money. He would goof off, going over to play cards with Angelo after calling in sick. He owned a used Cadillac, then couldn't make the payments. She had hoped that the baby would cause him to have a sense of purpose, to encourage him to change his ways, but it didn't.

Perhaps Los Angeles was the problem. Everything was a hustle. People had no depth, no values, no integrity. Ken did. He was a very moral man, yet he was young and easily influenced by others. He desperately wanted approval, and apparently he didn't get it from just doing his job and following the work ethic. Whatever the case, Kelli realized that they were finished in that city.

The answer for Kelli was the logical one for her needs. She was going home to Bellingham. She loved the land up there. She delighted in the water, the birds, the peaceful changing of seasons. Money would be tight and life might be hard, yet there was an acceptance of people for themselves, not some artificial, arbitrary value. People pulled together; no one was concerned about the size of your car, the quality of your home life, or anything other than the fundamental goodness of your heart. She had been deeply hurt after her failed marriage, but that no longer mattered. She would find someone else if that was necessary. She would make new friends and solidify old relationships. Her baby would know a good life with loving grandparents. It was the right place for her.

The decision to move was devastating for Ken. Once again his loved ones were abandoning him. First he was rejected by his real mother, a teenager who never wanted to be pregnant by a man who didn't want children. Then his adoptive father, whom he adored, died. The death, to a boy of thirteen, was very much an abandonment. He could understand what had happened, yet he had memories of going to the attic for days after the funeral, weeping and talking to the man who was no longer there to answer back. Finally there was the failed marriage and a wife who had cheated on him.

Now Kelli and their baby were leaving him. He was being rejected, thrown away. His world was again being shattered. He had always tried to love and earn love. He sent Kelli poetry and flowers. He adored their son, Sean. He tried . . . He tried . . . He tried. . .

But there was no turning back for Kelli. She wanted either to have a true family or to be on her own. She needed Ken to help her establish a plan for working together, budgeting their money, and building a future. She wanted someone who gained his greatest joy from sharing with her, not running off to play cards with his cousin all the time. She felt Ken should be responsible at work, especially now that he had a son. Yet he continued to spend money foolishly, to be less than honest about where he spent his time, and generally to act in ways she could not accept from a husband.

Kelli's father and stepmother had a large home in Bellingham with plenty of room to house Kelli and Sean for a few days. Her father was a city employee and made enough money to cover the expense of the extra mouths. Kelli would get on welfare, then move out and find a job so she and Sean could become self-supporting with a small place of their own. Life would be difficult but she would be out of the madness.

In March, three and a half weeks after Sean's birth, Kelli and her sister loaded Kelli's old car and left California. The women and Sean traveled north, stopping just one night in a motel to save money.

They arrived the day before Easter. She changed her plans for the night, spending the time with her mother and stepfather. Then she went to her father's home just as the family was leaving for Easter dinner. The house was all set for the two of them, properly baby-proofed and warm. At last she was home.

Ken Bianchi hated Los Angeles the minute Kelli and the baby were no longer there. He desperately wanted to follow, but Bellingham was another unknown for him. If Kelli rejected him when he arrived, he would know no one. He would be even more alone than in Los Angeles.

He began telephoning and writing her, begging her to take him back. He wanted a new chance, a new beginning on her terms, in her hometown. He promised never to lie about his activities, to avoid such scams as the psychological counseling service for which he was far from qualified. He said he would take a job and work hard at it. He would be the man she knew he could be if she would just give him the chance.

Finally Kelli agreed. Ken would leave California and drive north to be reunited with the woman he loved. It was May and he drove straight through, stopping only for gas, grabbing food from vending machines while his tank was being refueled. He arrived on May 21, 1978, the day before his birthday.

The reunion was warm and happy. Kelli had never wanted her relationship with Ken to end. She loved the man and delighted in the way he handled Sean. Perhaps with the pressures of Los Angeles behind them, Ken really would settle down. Bellingham was the kind of community that would give Ken a chance to prove himself. If he had learned his lesson, grown more mature through the separation, and was willing to work, there might be a future for them after all. She wanted it and she wanted to feel comfortable marrying him. That night together, their first in weeks, proved to be glorious.

The city of Los Angeles was rapidly becoming a community of armed citizens. A tourist from New York, staying at the Mayflower Hotel in downtown Los Angeles, pulled a revolver and aimed it at a shocked bellman who had joked that he was the Hillside Strangler. The father of one of the city's public defenders carried a broken baseball bat in the family car so his wife would have a weapon. And in Pasadena, a supermarket clerk named Roxanne Barnwell was also traveling armed.

Roxanne Barnwell had more reason than most women to fear the Hillside Strangler. She was not convinced that the killings were random acts. Her home was located near where both Cindy Hudspeth and Kristina Weckler had lived before their deaths. Each day, on her way to and from her job, she had to pass near the area where Judith Miller's body had been dumped.

The fear in Pasadena was great. Roxanne would listen to the radio and hear reports of an investigation that was obviously getting nowhere. Then she would talk with coworkers who were concerned about the possibility that they or members of their families would be raped and murdered. She knew she wanted to live. She was not a violent woman, but she would rather fight than be led passively to her death. She decided to start carrying a handgun for protection.

One Monday night Richard Reynolds, a cardiopulmonary technician at Lavina Hospital in Altadena, approached the white Thunderbird Roxanne Barnwell drove to and from work. Reynolds had a history of sex offenses, the most recent one having been in 1967, when he was arrested for assault with intent to commit rape. He had either gone free since then or had decided to return to his old habits. Whatever the case, he used a gun to force his way in beside the attractive woman, ordering her to drive him to wherever he planned to assault her.

Roxanne Barnwell was not the type of woman to allow herself to be intimidated by any man. She was armed and had always intended to use the weapon if confronted with danger. At the same time, Reynolds was expecting his show of force to so intimidate his victim that he would have no problem.

Suddenly Roxanne pulled her gun, turned to Reynolds, and fired. The shocked attacker also fired, though there is a chance that he shot after death, the trigger pull a reflex action. He had not expected to have to fight his intended victim. Whatever the case, both were dead in the car when police arrived at the scene.

Finally the police felt the case was solved. The man had been a known sex offender. He had a strong connection with Lissa Kastin and the initial investigation indicated that his whereabouts were not known the night of her murder. However, the more intensely the matter was explored, the less he looked like a good suspect. Some officers theorized that a van had been used to transport the girls. Reynolds supposedly had access to one, but upon checking, it was found that the van was registered to his brother and had been disabled for several months.

The forced abduction did not fit the known pattern of the Hillside Strangler. Even worse, when all of the murder nights were checked, Reynolds turned out to have conclusive alibis. After a few days' investigation, Reynolds had to be ruled out.

"We had reached a dead end," said Lieutenant Phil Bullington of the Los Angeles Sheriff's Office Homicide Squad. "None of our leads had proven conclusive. We had checked everything that could be checked and we just didn't have enough evidence against anyone to consider making an arrest. We were just waiting for that magic telephone call which would provide us with something new, something which would finally lead us to the killer."

That call did not come until January 1979. It originated from Bellingham, Washington, a small town of which the majority of the officers had never heard. And when it came, it would lead to one of the most unusual investigations ever conducted into the mind of a mass murderer.

PART THREE

*Murder and
the Mind of Man*

PART THREE

CHAPTER 6

Kelli Boyd's world was shattered with Ken's arrest. Her father worked for the city government and she had been raised with the attitude that the police were deserving of respect. Even Ken had to admit that, given the circumstantial evidence known to the police after the girls were found, he was the person who should be arrested as a suspect. Yet he was saying he did not do it and Kelli was convinced of his sincerity.

Her first step was to hire Dean Brett as Ken's attorney. She had no money and there was no public-defender system in Bellingham at the time of the arrest. Attorneys who agree to take cases where no pay is expected from the client must collect their fees from the city, the county, or the state. Brett did not like to work this way, though he had done so in the past. He did not really want to accept the arrangement with Kelli and he initially agreed only to work for her through the weekend for little more than a retainer. A murder case can cost as much as $100,000 by the time all appeals are handled, background checking is done, and court fees are paid. Brett estimated the total value of everything Kelli and Ken possessed to be perhaps $1500. Kelli was only certain that she could raise a few hundred dollars.

Once Ken had a lawyer, Kelli could do little but answer the myriad calls she was receiving from family, friends, reporters, and police. She was also shocked to discover that the Los Angeles police were flying into Bellingham to talk with her about the Hillside Strangler murders. The idea that Ken could have been involved seemed impossible, yet a few days ago she would have said he could never be arrested for murdering anyone.

What Kelli didn't realize at first was that Terry Mangan had arranged for both the Los Angeles and Rochester authorities to be contacted. "These murders were too sophisticated to have been the first ones he committed," explained the chief. "They were well planned and carefully executed. The mistakes were ones made by somebody who was not familiar with how close people in a small town can be. If he had done this murder in a different city, we might not have been lucky enough to get to the crime scene so quickly. I had to assume that he may have killed elsewhere and I was thinking about Tony Johnson's daughter, who had been murdered in that series in Los Angeles. We just felt we had to alert the people down there."

The Strangler Task Force in Los Angeles didn't know what to expect from the Bellingham Police Department. Detectives in major cities often view small-town police officers with the disdain reserved for poorly trained security guards—laughable bumpkins who are likely to blow their toes off when drawing their guns. They might have lucked into catching Bianchi and he certainly was a better suspect than most they had had recently. But whether or not Bianchi could be linked with the Los Angeles crimes was unknown. They had their doubts about the value of the entire trip, yet they had to go.

On January 14, 1979, Kelli Boyd was faced with Sergeants Dudley Varney of the Los Angeles Police Department and Frank Salerno of the Los Angeles Sheriff's Department. She agreed to be questioned by them; Dave McNeal, a detective with the Bellingham Police, was also present.

At the moment of questioning, Kelli Boyd was an unknown factor in the case. What did she know? Was she involved with the murders? Was she the innocent dupe of a madman or a cunningly brilliant mastermind of the entire horror story that was known as the Hillside Strangler case? And if Bianchi was innocent, would Kelli eventually sue them for bringing her, a second innocent party, into the case? It was a difficult situation for everyone and had to be handled with tact and skill.

The questioning began with the taking of Kelli's description. Born: August 17, 1955; height: five feet one and three quarters; weight: 125 pounds; blond hair; blue eyes; on and on with the vital statistics. The idea was to get her to relax, talking about something familiar. They would also have a description to compare with any eyewitness accounts of other murders. The crimes being investigated in Los Angeles involved two people; a woman might have been one of them. It couldn't hurt to have the information taped for the record.

"Where did you meet him?" one of the officers asked Kelli.

"California Land Title Company, where I worked and where he did work."

A connection. A link. Yolanda Washington had applied for a job at the company at one time. No one knew if she was serious or how long she would have stayed. Still, it was something. Not much. A piece, a tiny piece of the puzzle.

"Is this in Los Angeles?"

"Universal City."

Hollywood area. Another link.

"What were you doing there, what kind of work?"

"Secretary."

"What kind of work was he doing?"

"He worked . . . At first he worked in a different office where my sister worked, and I went over there for training, you know, when I started in the business I knew nothing about it and I met him there and I thought he was a real nice guy, and he helped me work on my car once . . . and that's mainly how we got acquainted, and later he was transferred to the main office, where we worked together with everyone else."

Kelli Boyd called Ken a nice guy, a term others would use during the first few days of investigation. Everyone liked Ken Bianchi. Some people thought he was too talkative. One of the American guards along the Canadian border worked with Bianchi when the latter was in the Whatcom County Sheriff's Reserves program. He said, "He was a little off. Always talking about psychology and stuff, but in a way that made you know he didn't know what he was talking about. Nice guy, though. Wouldn't want him as a cop. I wouldn't have trusted his backing me up. Not aggressive enough. Just a nice guy. A bit of a nut, but not the kind to murder anyone."

Kelli's questioning continued.

"Where were you living at the time you first met him?"

"Franklin Avenue in Hollywood."

"Do you know where he was living?"

"He was living on Garfield Avenue in Glendale."

Kristina Weckler was last seen on the 800 Block of Garfield in Glendale. Cindy Hudspeth was last seen at 800 East Garfield. Jane King was last seen at Franklin and Tamarind. More links, more reasons that the trip was warranted, that Bianchi should be investigated in much greater depth.

"Were you ever to his apartment?"

"Yeah, I moved in with him there after I moved out from Franklin."

"When was that?"

"About May, I think of '77, I think."

"That was about a year and a half ago?"

Kelli was shown photographs. One of them was of Ken's used Cadillac, the car that had been repossessed when he couldn't maintain the payments. A Los Angeles County seal was plainly visible on the windshield. Kelli identified it, adding another link. The seal made the car seem official. It was the kind of vehicle identification the public would assume a police officer might have. The seal was another link with the way the crimes seemed to have occurred.

Kelli answered each question fully and truthfully. She knew that the only way she could help an innocent Ken was to never be trapped in a lie. She had to be completely honest. And if Ken was guilty—a growing fear within her—then telling the truth would be her protection, her defense. She would not risk arrest herself. She could continue to care for Sean, the truly important innocent in the case.

Ken had a badge, Kelli said. It looked like a police identification badge rather than being star-shaped, though Kelli wasn't certain what it meant.

The talk turned to Angelo Buono. What did Kelli know about him? What did she think about him? What did Ken do for him?

Kelli expressed her disdain for Angelo. She had never felt comfortable with him, never viewed him as being particularly nice or honest, though her bias did not prompt her to investigate his actions. For all she knew, he might have been innocent of any involvement with anything dishonest, but she didn't think so. Her attitude was that she was not going to tell Ken whom to choose as his friends, though she didn't have to share that friendship.

"Did Ken ever have large sums of money that you—"

"Never large sums of money, but I know there were a few times we were pretty broke and he said, 'Well, I'll go over to Angelo's. He owes me some money and I'll see if he's got it.' And he'd come back with twenty or forty dollars."

Kelli told of Ken going to the Glendale Library to use the telephone; he called from there frequently. Another link. The out-call modeling service had been contacted by a telephone from a library.

There were other surprises, not links, just unknowns to be checked. For example, Kelli mentioned looking for pictures of Ken's ex-wife to show one of the Bellingham police officers. As she looked for them, she said:

"I looked in his bottom drawer and I found this right on top of his long underwear and stuff, the pink shorty pajamas, bottoms, like bloomers, they weren't like underwear, they were bloomers. But I had never seen them before and I brought them out and I showed them to Dave"—the Bellingham detective—"and he said, 'Yeah, we saw those the first night we were here. They were rolled up and stuffed under the long underwear.' They weren't mine. They weren't my sister's. I don't know whose they were, but, you know, it's kind of strange that they were there."

Women's clothing. Did the garments once belong to the victim of a murder? Were they links in an unsolved killing? Or did Ken have them for some other purpose? Kelli said he wasn't bisexual and he had never dressed in women's clothing. There was nothing abnormal about his sexual appetite, so what did it mean?

There is an independent spirit about Dean Brett, the man Kelli Boyd hired to be Ken Bianchi's lawyer. He has the appearance of a pioneer intellectual, a man who would enjoy building a shelter by day and studying books by firelight throughout the night. He views himself as one of the more liberal attorneys in Bellingham and, while not a criminal lawyer, he had handled some criminal cases due to the lack of a public-defender system.

Brett had a strong aversion to the way all government agencies function and he particularly abhorred the general lack of competence he saw among lawyers working for cities and counties. A law-school graduate working as a public defender or county prosecutor will draw a paycheck even if his work is of low quality. Such a person faces neither testing nor ever-growing challenges, and this is contrary to Brett's goals for himself.

The defendant in a murder trial has the right to see all evidence available against him. In addition, his lawyer can obtain a certain amount of assistance by hiring one or more investigators. However, Brett wanted to dig further. He wanted to have a complete understanding of Ken Bianchi, the man who, increasingly, seemed to be a prime suspect, not only in Bellingham but also in a dozen murders in Los Angeles. Who was Ken Bianchi? What were his roots? How had be experienced childhood? What brought him to circumstances where he was suddenly fighting for his life, accused of crimes he fervently denied committing?

Dean Brett began contacting every person and agency he could discover that had been involved with Ken Bianchi over the years. The records compiled in this manner revealed a fascinating story which psychiatrists and social workers will be discussing for many years to come.

Life had never been easy for Frances Buono, Ken's mother. Her parents were immigrants who had settled in Rochester, New York. They were devout Catholics for whom any form of birth control was sinful. Large families were gifts from God and Frances was a middle child of eight children.

Frances Buono saw her childhood as being happy, though life was difficult. Her father was typical of many Italian immigrants arriving after the turn of the century. He was an upwardly mobile laborer, striving for a better life for his children. It didn't matter that he had to work seemingly endless hours, often coming home from work so exhausted that he could do little more than drop into bed. The children and the future of the family were all-important. He encouraged the children to go to school, yet was unable to help them at home. His wife was also constantly busy with the endless chores of a large household.

The values instilled in Frances Buono were fairly simple ones which she felt should have been easy to achieve. They included marriage, ownership of a home in a comfortable, middle-class neighborhood, and a large family. The husband would be the provider, the wife would raise the children, and the future would be happy.

Nicholas Bianchi was a man with a background similar to that of the woman he eventually married. Both were born in 1919, both were first-generation Americans raised in Italian Catholic families. His childhood was somewhat easier, though, as his father was a shoe cutter working for the Hickey-Freeman Company. Nicholas was one of only five children, so the earnings from his father's skilled trade bought a somewhat easier life for the family.

Nicholas Bianchi had had an upsetting childhood, though the problems were more emotional than financial. He had great difficulty speaking, stuttering so much that he was ridiculed by the other children in the neighborhood. He tried to be open and friendly, hoping his attitude toward others would compensate for his problem. However, he was cruelly teased by the other children and became withdrawn and shy, and eventually leaving school in his second year at Jefferson High. He first became a laborer with the New York Central Railroad, where he learned that to adults a man's work can be more important than the difficulty he might have with speech.

Nicholas decided to better himself. He tried to join the army, but some of his emotional problems prevented that.

His phobia about worms and insects, as well as other nervous traits, made him unfit for duty.

The military rejection was difficult to take, especially with the Second World War approaching. He decided that if he could not serve his country, the least he could do was learn a trade and develop himself economically. He joined the American Brake

Shoe Company and worked twelve hours a day in the Engineered Castings Division, determined to earn more money and ensure a better future.

Frances Buono also left Jefferson High in her second year. She and Nicholas had been childhood sweethearts and she had little incentive to graduate when he left to go to work. Her family needed the money she could earn, so they were pleased when she took a job with Speedy's Dry Cleaning Establishment. She worked hard and earned the respect of her employer, eventually being moved to the position of manager of the company's west Main Street store.

By December 1941, Nicholas and Frances felt that it was time for them to marry. They were deeply in love, and they both worked hard at jobs they enjoyed and shared similar dreams for the future. The house they wanted would be theirs. They would have children running everywhere; both of them realized that they had much love to give. And so Nicholas Bianchi and Frances Buono were married on the twenty-seventh of the month by Father Michael Tydings of St. Anthony of Padua Church.

Weeks passed and then months. The marital relationship was happy, the couple very much in love. It was only in the bedroom that emotions were high. Both of them wanted children of their own, yet nothing seemed to be working as it should. Finally they decided that they had to get help. They went to the doctor and found that Frances was in danger, that she had to have a hysterectomy to save her health. Of course, the operation would also destroy her chance of ever having a child of her own.

Frances Bianchi was devastated. Her life seemed to be over. She had lost her self-respect. She became a mild hypochondriac, imagining that every normal ache and pain represented some sort of illness. She was also severely depressed, her will to live shattered. No matter what else occurred in life, nothing could replace the sense of failure at not being able to have the child she and her husband so desperately wanted to love.

Friends who saw the way Frances Bianchi dealt with family and neighborhood children, as well as the gentle relationship between husband and wife, felt that the couple should have a child; it was unfair that other parents had children they did not want.

Eventually they decided to adopt a baby, making that child their own through the legal system and the boundless love in their hearts.

Not much is known about Ken's real mother during this period. However, investigations by the Monroe County, New York, Children's Court and other agencies indicate that the woman was a teenager when she got pregnant by a twenty-four-year-old man whose Italian Catholic background was similar to that of the Bianchis. The teenager was unmarried at the time, then married a man who was not the father, apparently not telling him about the pregnancy until after the marriage. The teenager was five feet four inches tall, with brown hair and blue eyes, and extremely attractive. She was also extremely nervous, constantly biting her nails and chain-smoking. According to the Monroe County adoption report, "She appears to be a pathetic creature of limited intelligence. . . ." She was also called promiscuous from the time she was fourteen years of age, having been frequently involved with the juvenile-court system.

The man Ken's mother married was in the army, stationed at Fort Dix. He had had a nervous breakdown in the past and been separated from his wife shortly after their marriage. The teenager had become interested in a Buffalo, New York, man who was forty-three. She apparently planned to make him her next husband.

Ken's mother was allegedly an alcoholic. This may or may not have been the case, though there were indications that she spent a great deal of time drinking in bars.

The picture which was emerging was of a child conceived out of ignorance of birth control rather than being wanted by his natural mother. The physical appearance of pregnancy probably adversely effected the teenager's personal life and she undoubtedly resented the growing fetus. Studies have now shown that a pregnant mother's stress and personal problems can affect her infant. There is also evidence that alcohol and drugs taken by the mother can effect the baby.

Was Ken Bianchi damaged at birth? There was no obvious indication of it. He was a full-term, breech-birth baby and weighed 6 pounds 4 ounces, again completely normal. There were no signs of illness or any abnormality.

If a fetus can experience emotional trauma related to the mother's anxieties, then Ken Bianchi's troubles were magnified after birth. His mother placed him in a foster home where the elderly woman was not interested in him. The foster mother passed him from neighbor to neighbor for care during the day so she would not have to be bothered. She was also believed to be a heavy drinker. A second foster home was eventually found, but not until several weeks later.

Once again the questions are many concerning the impact this all had on baby Ken. He was unwanted by his real mother, abandoned to a second woman who did not want him, then further shunted from person to person. Experts in child abuse feel that such a situation definitely affects a baby. Pamela Reagor, Ph.D., a Southern California psychologist and expert in child abuse and its results, feels that the emotional results can range from extreme insecurity to mild antisocial behavior. However, being adopted into a loving environment almost always counters any long-term problems.

Child abuse, if carried out long enough, can lead to what is known as altered ego states. The abuse—physical, emotional, or both—can lead the child to violence, then force the memory of the act from his or her mind. Dr. Reagor feels this type of change takes far longer than just the first four months of life. However, because the entire field of child abuse has not been investigated to any degree until recent years, little is known for certain about how much abuse is necessary to create an adult capable of violence.

Frances and Nicholas Bianchi were aware of baby Ken and the situation his mother was in. They realized that she would be willing to give up the child permanently and approached her concerning a private adoption. They agreed upon terms, then made legal arrangements through the courts.

At last Frances Bianchi had found a reason for living. She went to church and said a novena for this baby. She promised to raise Ken in the Catholic faith and have him attend Catholic schools if God would give her the chance to be his mother. She wanted to fill his life with love, giving him a relationship his real mother could not provide. She was thirty-two years old and her husband was thirty-three. They had been together approximately ten years and this was their first chance to have a child. It was also possibly their only opportunity.

No one, perhaps not even Frances Bianchi herself, can describe her feelings when she was awarded temporary custody of Ken at the age of approximately three months. At last she had a baby, a real baby, a son whom she could love, nurture, and help reach manhood. Yet the baby was not hers. The baby was a ward of the court, in a sense, even though she had taken the responsibility of his physical well-being. She was legally a temporary mother. Full adoption proceedings did not take place until 1952, when Ken was just short of a year old.

The result of the situation was a mixture of love and fear. She was committed heart and soul to this baby, yet frightened that he might be snatched from her arms at any moment. If the courts decided she was unfit, there probably would be no second chance. Ken was to be her baby or there would be no baby in her life.

Gradually Frances Bianchi's fears were translated into ailments. She began taking the new baby to the doctor's once with great frequency. He had allergies, responded to pollutants in the air, and otherwise had trouble adjusting to life. Yet always there seemed to be a way to protect him. Between December 4, 1951, and May 22, 1952, the baby was taken to see doctors eight times. Nothing serious seemed wrong with him. His weight was good, he was growing strong, and the only apparent problem was a respiratory infection that was responding more slowly to treatment than is usual. However, it was responding.

The fears that Mrs. Bianchi had for her adopted son were many. She constantly worried about the state of his health, creating a climate of endless anxiety within the home. She seemed to live in fear that this one chance at the all-important motherhood might be snatched from her grasp. If the court did not take him back, the incompetent medical profession might.

The anxiety was contrasted with the way the family lived in a lower front apartment on Saxton Street. Frances and Nicholas could not yet obtain the home they wanted, but she could show the world her skills at providing a happy environment for her new baby. According to the adoption report:

"This is an unattractive residential section just one block from a busy intersection at the corner of Broad and Saxton Streets. There is no yard and the windows open practically over the sidewalk.

"The apartment consists of four rooms which are freshly re-decorated. Mrs. Bianchi states that she did the redecorating her-self. She has individual taste in her choice of paper but has shown good artistic sense even though most people would not prefer pa-per with a Chinese design in the living room. The home depicts good housekeeping and women's ability to make a cheerful envi-ronment out of something which could otherwise be very drab.

"Kenneth has his own bedroom which is equipped with a child's maple furniture. The room is cheerful and colorful with cut out pictures and toys arranged around the wall so as to at-tract child's attention."

The family quickly moved to a larger apartment on Saratoga Avenue. The new home was in a far more attractive area and had such advantages as a fenced-in yard. Now the Bianchis didn't have to worry that their toddler might go into the street when their backs were turned.

No matter what inner tensions may have existed for the Bianchi family, the adoption of Ken positively changed their lives. Friends said that Nicholas seemed to make the baby the center-piece of his life. He was calmer, less likely to stutter, when talk-ing about the new addition to the family.

Doctors were involved in evaluating the Bianchis. Were the parents emotionally stable enough to provide a proper environ-ment for a growing child? According to the report gathered at the time, Ken's adoptive mother "has had far fewer complaints about herself since she has had the child in the home. He said that she has frequently called him but he always refuses to see her unless he believes it is absolutely necessary. [The "he" is a doctor with whom Mrs. Bianchi had been involved prior to the adoption.] He thinks she will always be excitable but doubts that this will affect the baby in any way. He thinks that her love for him will compensate [for] any emotional upset as her love is true and not artificial."

One of the doctors also stated that Mrs. Bianchi's "attitude and emotional stability may improve after she is through the menopausal period which was induced prematurely by the operation."

The life of Ken Bianchi had finally achieved stability. No longer would he be passed from hand to hand, rejected by each surrogate mother who came into contact with him. He had been adopted by a couple who loved him. Mrs. Bianchi had feared going through life without a baby, now she could finally begin to relax.

Ken Bianchi did not relax. Almost from the time of his adoption, he had a number of problems. Asthma was one of them and the family moved to Los Angeles for a while, to see if the greater sunshine and warmer climate might help. This was not a particularly happy time for anyone and, in January 1957, Ken fell from a jungle gym at the Century Park Elementary School, striking his nose and the back of his head. He had been prone to falls and the family was angered that better supervision had not been provided.

The boy also began having *petit mal* seizures and a tendency to roll his eyes when he was upset. Mrs. Bianchi was certain that he had epilepsy. The doctors felt that epilepsy could be ruled out. Their feeling was that the various problems were psychological, which greatly angered Ken's mother.

The following year, with the Bianchis back in Rochester, Ken was admitted to Rochester General Hospital. He had a tendency to urinate with great frequency, dribbling in his pants. Mrs. Bianchi had tried every type of punishment she could imagine to teach her son that this was wrong. She even went so far as to spank him before he went to the bathroom to ensure that he did enough to not dribble in his pants, according to reports made by social workers. However, none of this stopped the problem and she was convinced that an operation was necessary. According to the hospital report,

"Dr. Townsend referred Kenneth Alessio Bianchi, a seven year old adopted boy, to Social Service. He had been admitted to the hospital on 12-15-58 with a diagnosis of genito-urinary problems. His diagnoses now were: 1. Diverticulum, 2. Horseshoe kidney and 3. transient hypertension. Dr. Townsend said that although there were physical findings for this boy, he also had many emotional problems. He proved to be "a little minx" on the floor. Everything went fine during the day except during visiting hours when his mother was there and then everything was wrong, especially for his mother's benefit. He would have one complaint after another and Mrs. Bianchi would take these up with any available nurse or doctor who happened to be handy. Having this child hospitalized proved to be a trying experience and Dr. Townsend wondered if his social or home environment could be considered at all adequate."

The hospital staff felt that Mrs. Bianchi was unusually emotional and troublesome and that Ken's behavior was abnormal. Yet the question of what really happened remains. Was Ken acting like any other manipulative child, being nice to the staff because they responded to his friendliness, and constantly complaining to his mother because he enjoyed watching her get mad at the others? Many children will do this without either the child or the parents being in any way abnormal. Whatever the truth, the hospital staff and investigating social workers felt that both mother and child should see a psychiatrist. But they did not.

In 1959, Mrs. Bianchi's world developed new problems. She and her husband decided to buy the home they had always wanted, even though the payments were more than they could afford. The social workers involved with Rochester General considered this behavior by Mrs. Bianchi "more and more irrational." Yet was it irrational or normal for the way she was raised?

Marriage, family, home, and church were the important aspects of the Bianchis' lives, and their dream was realized with the purchase of the house in Greece.

Greece was a suburb of Rochester which was filled with modest, middle income homes. It was a nice place to raise children, a respectable place to live. It was the kind of residential area that would have seemed like heaven to either of the Bianchi parents.

What is the price of a dream? How much should someone pay for ultimate happiness? The suburban Rochester home made everything in life all right for the Bianchi family. It was a place Frances Buono had grown up fantasizing as her own. Certainly it was expensive. Everything was expensive. Two mortgages would be difficult to pay, even with all the overtime that Nicholas was taking on. Yet that did not matter. What was important was that Ken could grow up living the dream that had brought Mrs. Bianchi's parents to the United States in the first place.

Irrational behavior? Perhaps. Yet it was the kind of irrational behavior shared by millions of American immigrant families and their offspring.

The real problem was not so much the house but the tension meeting the payments created. Nicholas Bianchi had to work constant overtime and Frances also needed to work a part-time job. The tension seemed to effect Ken, though no one could be certain what this meant. Usually the medical reports indicated that the boy might be more of a con artist than truly troubled. For example, while still living in California, Dr. Ralph Bookman commented:

"The eye-rolling apparently occurs when the child is frightened or possibly it is a habit which the child has developed, as was what was suggested to them by Doctor Weeks."

The doctor said also, "The mother states that the child's father lets the boy do anything he wishes, and there is quite possibly a conflict between the parents in their behavior and attitude towards the child."

The Greece School District maintained records on Ken which included the perceptions made during a parent-teacher conference on December 16, 1958. That notation said, "Mrs. Bianchi in. She is very nervous person, easily upset. As a result, Ken is also nervous and wets his pants. Check his health record. Mother needs to be calmed down."

Some psychiatrists and psychologists say that when one parent is dominant and the other somewhat passive, the child can have emotional problems upon reaching adulthood. However, these problems are so numerous that critics of the theory say it is actually a "catch-all" when no other cause for the problems are easily identified by the doctor.

Mrs. Bianchi gave the impression of being the dominant parent, yet was her concern such that there was a problem? Her actions were taken out of love. On September 13, 1959, she even went so far as to write the school and request that she be notified "if

Kenneth should have a fall or injured in any way regardless how slight the injury may be." She feared his losing more school time if it was misdiagnosed, a legitimate concern by a parent interested in her child's welfare.

On September 15, 1962, a report was made by the Rochester Society for the Prevention of Cruelty to Children, Inc. The Bianchis had been repeatedly reported to the authorities because of concern over Ken's emotional state. Among the comments made following the investigation were:

"Worker found mother to be a deeply disturbed person, socially ambitious, dissatisfied, unsure, opinionated, and overly protective. Mother seemed guilt ridden by her failure to have children. She had a hysterectomy in 1951, and suffered post-operative depression. The possibility of adoption of a child was suggested to mother. This solution to her dissatisfaction was embraced by her with great enthusiasm and religious fervor. Worker felt that mother had smothered this adopted son in medical attention and maternal concern from the moment of adoption, at the age of three months."

The Bianchi family problems had become more intense by the time the agency investigated the home. According to the report, "Mother's ambitious effort to place in a higher strata [sic] of society met with financial disaster. Soon after our initial contact with this family, the parents lost the middle class home they were attempting to buy, and had to move into less desirable quarters. Mother went to work. Worker observed that during the time mother held a job, mother, as well as the boy, benefited emotionally. Mother was unwilling to accept the suggestion that possibly she, as well as the boy, might need psychiatric treatment, rather than medical treatment, and has shopped around for doctors endlessly.

"During the time that we were active with the family, psychiatric opinion was that mother was not capable of following through with a plan of treatment for herself or the boy psychiatrically at that time."

Later the agency stated: ". . . it became evident to the family that they could not pay their bills and keep up payments on the house they were buying. In 9-59, the family disposed of the home and moved to 65 Villa Street. In the meantime mother took a job at Bell Aircraft Company to help alleviate the family's financial difficulties. Arrangements were made for the boy to be cared for by a neighbor, and during this period the family functioned smoothly. Kenneth was noted to be markedly better with the enuresis disappearing. Family tensions were greatly reduced with mother working and out of the home. Father seemed to be happy with the new location and the elimination of his financial worries."

A lengthy report by the Society for the Prevention of Cruelty to Children focuses, in part, on the frequent attempts Mrs. Bianchi made to have Ken tested because of his constant urination. Each test involved the probing of Ken's genitals. There was discomfort, possibly humiliation, fear, and pain involved, though what effect this may have had psychologically remains unknown. Some psychiatrists feel that repeated probing such as this can psychologically be much like rape. Others say that the mother's attitude would prevent such feelings and it was obvious that she was having him tested because of loving concern. The question remains as to how all this may have affected the small boy.

There were other reports. Strong Memorial Hospital of the University of Rochester did a preliminary report on Ken and his mother on February 3, 1959. In that report, there was much discussion of Mrs. Bianchi's defiance toward doctors (". . . Mrs. Bianchi seemed very paranoid, feeling that everybody was against her in all her contact," then ". . . defiant in telling me that this was something she would not stand for") and also of Ken's problem controlling his urine. Under "School Adjustment" the report stated, in part: "He has not been in school for the last two months because of his inability to control his urine that started again and then he started having sore throats and so she felt she should keep him home."

Dr. Dane Pugh commented on March 13, 1959, in that same Strong Memorial report: "The impression is gained that this mother is herself a seriously disturbed person, and her discussion about the handling of the child by various medical men indicates some apparent paranoid trends. It is apparent that she has been strongly controlling toward this boy, keeping him out of school very frequently, particularly in the last several months, because of her fear that he would develop a sore throat and begin to wet. It is not clear whether this mother can carry through successfully with a psychiatric evaluation, but it is felt that diagnostic study should be offered, in order to clarify more fully the degree of personality disturbance on the part of the boy, the operation of any emotional components if present in the boy's presenting symptom, and the nature of the family relationships, including the degree of disturbance on the part of the mother in particular."

By the time Ken Bianchi was in the fifth grade at Holy Family School, he seemed to have endured an endless stream of doctors, testing, and other pressures. Seldom did his mother agree with any of the reports, though they were frequently similar. Then, in 1962, Ken was seen by the DePaul Clinic in Rochester. Under "Child's Problems" was written:

"The boy drips urine in his pants, doesn't make friends very easily and has twitches. The other children make fun of him and mother is extremely angry at the school because they do not stop the other children. The mother sounded as if she were very overprotective of this boy. When the boy fell on the playground in kindergarten early in the school year, she kept the boy home the total year."

The DePaul Clinic interviewer, an individual named Connors, added: "She indicated that she has become so upset because people keep on telling her to take her child to a psychiatrist. She does not think he needs a psychiatrist and she went into great detail about how the doctors these days are just out for money and she does not trust any of them. She found that she, herself, had become so upset that she was crying a great deal and recently went to see a psychiatrist herself. She said she was late for her first appointment and had only 20 minutes to spend. The next time she spent a whole hour with him but all he did was pick his nose and clean out his ears. This made her very angry and also he recommended they would put Kenneth through the brain wave tests etc. which frightened Mrs. Bianchi off. She could not give me the name of the psychiatrist she saw and I pointed out to her that she seemed to be holding back information from me. I recognized that probably she didn't trust me yet and she said that many things she knows is 'water over the dam' and she doesn't think it important to tell me. I indicated that I felt it was important enough to know what concerned her and what she was attempting to do about these things."

The staff at the DePaul Clinic was constantly upset with Mrs. Bianchi. The reports frequently had such comments as:

"I felt that this woman was really not motivated for any help for herself or really for the boy for that matter, but I felt that if the school was going to be faithful to this boy and his mother in years to come it would be good if we could see him here at the Clinic." "In some ways, I feel she is bringing the boy here to prove that there is nothing wrong with him." "The mother is obviously the dominant one in the family and impresses one as a quite disturbed woman." "Mrs. Bianchi tends to displace her anger especially on doctors and hospitals and project the blame for the boy's problem onto other sources."

Later there was a discussion of Ken Bianchi, then approximately eleven years old. It read: "Dr. Dowling reported that Kenneth is a deeply hostile boy who has extremely dependent needs which his mother fulfills. He depends upon his mother for his very survival and expends a great deal of energy keeping his hostility under control and under cover. He is very eager for other relationships and uses a great deal of denial in handling his own feelings. For example, he says that his mother and father are the best parents in the world.

"He is [a] very lonely boy who wants to move away from mother. He is very constricted however, and feels [sic] being hurt if he should move away from her. Mother seems to allow him only one friend in the house. There seems some basic confusion around his own identity. He tries very hard to placate his mother, but she always seems to be dissatisfied. To sum up, Dr. Dowling said that he is a severely repressed boy who is very anxious and very lonely. He felt that the only outlet whereby he could somehow get back at his mother was through his psychosomatic complaints. Dr. Dowling felt that without this defense of the use of his somatic complaints he might very well be a severely disturbed boy."

As Dean Brett and others involved with the case read the records, a picture began to emerge of a boy who might have been genuinely loved too much by a woman who exaggerated his problems out of her own fears of losing him. The child seemed desperate for his mother's approval, at the same time feeling great rage for the way he was being treated by her. He suppressed his anger. He denied he had any problems. At the clinic he refused to say anything against his parents directly, even though he constantly talked of his underlying nervousness.

Another diagnosis from DePaul stated: "Dr. Sullivan reported that Kenneth is a very anxious boy who has phobias and many counterphobias. He uses repression and reaction formation. He is very dependent upon his mother. He has tics since he is overly concerned about his health. His mother has dominated him and indulged him in terms of her own needs. Her anxious, protective, clinging control has made him ambivalent but he represses his hostile aggression and is increasingly dependent upon her. Dr. Sullivan felt that the boy was very lonely and has been kept from adequate peer relationships. The mother appears to be very controlling both toward the boy and the father."

On January 30, 1963, additional observations were made at the clinic. These stated, in part:

"He was anxious, passive, cooperative, conforming and easily threatened. He covers his anxiety and his lack of confidence. He appears to be a rather lonely boy who clings to home rather than face the dangers of the outside world. He is easily threatened, fears authority and aggressive people whom he tries to pacify.

"About himself, he said he has a horseshoe kidney which makes him wet his pants sometimes, but he is getting over it. He is nervous most of the time. He feels sad when there is no one to play with. He revealed his fear of adults, particularly with aggressive people. He doesn't know what he wants to be when he grows up but his wishes were that there would be no more school, that he wouldn't have to work hard, that he could live forever and he would enjoy life more. His fun is putting on scary plays with his boyfriends in which he is the monster."

Later the report states: "He said he hates school because it is hard and the teacher yells at him. He went on to say that the teacher shouldn't 'take it out on other kids.' He said that the children sometimes blame him for doing things that he hadn't done and the teacher believes it so he gets blamed. He gets nervous when he has to do school work and is not able to do it.

"He said his mother will do anything to help him, even if she is sick. She hollers a great deal and is the boss. She does the punishing. He developed facial tics talking about his mother. He said she bosses his father who does what she says.

"He indicated his father is nice and helpful and doesn't get angry at him."

The more Ken seemed to retreat from his emotions concerning his mother, the closer he apparently grew to his father. The older man was almost a fantasy figure because he had to spend so many hours at work. However, they did begin to see each other more as Ken entered his teenage years. They bought new shoes together, both of them delighting in the fact that Ken's feet were the same size as his father's, even though Ken was just thirteen. They were so proud of the new shoes that Ken threw away his old ones, leaving him the owner of one new "dress" pair and some old, well-worn tennis shoes.

Father and son decided to go off together on a fishing trip, Ken taking both his new shoes and his sneakers. The tennis shoes were better for slogging through the mud and Ken forgot to bring home his new pair of good shoes. Several days later, before anything could be done about retrieving them, two police officers knocked at the door of the Bianchi home. Ken's father had been found dead at work, his body sprawled by a telephone booth from which he had planned to call someone. All the stress and overtime had finally taken their toll.

What happened next is unclear, the garbled memories of an emotional experience and many years passage. Apparently Mrs. Bianchi became hysterical and Ken rushed inside the house. One witness says he attacked the police for hurting his mother; finally he was restrained long enough for them to explain why they were there. Other witnesses say that he became hysterical, not violent, wailing and crying, then fleeing to his room.

Whatever the case, the death was traumatic. Ken and his father had just started to learn to love one another and now Nicholas was gone. For many days Ken would climb the stairs to the darkened attic, crying and talking with his dead father. He wanted nothing to do with the family. His grief was intense and he tried to handle it alone. The only exception was to be his presence at the funeral.

The undertaker arrived to obtain clothes to dress the body. While discussing the burial, Ken realized that his new, good shoes were gone. He was heartbroken about not having them for the funeral.

The undertaker learned that Ken and his father wore the same shoe size. He suggested that the father's new shoes be left behind for Ken to wear at the funeral. He had talked about keeping some of his father's clothing so that he would have something personal, and the undertaker explained that the feet could be covered with slippers. They would not be shown, even with an open casket, so Ken should wear them.

Ken seemed thrilled with the idea of being able to wear some of his father's clothing to the funeral. At least this is what others thought. However, other people who have shared this kind of death experience in much the same way, say that they were bothered by having to wear the dead person's clothing. During this period of shock and high emotion, it is as though they were living with the shell of a man when his essence is gone. The smell is his, the item is familiar, yet the man himself is gone forever. The situation can make the acceptance of the death much harder, though whether or not this was the case with Ken is unknown.

Dean Brett could only wonder what it all meant. Ken had reported being picked on by teachers and students as a child. He was frequently accused of doing things he said he never did. This was much like his argument concerning the murders in Bellingham, which he continued denying despite the growing body of evidence against him. Had he always been a liar? Was he an innocent man somehow being trapped by circumstances that were beyond understanding?

The answer, Brett felt, was to find a way to probe deeper into Ken Bianchi, the man. He has been using John Johnson, a social worker who had formerly been at the University of Montana, to work with Ken. Johnson mentioned a husband-and-wife team at the university who had studied people with dissociative reactions—periods when they take an action but do not remember it. The professors used hypnosis to help focus the subject's thinking. Brett decided to seek still more help than he had received, and this couple seemed one possibility. What he did not realize was the potential for evil that can lurk within the average person and the triggers which might bring it forth. He was about to discover the frightening truth about Ken Bianchi, and the reality would be as shocking as the crimes he was trying to solve.

CHAPTER 7

It was supposed to be a typical interrogation interview. The Sheriff's Department registered it under file number 079-16127-2010-999. The proper people were present: Dean Brett, counsel for the defense, Sergeant Frank Salerno and Deputy Peter Finnigan, Homicide Bureau, Detective Division, Los Angeles County Sheriff's Department, Dr. John G. Watkins, professor of psychology, University of Montana, and, of course, the defendant, Kenneth Bianchi. An audio tape recorder and a video tape recorder had been set up to record the event. It would be a relatively routine interrogation of a murder suspect, though a few more individuals than usual would be present. The date was March 21, 1979, and Ken had already read the DePaul Clinic report, giving him a better insight into how others had viewed his past.

Ken was nervous about the interview and having to interact with a man who was nationally known in his field. Watkins was past president of the Society for Clinical and Experimental Hypnosis and past president of the hypnosis division of the American Psychological Association, and held numerous other honors. Bianchi wanted the man's approval and remained extremely respectful during the first few minutes of the talk. He also tried to explain his feelings as much as possible. "I've been drawing pictures and ideas about my life that I could have swore up and down was just real rosy and, you know. . . ."

Bianchi explained that the DePaul Clinic report showed him a different side of his relationship with his mother. "You could have talked till you were blue in the face about my mother, you could have talked till you were blue in the face, try to discredit her. And I would have fought tooth and nail, thumb screw, I mean I—I would have disagreed with whatever you had to say about her. Because I've always had a respect and a—and deep love for her. But now looking at one report when I was eleven years old and seeing that I had problems, some more serious than others, which could develop into serious problems. Maybe they wouldn't, who knows? But it leaves a question there that I probably should have had help, more professional help."

Bianchi said he often seemed to have a different perception of how he reacted to stress than those around him. "There have been times when I—I just handled a situation and I think I handled it really well, I stayed calm and everything else. And I get an interpretation from a third party who was witness to this, and they said, boy, you really came on strong. And—and boy you really did this wrong, and you really did that wrong. And I think back, and I think it's not the way I see it."

After several minutes of talking, Dr. Watkins said, "You know, if you really want to know who you are and understand yourself, you're gonna have to open some doors, and no promises as to what you're gonna find inside when you open the doors up."

Dr. Watkins explained, "I guess it's much harder when one fools oneself rather than when one fools other people about what the score is inside. If you hide yourself from yourself, if you don't know what you really are, you're giving me the idea that in a sense this rosy picture that you had before is a little bit like fooling yourself for a long time, possibly."

Bianchi expressed an interest in learning more about himself. He admitted that he felt as though he might have been spending his life denying aspects of his own existence. He said that he felt he might have more problems than he has faced, and Watkins said: "I guess if you do have a problem it must be because you've been denying some aspects of yourself, sort of denying awareness of their existence or what is. And if you have the courage, you can see that maybe there is something that's a problem that you haven't known about, about yourself. And you have a feeling you want to end out what it is, I guess that's the first step of courage, isn't it?"

Watkins explained that he would use hypnosis to explore Ken's mind. "Hypnosis is just one approach at trying to help people to find out what's going on inside themselves. It's not the only one but it is one—some of the others take a lot longer. Like many, many sessions of talking, going over dozens, and dozens, and dozens of hours. And over a period of time, sometimes hundreds of hours, why one can come to understand oneself. And some of us who are in this business have gone through that long-winded process ourselves, not that we know everything about ourselves, but we know some things that we didn't know beforehand. And hypnosis is probably a very natural phenomenon, it's, I suppose every one of us is hypnotized at least twice a day without realizing it. When you—you know when you wake up in the morning and it's kind of drowsy and you're kind of half awake and kind of half asleep, sort of—things get foggy. And maybe you're remembering some of your dreams at that time. You're wide awake, you forget 'em kind of, yet you're not quite fully in them either in a way.

"Hypnosis isn't sleep, and it isn't anything like somebody's got weak willpower or somebody's pushing power over another person, that's not what it is. It's kind of a natural relaxation in which we try to help people to recall things and experience themselves a little bit more, look at sides of themselves"

Ken became interested. He asked how far back someone could go with hypnosis. Watkins explained that everything we experience is recorded in the mind so that theoretically we could go back to birth. It is more common for someone to return to early childhood, though. The important point, he stressed, is that there is no pain involved. Ken would not be hurt by remembering.

Before hypnosis could be used for part of the questioning, Ken wanted to talk about some of the more frightening dreams he had experienced in the past.

"When I was a child we lived on Clifford Avenue and we lived upstairs and in my bedroom was a doorway to a walk-up attic. And I used to have dreams night after night that I remember like they happened yesterday. The dream was that the door—I would wake up and for some reason be attracted to the door. And it would be dark, pitch-black dark, I couldn't find any lights. There was something there, don't ask me what, I never saw it, I never touched it, I never felt it. It was something in there that put such a fear in me that I could remember waking up screaming."

"How old were you then?"

"Second grade, third grade, something like that. That dream eventually went away, I don't remember how or when. When we were living on Campbell and Reese Street, upstairs. I had my own bedroom. And I used to dream at night that I'd wake up and it'd be something in the room, be pitch-black. I couldn't scream, I couldn't move, I couldn't run, I couldn't get help, nothing. I was stuck with this, whatever it was.

"And it feared me, you know, really put the fear in me. And I wouldn't wake up screaming but I'd wake up, you know, sweating and really just hard time getting back to sleep again. And I had that for—for a while, I don't know how that ended. It just eventually disappeared, I guess."

Ken then told of other dreams, especially after his father died. He dreamed of his father almost nightly for two years after his death. The two would always meet in these dreams and Ken said, "I sensed him as if he were saying to me, 'I'm here,' you know, 'don't worry about it, everything's okay,' and I always woke up with a good feeling."

The conversation continued, Ken talking about his father's death and how everyone where he worked attended the funeral. He was relaxing, becoming more open with the doctor. The tension was going and he was comfortable with the situation. It was time for Dr. Watkins to use hypnosis to probe deeper into Ken Bianchi's mind. He began the introduction, a long, slow relaxation technique. He talked of Ken's body becoming heavier, he narrowed his attention to thoughts of relaxation.

"It's kind of nice not to have to pay attention to a lot of things, to ignore things, to expect just a sense of heaviness in the arm . . .

your arms feel heavy, too. They feel like the limbs on the trunk of a tree. And the sense of warm heaviness can move down into the trunk of your body, and on down into your legs, and your feet, sort of like the world is getting warm and heavy. And you feel good just kind of letting go . . . You have a feeling of deep calmness and peacefulness, and relaxation . . . Images of a blue sky, warm sun, soft grass. Restfulness and peace. Deeper and deeper."

Dean Brett and the others watched the proceedings, listening to the monotonous drone of words which were focusing Ken's attention, easing him into the state of total concentration we call hypnosis—nothing magical, just a focusing of the mind. Though it was hard for the observers to stay alert, they did. They had no idea what might come next; the induction of whatever was to follow seemed rather endless.

Finally John Watkins performed the most controversial part of the induction. He asked to speak to only a part of Ken, not the whole man. He said, "And now while you're relaxed, Ken, I want you to stay in your deeply relaxed state. But I would like to kind of talk to you. And I've talked a bit to Ken but I think that perhaps there might be another part of Ken that I haven't talked to, another part that maybe feels somewhat differently from the part that I've talked to. And I would like to communicate with that other part. And I would like that other part to come to talk to me. And when it's here and then the left hand will lift up off the chair to indicate to me that that other part is here that I would like to talk to. Part, would you please come to communicate with me? And when you're here, lift the left hand off the chair to signal to me that you are here. Would you please come, part, so I can talk to you. Another part, it is not just the same as the part of Ken I've been talking to. Would you lift the left hand to indicate to me that you are here when you are here and you're ready to communicate with me. Part, would you come and lift Ken's hand to indicate to me that you are here. All right, part, I would like for you and I to talk together, we don't even have to—we don't have to talk with Ken unless you and Ken want to. But I would like for you to talk to me. Will you talk to me by saying 'I'm here?' Would you communicate with me, part? Would you talk with me, part, by saying, 'I'm here?'"

A voice, deep, slurred, as though partially asleep, mumbled, "Yes."

"Part, are you the same thing as Ken or are you different in any way? Talk a little louder so I can hear you."

"I'm not him." The voice coming from Ken was still slurred, deeper than Ken's normal speaking voice.

"You're not him. Who are you? Do you have a name?"

"I'm not Ken," said the voice that was different from normal, yet coming from Ken's body.

"You're not him? Okay. Who are you? Tell me about yourself. Do you have a name I can call you by?"

"Steve."

Ken sensed Watkins's astonishment and repeated, deeper and more forcefully, "You can call me Steve."

Dr. Watkins gave no indication that anything was out of the ordinary. His voice did not change. He calmly said, "I can call you Steve? Okay. Steve, just stay where you are, make yourself comfortable in the chair and I'd like to talk to you. You're not Ken. Tell me about yourself, Steve. What do you do?"

The voice became intensely angry, as though the man in front of Dr. Watkins was trying to use his mouth as a weapon. "I hate him!"

"You what?"

"I hate him!"

"You hate him. You mean Ken?"

Then, slowly, with intense feeling, his entire body rigid, the man sitting in the chair said, "I hate Ken!"

"You hate Ken. Why do you hate Ken?"

"He tries to be nice."

Dr. Watkins was startled. The man in front of him said:

"I hate a lot of people."

"You hate a lot of people, now."

"He tried to be friends."

"He tried to be friends. Who do you hate?"

"I hate my mother."

"You hate your mother. What has she done to you, Steve?"

"She wouldn't let go."

Dr. Watkins asked him who else he hated. "I hate Ken."

There was a pause, then the man said, "I hate nice! I hate Ken!"

Dr. Watkins was talking with Ken Bianchi and yet he wasn't. In an effort to clarify things, he asked who Ken might be.

"That's the other person."

"The other person?"

"He tries to do good."

"Ken, you mean? Yes, you hate Ken. You hate Mother."

"Uh, his mother, she's—"

"His mother, she's not your mother then?"

"Well, she is in a way."

"Yes, what do you mean? Do you have a different mother?"

"I don't know. I guess not."

"What would you like to do about her?"

"Disappear."

"How do you mean disappear?"

"Oh, he—he likes her being around and I just want her to disappear."

"You want her to disappear. Do you get angry?"

"Yes."

"What do you do when you get angry?"

"Anything I can."

"Like what?"

"Oh, I make him lie."

"Yeah."

"I like doing that."

"You like to hurt somebody?"

"Yeah."

"Who do you like to hurt?"

"Oh, anybody that's nice to Ken"

"Anybody that's nice to Ken, huh? Being man or woman mostly?"

"Doesn't matter."

"Yeah, have you hurt somebody?"

"Yeah, I fixed him good."

"You did what?"

"I fixed him good." Steve continued talking about causing trouble for Ken. He spoke of starting arguments, then said, "I fixed him good when he went to California."

Dr. Watkins asked Steve what happened. "I can't tell you," was the reply. "I can't tell. You'll tell Ken."

"He won't tell me, so you gotta tell me."

"I was with him one night," said Steve. "He walked in on his cousin, Angelo. And Angelo had a girl over . . . Ken walked in—in the middle of Angelo killing this girl."

"Walked in on the middle of what?"

"Angelo killing this girl."

The statement was startling and Dr. Watkins felt he should probe more deeply. "Now, who's Angelo?" he asked.

"Oh, some—some turkey he knows, his cousin."

"His cousin?"

"Yeah, and it worked out perfect," said Steve. Then he added, "Later on I made him go over to Angelo's a lot and . . . and I made him think all these real morbid thoughts."

"Like what?"

"Like there was nothing wrong at killing 'cause it was like getting back at his mother, and made sure he didn't really know what was going on."

Dr. Watkins asked, "Did he kill a number of them?"

"Yeah, he—I made him do it."

"You made him do it?"

"He thought it was his mother, and he thought it was people he hated."

"Yeah, you fooled him."

"Oh, yeah, he couldn't figure out later what he had done and why."

"Well, did—did he forget it then, that he did it, or not?"

"Yeah, I wouldn't let him remember that."

The reels of tape kept spinning, recording what was a shocking example of a rare mental illness to Dr. Watkins and a possible fraud to the observing detectives. They had carefully searched the house that Ken and Kelli shared. They had found several cartons of books, perhaps a half dozen, on the field of psychology. Creating another person seemed like a con game, a ruse to plead insanity instead of facing the ultimate penalty for his actions. Yet even if this was a con, the new information was fascinating.

"Angelo, his cousin Angelo has killed people before and I made it like it was like a hunger to him."

"Yeah, but you made Ken do that?"

"Uh, yeah, I hate him so much."

"And—and—and how did Ken kill the girls?"

"Uh, he killed some of 'em and he—he helped with others."

"He helped with others. You mean him and Angelo together?"

"Yeah."

"I see. Well, how would he kill 'em? Would he shoot 'em or what?"

"Oh, I made him strangle 'em all."

"Yeah, you made him strangle 'em all, I see."

"I fixed him up good. He doesn't even have any idea."

"He doesn't have any idea at all, you really fixed him but good."

"Oh, I am so good."

Watkins asked Steve, "Did you do it or did he do it or did you just make him do it or how?"

"I did it," said Steve/Ken proudly.

"You did it?"

"Oh, yes, I did."

Watkins then approached "a girl by the name of Karen," bringing the discussion to the subject of the Mandic and Wilder murders. Steve explained that Ken and Karen had been good friends and that he had decided to get even. "I made him set up this stupid deal with them."

Steve continued describing what happened. "I made him kill them," he said, referring to the Bellingham coeds. "I told him that it was the people who made his father go away," he added, laughing.

The details of the killing were too sketchy for the officers to gain much evidence. He then said, "I put the girls—I killed the girls, and I put the girls in the back of the car." He said he carried them up the steps and drove the girls to a street. Ken did not come back until later when he found himself walking down the street and had no memory of how he had gotten there or of the murders.

The subject switched to Los Angeles and Dr. Watkins asked him to remember one of the girls he had killed there.

"That black girl," he said, laughing. "He picked her up downtown."

"Where?"

"Up on Hollywood Boulevard."

"Yeah, what kind of girl was she?"

"She was a prostitute. She was a hussy." He then went on to say that he was with his cousin Angelo at the time, both of them driving around until the woman became scared. Then Angelo said to get rid of her. He also said that Angelo's full name was Angelo Buono and he supplied the Glendale address. He also explained that Angelo owned an upholstery shop.

"You fixed Ken but good," said Dr. Watkins.

Steve laughed. "He's such a sap. I wish I could stay out. I wish I could stay out."

"How do you mean, you want to be on the outside?"

"He never lets me, you know. I mean, not enough. Not as much as I want to. Oh, yeah, I want to be on the outside."

"How come?"

"I could do what I want more, anytime I want. I can—get rid of him. He's—he's such an ass. He's soft. He can't handle it, you know. He's just—he's dumb, you know, just totally unaware. He's just—oh, I want to get out."

"And what would you do if you got out?"

"I'd kill Ken," said Steve. "I got to get rid of him, make him disappear."

"Who else would you kill?"

"I don't know. I don't know. I'd find somebody."

Dr. Watkins mentioned that Steve had always killed women. He asked if Steve killed men but Steve said no. "You must like to kill women more than men. Why?"

"Because Ken hates women. I mean, l hate women."

"Why?"

"They hurt . . ."

Steve discussed his other activities. He talked of hating Kelli, of managing to hit her before Ken could stop him. He spoke as if there was some sort of battle going on inside his body between Ken and himself, yet there was only one body. The violence he enjoyed and the gentleness he hated in Ken were the same. If the police did not believe much of what they were hearing, they were now certain that Ken Bianchi was confessing to crimes and implicating his cousin as the second man. But would the confession be valid?

When the interview was over, Dr. Watkins understood the type of man with whom he was dealing. He had seen others like him, though fortunately the others had not been mass murderers.

Dr. Watkins explained to Dean Brett that he felt Bianchi was what was known as a multiple personality. Such an individual seems to have several different people living within one body. Technically the phenomenon is known as an altered ego state through hysterical dissociation.

Children who become multiple personalities usually have several factors in common. They are usually a little more sensitive than other children their age; one of their parents is passive and the other is dominant; they may feel rejected by one or both parents, and abuse is common. Punishment, even when deserved, can be extreme—severe beatings can be meted out for accidentally spilling a glass of milk. Punishment can also be inconsistent: a beating for spilling the milk today, then a new glass and some cookies for spilling the milk tomorrow.

Sometimes the abuse becomes sexual in nature. A small girl is raped, by her father or by a motorcycle gang. A little boy might be abused in other ways. For example, the constant focus on his urinary problems and the probing necessary to make a medical diagnosis could have been taken as sexual abuse by the young Ken Bianchi.

Eventually the child responds to the abuse in whatever way is necessary. One personality may be created to handle all anger and violence, another to handle loving feelings if the child thinks it is wrong to express them. A third personality may do nothing but be skilled at running away when danger is near. A fourth personality may be a perfect parent or business person. There can be as few as two personalities and as many as there are severe traumas, Dr. Watkins explained to Dean.

Dean Brett did not know if Watkins's theory was correct, though he was somewhat aware of cases reported in books such as *The Three Faces of Eve, Sybil,* and *The Five of Me.* If the Bianchi case was similar, that would account for Steve. Steve would have been a protector when Ken was small, handling any perceived violence from his mother. He would also have handled the growing rage within, eventually exploding into violence. Ken would be just a part of the mind and he would do everything right in order to earn his mother's approval.

The Bellingham authorities felt that the case should involve far more testimony that just Dr. Watkins's work. It was decided to bring in a total of six psychiatrists and psychologists to see Ken. Watkins and one other would be paid by the defense, two would be advisers to the judge and thus impartial, and two would be working for the prosecution. It was hoped that all the psychiatrists could accept the concept of multiple personality when weighing their findings, even if they felt the initial diagnosis was invalid.

The problem for the courts and the investigators, if Dr. Watkins was correct, was that the actions of one personality are unknown by the other personalities until the condition can be changed through therapy. If Steve really was a violent alter personality, then Ken would have no knowledge of what he did, just as he claimed. This meant that the shock of facing the murders his hands had committed could be extremely dangerous for him. He might even become suicidal. Thus Watkins felt that before he left he must make a posthypnotic suggestion that would start changing Ken in ways most helpful for him.

Watkins said, "Let me tell you something, Ken. During the coming days and weeks, at your own speed, and in your own way, you will find out about Steve, who he is, what he has done and what has happened. And you will find out in such a way that you can become stronger and stronger and stronger with each passing day."

The suggestion was meant to help Ken. The result within the mind, if Ken was a multiple personality, would be a crossing over of memory. Ken would begin to accept the truth about himself without having to revert to being Steve when thinking of past violence. However, this would also change the way the other psychiatrists would see him. In the not too distant future, Ken Bianchi would become a different person, and that could be a problem.

CHAPTER 8

On March 28, 1979, Dr. Ron Markman of Los Angeles was in Bellingham, Washington, to examine Ken Bianchi. He had arrived to help both Dean Brett and the Los Angeles public defender's office, which would eventually be responsible for defending Bianchi against the California charges.

Markman is an unusual man in the medical field: he is both a psychiatrist and a lawyer, though at the time of the Bianchi case he had not yet finished his legal training. He works extensively with the court system and is never happy unless he's tackling a dozen projects at once.

Dr. Markman has been trained in the effects of child abuse and is aware of the background of multiple-personality patients. However, he has also seen enough con men in prison who have tried to excuse their crimes on specious psychological grounds that he is slower to make a diagnosis. He had already been involved with such cases as the Manson Family and the Symbionese Liberation Army members who kidnapped Patty Hearst, then converted her to their ways. He would prove to be the slowest of the psychiatric investigators to come to a conclusion related to the case.

There would be no hypnosis during the visit with Bianchi on March 28. Markman believed that the human mind can remember all actions a person takes, good or bad. Even the most repressed memories of a true multiple personality can be tapped without hypnosis. The personalities respond to stress, changing according to the perceived needs of the person, so again hypnosis would not be essential, even if Bianchi did fit Watkins' theory. All Dr. Markman wanted to do was interview Ken Bianchi about his life and about the crimes.

Ken began talking about his early years, including some of his first sexual experiences. He mentioned the first time he reached puberty and had a sexual experience. "I was in bed, I was halfway between sleep and awake and, oh, God, I was just thinking all kinds of weird things, girls, had to do with, with books I had come across with my parents. Nudist books, and a few other books, which were more explicit. And I was still a virgin when this happened. And uh, sure enough, um, I climaxed and came and it scared me, you know, I'd never experienced it. I'd never really talked, you know, your street-concern talk, you know, you talk about what happens but you never really get into detail. You never know how it feels when it happens. And it burned and I got a little worried, and it took me a little while to put it together, exactly what happened."

Markman tried to reassure Ken that the experience was normal. What he did not know was that Ken and his mother had different memories concerning the types of reading material in the home. Bianchi said his mother and father had magazines relating to nudity, body building, and the like in the house. However, his mother said that Ken would sneak Playboy-type publications into his room, that she and her husband never purchased them. It was a fairly minor point but a curiosity concerning the way each chose to remember those years when Ken was growing up.

Months later more details would come out concerning Ken and sex, details which cast his mother in a sympathetic light. Ken was a frequent purchaser of hard-core sex material in Rochester adult bookstores. He had a collection of pornographic movies he had purchased which he never discussed. Periodically he would borrow the family projector to show the films to friends at their homes, telling his mother that he was just showing old home movies the family had made.

One night Ken's mother discovered some of the films he had been buying. She didn't know what they were and projected one to find out. She was extremely upset and talked with Ken about it. However, even her anger and concern didn't stop him.

Many of the people involved with the case wanted to portray Ken's mother as irrational. It would have been simple to cast her as a "Witch" and Ken as a created monster. But the truth was more complex. Kelli Boyd and one of her friends found a stack of pornographic movies Ken had hidden at home years after the Rochester incident. She also found an old rabbit fur which had been treated for use as a table decoration and which Ken had taken to use for masturbation. It too had been hidden—at home, again proof of an ongoing secret sexual activity quite different from what he wanted others to know about. These discoveries further undermined Ken's view of his own childhood.

Bianchi also talked about drug use. He had smoked marijuana upon occasion but had never been seriously involved with the drug culture. His experimentation with drugs seemed to be normal, not sufficient to affect his personality.

Eventually the subject of Ken's parents became important. Dr. Markman wanted to explore what might have happened in those early years and how Ken had remembered the events. He was familiar with Dr. Watkins's interview, and wanted a fuller understanding of what Ken thought of his own childhood. Ken said:

"I always thought of my mother as understanding, loving, caring. She's always sheltered me, forceful, just a super great person, you know, who made very little mistakes. I've changed on my opinion, my idea of my mother, now, recently."

Bianchi then explained that since he had been able to review the DePaul Clinic reports obtained by Dean Brett, his attitude had changed somewhat. "I still love her, but she made a lot of mistakes. She was very stern on punishment, things I had apparently blocked out of my mind that have surfaced as of recently in regards to punishment that she went through. I remember she put my hand over the fire once on the stove, and there were lots of times when I really feel I should have been given more freedom than I had. And for something that I didn't really have a chance to even discuss, let alone being told it was totally wrong,

I'd be just sent into the room to stay there, you know, and it was a constant punishment, and I see now where she made a lot of mistakes with me. She really did. I never realized that she limited my visitation with friends, only one friend in the house at a time. I never realized this. I just, I see her in different light, now, than I did before. I still love her. I love her in a different way, but still love her. You know, she should have had help and if problems developed within me I should have had help in early age, and I'm realizing that now for the first time."

"If you add the letter s to mother, you get smother," said Markman.

"Smother."

"Did she do that?"

"Yes, she did. Too much. Absolutely too much. She, you know, it's one thing in protecting your child from harm and another thing protecting them from the whole world, you know. No exposure, no experience. And I never had, I feel I never had the chance to experience things that would have made me a different kind of person. She more or less took me and molded me to her specifications, instead of letting me experience the outside world, or letting me mold into my own type of person with a little guidance from her. Instead, it was a totally enveloped type of deal."

"Do you ever remember while you were growing up, if you felt that she was unfair or too cruel, that you hated her, or wanted her dead, or . . . Do you remember ever feeling negative feelings towards her that you can recall?"

"I think so. I'm not totally sure. I think when I was small I seem to recall one or two small instances when I thought she was just running my life, I was a kid. And I hated her. Hated her. Of course I didn't mean it, but I'm sure I told her I hated her, and got smacked for it . . ."

Bianchi began talking about his father. He mentioned an instance when he was growing up and had started smoking. He obtained a cigar and was in bed "puffing away on it. And I had, the window was open, and I heard them coming. Well, I threw the cigar out, out the window and tried to clear the air of the smoke, and Mom told Dad to come in and make sure I was okay and say good night to me. And he came in and he knew right away. And he says, let me smell your breath, and I held my breath and he knew. And he said, I know what you've been doing. He says, don't you ever do it again, he says, or you'll have to deal with me. And that's, that's the only time he's ever really been super stern and he walked out and never said anything to Mom. Boy did I feel lucky."

Ken laughed and continued. "I used to feel real bad, Mom used to yell at him a lot. She was the more dominant factor in the family. Very much so. I remember a couple of times when he'd have to sleep out in the car. One particular time it was in the middle of winter. Simply because he loved the horses and he'd bet on the horses wherever they were running in the United States. He had a bookie that would bet on them anyplace. And he apparently had bet too much of his paycheck, and she was pretty upset about that. I remember they had a big fight and he slept out in the car."

"She was taller than him, than he was?"

"No, they were about the same height."

"Same height? I think I read that she was taller in one of the reports that I've read."

"I don't think so. God, she's short. I can't imagine him being shorter. He was a big man. I have his wedding ring at home and it's too big for my thumb."

The talk eventually drifted to Ken's sex life with Kelli. He told of being turned off by her breast-feeding and spoke of not having had sex with her for several months. He admitted to cheating on her twice while in Bellingham. He did not discuss the unusual piece of evidence the police found in his possession at the time of his Bellingham arrest, though. This was a briefcase, in which he had a couple of hard-core sex books and several stained pairs of undershorts. He always had a large towel. The undershorts and the towel were all heavily semen-stained, indicating that he apparently had been masturbating with relative frequency.

The talk drifted to the crimes for which Bianchi had been charged in Bellingham and would still have to face in Los Angeles. "Are you capable of what they're accusing you of?" asked Markman.

"No. I really don't think I am."

"Ever been violent?"

"Not violent enough to kill anybody. Matter of fact, I was in a bike club. And I was a bouncer in a bar. And I could get violent enough. I was in one fight all the time I was at the bar and it just made me sick to my stomach, the one fight I was in, 'cause, you know, I had to hurt somebody, you know. And in the bike club—there were guys in there that—that used to fight left and right, get in fights galore. I never got in one fight in the two years I was in that club. Matter of fact, I got out because it was getting too heavy. There were a few gunfights with other clubs close by and I just, that wasn't for me. That wasn't my thing."

"What would happen if . . . in your own mind, the evidence was such that it demonstrated to you that you did do all these things?"

"Shock," said Bianchi, slowly. The possibility that he had taken a life was not one he seriously wanted to face. "I don't know."

"What was that first word?"

"Shock."

"Shock," Markman repeated, quietly.

"I don't know. I've thought about that because lately I've been looking at my life a little more realistically. I still can't envision myself killing somebody, but I'm looking at it as, as a po—a real possibility. Because of evidence and facts in the case. I don't know what I would do, I really don't. I really have no idea. I feel I'm a stronger person. I feel a lot stronger than I was, say a couple of weeks ago. And if I were to find out that I was responsible for all these killings a couple of weeks ago, I probably would just go to pieces. Now I—I think I'm stronger, I don't know. I—I think maybe I'd hold up a little bit better."

Bianchi talked of what he had learned through thinking, reading the records from the DePaul Clinic, and just sitting in his cell reflecting upon his life. He mentioned a conversation he had had with his lawyer.

"Dean and I talked a while back and [he] suggested that I may be sick. There may be something mentally wrong with me. That there is a possibility. He said he's not expert in the field— he didn't know. And I just said no way. Not me. But now, I feel differently. Now I've put together things that have happened in the past. I recalled a few things that have happened in my life, I've read the DePaul report as to what type of person I was at eleven years old. I've thought back on incidents that have happened to me, realized blank spots in my life. Places where I just should remember what's gone on and can't, and I just feel that there has been more to my life than I've let myself be aware of. And I really feel like there is something wrong with me. I'm not— I'm not normal. I'm not a normal person. For some reason there's—there's gotta be a reason why I lie, there's gotta be a reason why I steal. There's gotta be a reason for some of the things that I've done." He was referring to the charges against him concerning stolen property.

Gradually it became obvious that Ken felt he had lived a life that was filled with lies to others. He claimed to have gaps in his memory, something he discussed with most of the psychiatrists. He said that all his life he often found himself walking along a road, not remembering walking or driving to that location. Later, when someone talked about seeing him somewhere a half hour before he found himself out walking, he would not remember. He would be unable to recall anywhere from a few minutes to several hours of time. It always bothered him because he wasn't certain whether or not anyone else ever shared that type of experience. Now he talked again of forgetting, yet no one could conclusively say whether the statements about memory lapses were the lies of a man trying to escape punishment for murder or the nightmare reality of his existence as a true multiple personality.

"It's strange. I know to sit here and talk that stealing is wrong. I preached not to steal. I mean that was my line of work, was to pick up shoplifters. I preached not to steal to people, I've been doing it for a lot of years, but I've done it. But when I do it, the consequences don't faze me in the least. I just, I don't understand it. And I don't do it for any real reason. There are things sitting at my house—like the phones—they're not sitting there anymore, but, the phones—I have no idea why. None whatsoever. I have no use for four telephones. I had two phones to start off with in the first place. I could have had all the jacks in the world, you know, and just, I had no buyers for them. I have no idea."

Dr. Markman began exploring other areas in Ken Bianchi's life. One of the few studies of mass murderers which have been done over the years indicates that all mass murderers have certain behavior patterns in their childhood. They all wet their beds, played with fire, and tortured animals. Markman wanted to explore these possibilities. He asked about bed-wetting first.

"I remember one incident of wetting. I remember being told I had that problem, and I remember one incident . . . we were at a flower shop and I used to wear sanitary napkins 'cause I used to wet my pants. And I remember that I had wet my pants at this flower shop that we were at. It was actually a greenhouse . . . And . . ."

"How old were you?"

"Boy did I get scolded for that! I don't know . . ."

"Did you bed-wet also?"

"Six, seven. Apparently so, yes."

"How about animal cruelty?"

"Animal cruelty?"

"Didn't you ever have fun teasing or hurting animals?"

"I don't know. I love animals."

"Did you ever hurt them? Ever get involved in destroying them or . . . or—"

"Never! Never! Never! Ever!" Bianchi was upset by the question. He told of hitting a cat once while driving and how emotionally shattered he was. He spoke of his love for animals of all types. However, he would later speak of killing a cat and placing it on a neighbor's porch as a Halloween prank when he was a child.

When Markman asked about the matches, Bianchi did not recall any incidents of playing with fire. If they occurred, none of the investigators learned of them.

Finally Markman wanted to explore Bianchi's talk of lying. There was the question of whether the man suppressed reality or deliberately lied.

Earlier the doctor had been briefed about Ken's "cancer." Kelli had asked the Bellingham authorities to check Bianchi's physical condition after his arrest. She was worried that if he stopped his treatments his disease would worsen. However, a thorough check showed that he neither had cancer nor had ever gone for treatments.

No one was certain how Bianchi faked the cancer story. He apparently managed to steal legitimate report forms, either adding information to a blank or changing someone else's completed form so that his own name and address were on it. While Kelli sat in the car during this therapy, Bianchi would go in the hospital, sit and read or wander about, then return to the car.

When Markman began talking of the lying, Bianchi said:

"I think I've got it under control. I really do. I think I've got a handle on it. There are things, that I—once again, they're things that I—I've lied about to Kelli, for example. And then I'd lie about my lies. And there's no real solid rhyme or reason for it. I just— I go to tell her something and what should come out and what does are two different things, and I know it's a lie. Don't know why. And when I get caught at it, I find myself having to lie to cover up my lie. And it just got really out of hand. I don't believe it's a problem now because I'm really—I am, I'm working. I am working solidly on this one thing, I'm really working on it, is telling the truth no matter how how much it hurts. No matter how it feels to me. Just be completely honest and open and truthful and I've never been that way."

"How do you know that's not a lie?"

"Well, you don't. You're just gonna have to take my word for it, you know . . . No, I really feel, now, sincere enough and sure enough that I'm not afraid to get hurt. To tell the truth. I—I can think of times when I may have lied not to get hurt."

"So you are able to pinpoint times when you've lied? And you know it's you lying. And you know you're lying when you're doing it?"

"Yeah, sometimes, sure. Absolutely, without a doubt. There were a lot of times when I—I know I've—I've lied. Why? Beats the crackers out of me. I have no idea. There are other times when Kelli will turn to me and say, 'Do you remember when I asked you where you went the other night?' I said, 'Well, I went over so-and-so's house.' And she'd say, 'No, you didn't tell me that. You told me you went over [to] such-and-such place.' And I'll be damned if I know, you know, remember saying that. And, you can ask her. It's—it's just weird. It's . . . I have no idea. And I, beats me, maybe I just had a problem communicating. I don't know. Maybe lying has something to do with it. I'm not sure. This is a real confusing time with me. I'm just now trying to sort things out. My problems."

The interview continued but nothing was resolved. Bianchi admitted to being a liar and a thief at times, but certainly not a murderer. Dean Brett received information concerning the case being built against his client and knew there was strong reason to feel the man was guilty. The question which remained was what was truly happening inside Ken Bianchi's head and why. More importantly, how much more would come out concerning the murders?

The Los Angeles law-enforcement officers had at least as serious a problem as Dean Brett's. They felt increasingly certain that Ken Bianchi could be proven to be one of the murderers in the Hillside Strangler case. They also felt that whether or not he was a multiple personality, his testimony concerning Angelo Buono was probably accurate. The location of the shop, the nature of the man, and the relationship between the two made Buono seem a logical accomplice.

The task force was reconvened to open an intense investigation of Buono, including surveillance of his activities. The officers found that teenage girls spent a great deal of time at his home and that he seemed to enjoy the more exotic members of the Hollywood street scene. Unfortunately, concrete evidence in connection with Bianchi's confession had yet to be uncovered. So far, the closest to proof that they had was the few references made in the interview with Dr. Watkins.

During the first few weeks after the Bianchi arrest, very little was known about either Bianchi or Buono. Most of the law-enforcement officers felt that Bianchi was either a rational, extremely violent individual or the type of killer motivated by unknown reasons. They viewed Buono differently, though. If Buono was involved, and there was no proof other than the words of his cousin, then they suspected that the timing of the killings meant he was what is sometimes called a cyclical killer.

Suddenly the law-enforcement officers were faced with a dilemma. Ken Bianchi's testimony was not adequate to make an arrest. Far more evidence was needed before anyone could be certain enough to bring proper charges. The trouble was that if Buono was guilty and if he committed murder on a cyclical basis—as Bianchi's testimony seemed to indicate—then he was likely to take another life at any time. They could not arrest him and they could not provide adequate surveillance to fully protect the public. The only action they could take would be to release the information that Buono was a suspect, hoping that people would be wary in his presence.

The action of making a deliberate leak concerning the investigation was distasteful. The law-enforcement officers were concerned that they might ruin an innocent man. Enough people had been hurt already in this case. Yet wasn't such a gamble, including a possible lawsuit by Buono, worth even one life? If Buono was guilty, someone might die if nothing was done. They decided that they would have to risk it.

Before the decision could be reached concerning the release of information concerning Bianchi's link to the Los Angeles Hillside Strangler cases, leaks began appearing in the newspaper. A wire-service report from Los Angeles told that Jim Mitchell of television station KNXT had gained information that Bianchi's fingerprints were found in the Tamarind Apartments, where Kimberly Diane Martin was originally lured. The report, though inaccurate, was one of the first formal links made by the news media. However, all connections were publicly denied by Terry Mangan, who was concerned about not jeopardizing the case in either city.

Less than four months after Ken's arrest, on April 21, the Los Angeles police publicly acted against Buono. The home of Angelo Buono was searched by the task force for the first time.

There were other newspaper articles coming out during this period. Donald Lunde, a Stanford University psychiatrist with family in Bellingham, was vacationing in the Washington state area in early March. He made an off-the-record examination of Ken Bianchi and consulted with Dean Brett. Though he would not officially be called into the case until later, his opinion was valued because of his celebrated books in the field of murder and madness.

On March 30, the *Bellingham Herald* discovered the multiple-personality concept and headlined the story in an article bylined by Dick Beardsley and Bob Partlow. The story told of the arraignment before Whatcom County Superior Court Judge Jack Kurtz where Bianchi pleaded insanity in the case. According to the story, "'Dr. Markman suggested a possibility of a temporal lobe seizure disorder, which I understand is a multiple personality with an organic rather than a psychological basis,' stated Brett in an affidavit filed with the court.

"Among the tests a neurologist will be asked to conduct [are] an electroencephalogram, a skull series and an echogram and, possibly, a spinal tap." They would prove negative.

Organic damage, though a possibility, seemed less likely after the visit of Dr. Ralph Allison, then a Santa Cruz, California, psychiatrist. In an effort to understand the case, Judge Kurtz had first turned for expert advice to Dr. Cornelia Wilbur, the psychiatrist who became prominent for treating the woman known as Sybil. Because she practiced in Kentucky, however, Dr. Wilbur recommended Dr. Allison, who was considered the West Coast expert in the field. Dr. Allison had conducted a seminar in the field at the American Psychiatric Association convention and was doing extensive writing on multiple personality.

CHAPTER 9

Ralph Allison is a large man, six feet four inches tall, weighing perhaps 250 pounds. He has the boyish face of a man who was raised on a farm, and a gap between his two front teeth reinforces an impression that he is not very bright. However, when he speaks, his brilliant mind instantly becomes evident. He is one of the most innovative theorists in the field of abnormal psychology and altered ego states; his treatment programs are radically different from traditional psychiatry. Both his physical appearance and his brilliance came as a surprise to Ken Bianchi.

On April 18,1980, Ralph Allison began talking with Bianchi in the presence of both Dean Brett and John Johnson. As usual, the room was securely guarded and both audio and video tape-recording equipment had been provided.

Ralph Allison started by talking with Ken, getting his general background and learning about his early life. Then he decided to use what was actually a therapeutic technique meant to uncover the source of his problems. Dr. Allison and Dr. Watkins both took actions which were meant to help Ken get well and face life as a normal person. Unfortunately, this began to change Bianchi's thinking pattern and thus made it more difficult for the other psychiatrists to understand what Bianchi might have been like during his long rampage.

One of the techniques Dr. Allison utilized is known as age regression. The subject is taken back in time to an early year when personal traumas first occurred. The hypnosis focuses on the subject's memory so that he or she can relive the event as though it had happened just recently.

The hypnotic induction is a fairly long process, but after it has been accomplished once, the hypnotist can suggest during the hypnosis that the subject return to the relaxed, suggestive state quickly during future sessions. Sometimes a code word triggers the desired response; otherwise a shorter induction speech is used. Since Allison knew that he would be meeting with Bianchi more than once, he had planned for the next induction to go quickly. Once this was done, Dr. Allison stated:

"Okay, Ken. I said before we took a break here, what I want you to do is think of this index finger here, left index finger, as being hooked up to your unconscious mind through your arm, up to your head, and you can keep your eyes open or closed. It doesn't matter. But just let that finger be there, and I am going to count up the years from zero on up. Now how old are you now?"

"Twenty-seven."

"Twenty-seven. Okay. So I'll count from zero to twenty-seven and I want you to just allow that finger to raise if I mention an area at which something important happened that is quite closely connected to the reason why you're in jail now. So I'll start right off with birth, six months, one year, two, three, four, five . . . twenty-four, twenty-five, twenty-six, twenty-seven." As he spoke, Ken raised his finger at the age of nine.

"Now, stay in the same state of mind," Allison continued. "Let your unconscious work, because now I'm gonna count backwards, and as I count backwards, I would like you to think of yourself as just getting younger, and younger and younger, and then when I stop at a certain age I want you to feel as you were at that age. Not as you think you should have been or what you hoped you might have been, but as you really were, and being able then to talk to me about whatever kind of problems occurred to you at that age, as if you are going through those problems very recently, but are now able to express them to me as if I was a counselor there for you at that time. I'll just count backwards slowly, and you allow your mind to gear into those age states as you get younger. Twenty-seven, go down to twenty-six, twenty-five, twenty-four . . . eleven, ten, and nine. If I could talk to the nine-year-old Ken in any way that is comfortable for you, being nine years old; being aware of me, not being barred by anything else, not being upset about what's in the surroundings, I'd like you to be the nine-year-old Ken telling me about what kind of important things have been going on with you in recent days. What's been going on, Ken?"

"I've been playing, I've heard a lot of fights between my mom and dad."

"What about?"

"Hits me a lot."

"Your mom hits you? How does that affect you, Ken?"

"I don't want her to hit me. There's no reason for her to hit me."

"How do you cope with it, Ken?"

"I want to run and hide. I run outside. I just want to get away. I try to stay on her good side. I try so hard."

"And when you try hard, what happens?"

"She doesn't know, she doesn't appreciate it."

"So what do you have to do?"

"I've gotta do whatever Mommy says."

"What kind of things has Mommy told you to do that you didn't feel it right to do?"

"Clean up my room. But I didn't make that bad a mess. I wanted to play with the kids. The kids won't come near me. They're afraid of my mommy."

"Well, why are they afraid of her? What has she done to hurt them?"

"They see her always yelling at me. They're afraid of her. They don't understand."

"What would you like them to understand?"

"That they shouldn't be afraid. That she wouldn't hurt them."

"How do you know that?"

"Because she's only mad at me and Dad."

"I don't know. She—she picks on me so much. She picks on Dad, too. Always yelling and screaming. She can't talk in a normal tone of voice. She—she's gotta yell and she's gotta scream."

"What does it make you want to do?"

"I just want to die. I don't want her to be my mommy any-more."

"So what have you done to try to deal with it better? How do you solve it for yourself?"

"I—do everything she tells me to do. I don't want to get her mad."

"But there must be some things that you feel you ought to do that she doesn't want you to do. And you still need to do. What do you do with those things?"

"I don't want to get hit. When I do what I want to do I get hit. I don't want to get hit anymore. She hits my dad, she hits me."

Allison began asking about Ken's age and where he lived. Bianchi discussed the street in Rochester and the fact that he had just turned nine. Then the doctor asked how he celebrated his birthday.

"I thought I'd have a cake and a lot of friends over and Mom got mad at me. I didn't have any of my friends over. I was going to have a party and there was no party."

"What did you do?"

"I cried."

"Did you feel better?"

"No, I still wanted to see my friends."

"Do you know any particularly good friends that you really feel are on your side and real close to you?"

Bianchi then described a next-door neighbor named Billy who was his best friend. He was the same size and general appearance, though he never wore clothing that was quite so nice. Allison continued:

"What happened to you during this year to ease the pressures or help you get on to the next year?"

"I just go along. I like hiding. It's easy to hide away from everything."

"Where do you hide?"

"Under my bed, in my closet, behind the house. The bed is the best place."

"Did you ever hide inside your own head?" asked Allison. The question was subtle, spoken without emotion or a hint of what it might actually mean. A multiple personality hides within his or her own head, each of the parts of a normal mind fragmented, living a separate existence. Bianchi's answer to this question could be a vital clue to the reality of his various personalities.

"Sometimes, just to get away."

"What do you do in there?"

"Talk."

"Anybody else there to talk to?"

"My friend."

"Who's that?"

"Steve. He's my second-best buddy."

"Does he have a last name?"

"He did have a last name."

"What was it?"

"I can't remember . . ."

Then Bianchi spoke the name, but it was unintelligible because of the softness of his voice. Allison acted as though he understood, but he is no longer certain now that he heard the name or just said he did to keep Bianchi talking.

"Where'd he get that name?" asked Allison. "Do you know his parents?"

"He didn't have any parents. Steve was alone."

"How'd you happen to meet him?"

"I ran away once, hid under my bed. Mommy was hitting me so bad. I met Stevie."

"How did you first meet him?"

"I closed my eyes. I was crying so hard and all of a sudden he was there. He said hi to me, told me I was his friend. I felt really good that I had a friend that I could talk to."

"What does he look like?"

"I don't know."

"What kind of things does he like to do?"

"Steve and I have the same things in common."

"Such as . . ."

"We like to play the same games. He likes to hide, too. The only thing is, he is against my mommy. He doesn't like her. He's right. In some ways he's right. He tells me not to be afraid. He tells me to be strong. I feel better after I've talked to Stevie."

"Does he suggest anything that you might do?"

"He told me to run away. Told me to run away from home. He told me to not to take it. That I didn't have to take her yelling at me, the screaming, the hitting me, the screaming at my dad."

"So, did you? You didn't run away and see how it would work, huh? Does he suggest anything you do while you're there?"

"He told me when she hits me I should hit her back."

"Have you done that?"

"No."

"Why not?"

"'Cause she hits harder."

"Has there been anything that you *have* followed that he's suggested?"

"I guess."

"What?"

"I don't know. I couldn't do it. Maybe he was right."

"Couldn't do what? What?"

"I couldn't hit her. I couldn't run away. He knows she loves me. I love her, you know?"

"Does Stevie love her?"

"No. He didn't want to have anything to do with her. He just said she's bad news."

"What does Stevie think about your dad?"

"Stevie feels sorry for my dad. I do too."

"Were there any others that you met like that besides Steve?"

"No. Stevie was my second-best buddy."

"Second-best buddy. Okay. What kind of things have you and Stevie enjoyed doing together?"

"Playing out in the dirt, play hide and go seek, running through the neighborhood. We used to go down to the playground. We'd have such a good time. We could share secrets."

Ralph Allison listened to this report with a growing sense of understanding. Imaginary playmates are a normal part of growing up for all children. Often they try to bring their parents into the fantasy, insisting upon one cookie for themselves and one for the playmate. Or the child wants a place set at the dinner table for the imaginary playmate. Whatever the game, the child understands that it is all "pretend." The imaginary playmate never becomes so real that the child senses its physical presence in the way he or she relates to another actual child.

Some children are immensely lonely when they invent the playmate. Often they have been abused, either psychologically or physically. They are not allowed to have normal friends around the house, or the rules for such friends are extremely restricting. The imaginary playmate becomes more real. Fairly soon it is alive inside the head of the child. Often the playmate can do those things the child fears. If a father beats his son for enjoying the flowers, for example, the child may turn a playmate into a "real" person who can enjoy the gentle beauty of a dandelion or a rose. Then the father can only hurt the imaginary child, not the real one.

In some cases, as the child grows older, the playmate becomes permanent, rigid. Eventually that pretend friend becomes a real person living inside the child's head. It is what is known in psychological terminology as a rigid ego state—a distinct personality with its own memories and its own moral code, often quite different from the real child who created it. The alter personality is formed. The story Allison was hearing from Ken Bianchi, regressed to age nine, seemed to indicate that this particular imaginary friend had become quite real. "Does Stevie have a home? A house where he lives? Where?"

"Stevie lives with me."

"Does he have his own particular bed or clothes or closet?"

"He sleeps in my bed. We share the same clothes."

"Does he have a different taste in clothes than you do?"

"Yeah, a little bit different."

"Well, what does he like a little differently than you do?"

"Instead of wearing his shirts tucked in like Mom always says we have to do, he likes to wear his shirts out."

Another alarm went off inside Dr. Allison's head. Ken apparently has to be the good little boy. His imaginary friend is the rebel. Mom wants Ken to wear his clothing properly. Stevie likes to wear it out, something that Ken would never do. Naturally his mother will see it and want to punish Ken, but then he can blame Stevie, the imaginary playmate who was rapidly developing a unique life of his own.

"You'd just as soon wear them in?" asked Dr. Allison.

"Yeah. That's what Mom wants me to do. She says always tuck in your shirt."

"Okay. What else can you tell me about Stevie that makes him any different than you?"

"He's free. Mom can't touch him."

"Has Mom ever seen him?"

"No, it's just our little secret."

"So there's no way that he can get punished by her, right?"

"No way. He knows it too."

"Does he like different foods than you do? Does he eat along with you?"

"Yeah, but he doesn't like school either. School's so boring. Stevie always wanted to go out and play and so did I. Playing's more fun."

"Rather play with the boys or the girls?"

"I'd rather play with the boys."

"Why?"

"Girls are too squeamish. They're okay, they're just so fragile."

Dr. Allison discussed intelligence with Ken. Stevie was described as being smarter than Ken. The doctor then asked how he reveals that fact.

"He always seems to know what's gonna happen next even before I do."

"Does he warn you about dangers or problems coming up?"

"Sometimes. He can tell when Mom's getting mad."

"And you can't?"

"Not usually. I'm so dumb."

"So you get caught by surprise, huh?"

"Yeah, and then I get the worst end of it."

The two talked about games and Ken mentioned that Stevie liked to play jokes on people. "He likes to hide behind a tree at night just when it's getting dark, and when some kids are coming down the street, jump out and scare 'em. He's crazy like that."

"Do you like to do that? Would you do anything like that?"

"No, it's fun to watch, but I don't want to do that. It's not that much fun scaring people."

Again Allison noted that Ken likes to be the observer. Stevie takes the actions which might be construed as being naughty or bad.

"Do the kids really get scared when he does that?"

"Yeah, they sure do."

"And they go and complain to your mom?"

"Nope, not at all."

Allison then decided to move Ken forward in time, to learn about traumas during later years. He knew from the reports that Ken was upset with the loss of his father at age thirteen. While Ken was still hypnotized, Allison said: "I want you to start growing older as I count from nine, where you are now, to ten, eleven, twelve, and thirteen. Focus in on thirteen. I want you to tell me whatever you can about the problems that are going on at thirteen. Whatever Ken is having trouble with at thirteen. Where are you, Ken? Where are you living? What are you doing?"

Ken talked of living on J Street in Rochester. He had just passed the eighth grade but had not done well with his classes. He was then asked what was troubling him.

"Mom and Dad. And the neighbors upstairs. The neighbors upstairs are always fighting. Mom and Dad are always fighting. The whole house is just . . . everybody's fighting. The people upstairs are constantly fighting with my parents."

"How's that affecting you?"

"I don't like being around that kind of stuff. It just bothers me, you know, to see people fighting all the time."

Ken told that he sneaks out of the house and goes for walks when the fighting takes place. He goes to see friends. Then Dr. Allison asked about Stevie. When Ken said he was still there, the doctor asked what he was doing.

"He's angry with me."

"Why?"

"'Cause he doesn't understand how I put up with it. All the fighting. Why I don't really run away. I don't think Stevie and I are best friends anymore."

"What's happened to this relationship?"

"I don't know. I don't see much of Stevie. We just sort of parted."

"Where did he go?"

"Away."

"Did you have a farewell party for him or . . . in a boat or plane or car . . ." The doctor was trying to establish how Steve had left: did Ken feel he had physically left or just gone into another part of the mind? It was a question he couldn't specifically ask without leading Ken.

"No, we just parted ways. I just—one day he wasn't there. He comes back once in a while to visit, but it's not the same. We used to be such good friends."

"How has he changed that makes it difficult to be friends with him?"

"He's not funny anymore. He's mean. Everybody's mean and now my best friend is mean. I don't understand that."

"You're thirteen. Is he thirteen too, or is he older or younger than you?"

"Thirteen."

"Is he, uh, interested in girls yet?"

"Oh, yeah."

"How so?"

"He likes them."

"As much as you or less than you, or more than you?"

"I like them because they're girls. He was telling me that he likes to hurt 'em."

"Why?"

"I don't know. He gets his kicks that way. He thinks it is really great. I don't understand that at all."

"What ways would he hurt them?"

"Punching 'em. He told me of one girl that he knocked right down to the sidewalk."

Age regression often sounds like a fantasy to people who have never been trained in hypnosis. It is actually a way of focusing the mind on a narrow portion of memory—in this case, one year of a man's life. The fact that the person recalling the events often speaks as he or she did when at that age shows how intense the reliving can be. However, repeated studies by professionals in the field have shown that the memories of events reported in this way are accurate. The emotions experienced at that time are also accurate: the person is often willing to admit embarrassing thoughts that are repressed in adulthood.

Dr. Allison decided to move on to the death of Ken's father. The grief was typical of a child, in that Ken felt abandoned. His first comment was, "Why did he leave me?"

"How did he leave you?" asked Allison.

"Why did he leave me?" Ken protested.

"You tell me how he left you first."

"He died."

"Tell me what happened."

"He just went to work and he was dead."

"How were things going with you two at the time he died?"

"I didn't see Stevie at all. I don't know where he went to. Sometimes I thought he was back again, but nope."

"And then after your father died, did you see Steve again?"

"No"

"No?"

"I never saw Stevie again."

"What did you think happened to cause your father to die?"

"God wanted him more than we did. God doesn't know. I really needed him."

"Well, God must have had his reason, but we don't know what it is, do we? That left you awfully lonely, didn't it? That left you and Mom."

The fishing trip that Ken and his father enjoyed had been the high point of their relationship. The man and boy had been alone together, talking intensely for the first time. Even the fact that they forgot to bring back Ken's new shoes did not dampen the pleasure. They would return to the location in a few days and retrieve them.

The warm glow of the loving experience was with Ken when his father returned to work. Their talking was limited at home in Rochester because of his father's schedule, but Ken was anticipating their next time together. This added to the shock of hearing that his father had dropped dead of a heart attack while at work, the promise of the new relationship shattered in an instant.

The conversation continued, Ken being upset because Stevie had left him. Then he discussed his feelings about his mother.

"She always wants me home. I can't be Dad. I keep telling her I can't be Dad. I'm just a kid."

"So she's trying to get out of you what she needed out of your dad, huh? Did she calm down as far as hitting you and telling you what to do, or what?"

"No, she still hits. She tells me everything what to do. I can't even walk out the front door without her telling me to do it."

"Have other people shown up that are like Stevie?" asked Allison. If Ken was a multiple personality, as he suspected, then perhaps the trauma had resulted in the creation of a new personality whose job it would be to handle the stress of his father's death.

Allison decided to bring Ken's concentration forward in time to the present, then ask to speak to Steve. However, he felt he needed to first reassure the thirteen-year-old Ken as he would any child going through the grief process of death.

"Your dad is gone away," said the doctor. "He loved you very much. He still loves you. I'm sure God is having him look after you in whatever way he can and help you in whatever way he can. He was just beginning to be a close father to you, and I'm sure he misses you as much as you miss him. Maybe you can listen for him. Maybe he can get through and talk to you a little bit. Maybe you can get some of his wisdom and his judgment, some of his knowledge about how to cope with these things. You just never know, 'cause I'm sure he misses you, too."

As Dr. Allison brought Ken forward in time, he left the small Ken, crying and lonely for the father who would never return. However, when he returned in Ken's thinking to the present, he was not expecting what happened next. He asked to speak to Steve and suddenly Bianchi leaped from his chair to attack John Johnson, the social worker who was also operating the videotape equipment.

The change was shocking. It was as dramatic as the difference between Clark Kent and Superman. Steve/Ken began shouting:

"You! You're the motherfucker that's been trying to get me to leave him!"

Because of the hypnosis, Dr. Allison retained a degree of control over the situation. His voice, firm, commanding, showing no sign of panic, said, "You can't do that." He inwardly prayed that it would work. If he was wrong, someone could be seriously injured.

"Fucker!" said Steve, moving back toward his chair. Allison's voice and the fact that several men were in the room seemed to have a controlling effect on him.

"What's your last name?"

"What business is it of yours?"

"Just trying to find out who I'm talking to. Do you know who I am? How old are you, Steve?" His voice was casual, despite the inner fear.

"What're you writing? A fuckin' book?" The voice was hostile, defiant. However, he was physically more relaxed.

"No. I'm writing a report for the judge. He asked me to talk to you."

"Fuck it! Ask him how old I am."

"I know Ken's twenty-seven."

"That fuckin' asshole. Fuck him."

Ken would never swear; his mother would never have approved. Steve, on the other hand, could not seem to string a half dozen words together without swearing.

The two men sparred verbally for a few minutes. Then Steve made a comment which Allison could use to further explore his feelings. "Fuck him, his mother too. Fuckin' cunt."

"She was quite a bitch, wasn't she?" said Allison, urging Steve/Ken along.

"She was a fuckin' cunt. You know, he—he still puts up with her shit a little bit. You know, I mean, granted, you know, I can't come out, but I could see what he's doing, and fuck, man, he has got to wise up, you know. He just—I want to get out, I want to stay out, and fuck it, that's all there is to it. I'm just a better person than him."

Allison wanted to laugh when he heard Steve say that he was a better person than Ken. If Ken Bianchi was the right man to charge with the Bellingham and Los Angeles crimes, then the Steve aspect had committed numerous horrors during the past few years.

The urge to laugh passed. Allison dared not antagonize Steve/ Ken further. He pointed out that Steve did get himself into trouble, to which Steve replied.

"He got himself into a jam. It's—I fuckin' killed those broads. You know, to smarten 'em up, to show him that he couldn't push me fuckin' around."

"Which broads?"

"Those two fuckin' cunts, that blond-haired cunt and the brunette cunt."

"Here in Bellingham?"

"That's right."

"Why?"

"'Cause I hate fuckin' cunts"

"Why those two? You didn't even know 'em."

"He knew 'em"

"Oh? I thought he only knew one of 'em a little bit"

"He knew one of 'em. The other one came along for the ride. Cunts are so fuckin' stupid. You don't understand that."

"That's what I'm trying to learn."

Allison asked how Steve committed the crime. He was in the city to gain facts as well as to advise the judge. These interviews were helping Dean Brett to better understand his client and how the case should be handled.

"I strangled 'em."

"With what?"

"Fuckin' plain as that."

"With what?" Allison repeated. In police cases, a confession has little value unless the suspect provides enough detail so that the information is different from what is known by the press.

"I strangled 'em with fuckin' cord. Nothing to it."

"Did you bring the cord along or was it there?"

"Nope, brought it along."

"Where did you get it from?"

"Got it from my basement."

"Why did you have them go there? How did you have them go there?"

"Oh, it was a cinch, man. You know, he used to be such a fuckin' sap, you know, I just—he left, I came. I did all the calling. I found out what her phone number was, I called Karen. I set it up so she could bring her girl friend."

"How much money did you offer 'em?"

"Couple hundred bucks."

"That sounds like a pretty high price."

"It's a sap deal, you know. I never had the money to pay 'em."

"No? That's why their friends were kind of wondering about why you'd offer so much money. Why at that time did you choose to kill somebody?"

"Because I was trying to get—so hard to come out where I belong, you know? Do you fuckin' understand that?"

"Where do you belong?"

"I belong out. Ken belongs gone. I belong out in the world where I can do what I fuckin' want to."

"What about his girl and baby?"

Steve had only disdain for everything he claimed was part of Ken's life. Then, as Dr. Allison questioned him further, he said something which gave another indication that he might be an aspect of multiple personality. Frequently in such individuals, the violent personality has an unrealistic view of the world. He or she feels as though life can be endless. The personality feels that if the other personality can be eliminated, the violent personality will be immortal. This feeling seemed to be evident when Allison said, "What did you hope to accomplish by killing those two girls?"

"Get him out of the way!"

"Then what would happen to you?"

"Nothing would fuckin happen to me."

"How did you expect him to disappear? By being executed? Or disappear in some other way?"

"He would disappear in some other way."

"Did you ever think that the body there might be executed by the law? For first-degree murder?"

"So fuckin' what?"

"Well, that would sort of put an end to a lot of activity, wouldn't it?"

Steve apparently was taken by surprise at the idea that if the body was destroyed, he might not live either. "I guess," he said slowly.

"Did you think about that before you killed them?"

"Fuck, no!"

"Did you realize that it was right or wrong to kill them? Which way did you think it was?"

Dean Brett listened closely for the answer to this question. One aspect of an insanity plea involves whether or not the defendant understands the difference between right and wrong. His case for the plea increased when Steve said: "It wasn't fuckin' wrong! Why is it wrong to get rid of some fuckin' cunts?"

"Why did you think it was right?"

"Because it makes the world a better place to live in."

"Did you realize there's a law against killing girls?"

"Fuckin' laws. Laws are nothing but fuckin' writing on paper."

"Did you realize there is a law on paper that says you would get executed if you kill girls?"

Steve/Ken, bored, replied. "I know."

"Did you know that?"

"That's bullshit."

"Did you know that the State of Washington has a law against killing girls?"

"Fuck it. No! You satisfied now?"

"I'm just asking a question."

As the two men continued talking, Steve became angry with all the questions. Then Allison turned to Los Angeles and Angelo Buono. Bianchi called his cousin "my kind of person," and Allison asked him why.

"He just, he doesn't care a fuck about life. It's great. Other people's life. Doesn't give a fuck. That's great. That's a good attitude to have."

"Uh-huh. Has he killed anybody?"

"Yes . . ."

"How many?"

". . . he has. Five girls."

"Did you watch him kill them all?"

"You bet I did."

"You can be sure that he killed those five?"

"Positively without a doubt."

"Did you kill any down there?"

"Yep, I did."

"How many?"

"Four of them."

"Okay, that makes nine. Was there anybody else you knew that killed anybody else?"

Bianchi said there wasn't, then began reminiscing about the year period when the killings took place. He mentioned that the killings all began after he stopped living with Angelo. He also explained that they put the cords used in the murders inside plastic bags, which were then dumped in the trash.

Although Bianchi only discussed nine of the murders at this session, his subsequent statements to the police indicated an involvement with all of the Hillside Stranglings. In some cases there were positive personal links, such as the retaining of a personal item from a victim, as in the case of Yolanda Washington's ring. In other instances, Bianchi's testimony could only be corroborated with circumstantial evidence. Eventually, Bianchi would be charged with only five murders in California; he would receive five life sentences.

After some discussion of Bianchi's role, Allison paused to ask why Angelo Buono got involved with the killings in the first place.

"I don't know, man. You know, he just, ah, he was just an easy guy to get with the program, you know? I gave him the idea and he went with it all the way, you know. He's my kind of person."

"Well, how did you two decide to kill girls in the first place?"

"Just sitting around shooting the shit. I asked him if he ever killed anybody. He thought he was talking to Ken. He didn't think anything of it. He said, I don't know, why do you want to know? I said, well, what does it feel like? He said, I don't know. I said, well, we should find out sometime. He said, sure, okay. And we did."

"How long after that did you?"

"Week, week and a half."

"Who killed who?"

"I killed the first broad."

"Who was she?"

"Some black broad. I don't remember her name. Fuckin' names aren't important."

"Where'd you pick her up?"

"Downtown."

"How'd you happen to pick her up?"

"She was a hooker. Angelo went and picked her up. I was waiting on the street. He drove her around to where I was, I got in the car. We got on the freeway. I fucked her and killed her. We dumped her body off and that was it. Nothin' to it."

Allison knew that he had heard a confession to the Yolanda Washington murder. He then asked who killed the second victim.

"Angelo."

"Were you with him?"

"He did a nice job doing it, too."

Allison began asking for details. He learned more of the California victims how the girls were made to undress, then were raped and murdered. Bianchi described the Diane Wilder and Karen Mandic murders, explaining how he separated the two women, then killed them individually and carried them out to the car when it was over. Each detail matched the evidence already known to the police.

Finally the ordeal of listening to the foulmouthed Steve was over. Dr. Allison had enough information to make a preliminary diagnosis of multiple personality as well as enough evidence to convince Dean Brett that his client was guilty as charged. The doctor had Ken return to conscious awareness.

Ken remembered nothing of the interview but he was shocked by the fact that the filters had been torn from the cigarettes he smoked. Steve was a chain-smoker who couldn't stand filter tips. Ken couldn't handle unfiltered cigarettes. Steve had spent the interview time tearing off filters, then smoking the remaining tobacco. Steve also moved the pack from the location where Ken had left it when the hypnotic induction began. The shock of finding the tips torn off and the pack missing from where Ken last remembered it to be was further evidence of his lapses in conscious awareness. However, during that first interview, Allison decided to not go into great detail with Ken concerning what he had just witnessed.

The Allison interview continued the following day, April 19, 1980. Ken had had a troubled night and shared with the doctor a dream he had written down upon awakening.

"I was playing with my twin. Not identical. On either Ravena or Villa Street. We were running down the street playing games, laughing. We shared a lot. We were kids. Our mother came to the front door of our house and called me to come into the house. She didn't call my brother. I went in and tried to explain that he was still inside—outside. She wouldn't let me finish what I was saying. She slapped me and sent me to my room."

Bianchi explained that he called his twin by the nickname "Sticks." He said he didn't understand why. Then he went on to say that the person was one he had met in other dreams. Usually the dreams involved the two of them playing as children. They were not exactly friends, though they weren't enemies, either. He then talked more of his dreams over the years.

"When I used to dream of my dad, the dreams used to be so real that even when I'd—wake up, it was as if I'd actually experienced it. It was like thinking about what you did for dinner last night. It was that kind of reality, you know, that you feel you *had* done it, you know.

"Now, like going to dinner last night, you know you had done it. But it was always this feeling I had. And this was the feeling I had when I woke up this morning. I did what you said. I put my book last night before I went to bed . . . I always keep it near my bed so when I wake up I can just open it and jot it down. I might as well just read this to you and then we can talk about it.

"I was climbing a set of stairs in a house. A big house. There was a door at the top of the stairs. I reached for the doorknob and the door suddenly opened and there was my twin, me. He grabbed me, we pushed each other around. I managed to throw him to the floor and sit on him. I told him to get out of my life. Why does he keep fighting with me? He said he wanted to talk. I was leery. He assured me he would try and be reasonable. We both pulled up chairs and sat down. His legs were shaking. I asked him who he was. He said he was an old friend. I told him he was no friend. He said we used to be friends but that I probably wouldn't remember. I asked him what his name was. He said Steve. I said Steve what? He said Walker. His legs were still shaking. I mentioned something about why was he bothering me so? He said he was disappointed in me. I said I didn't understand.

He said we used to share many years ago. He said now he didn't enjoy the same things, and especially didn't care for my mom. I said, she's your mom also. He said, no way, never. He said I should have fought back years ago. I told him I couldn't. Not with my mom. He started to get angry. I told him he better not. I wasn't scared of him anymore. I felt sorry for him.

"He said he became so disgusted at my calm attitude that we parted as friends years ago. He said he came back once in a while ever since then, and when he could, he would send me away. He said he did it for my own good at first, and then he was so angry that he tried many times to send me away for good. He told me he couldn't send me away for good, so he decided to do everything be could to get other people to send me away.

"I told him I didn't understand how he was going to send me away. He said he could come into my body for periods of time, for one minute, for one day. And he would do this and do terrible things, and then leave me to take the blame.

"I wanted to know what kinds of things he did. He got up and started to pace. He walked over to me and put a hand on my shoulder. It was cold. He said, kid, you can't handle it. I said I could handle more than he thinks. He paced a lot more. He said he wanted me to leave. I told him I wasn't leaving until he told me, and then I'd think about leaving. He told me life wasn't what I thought it was like. He said there were no rules. You have to make your own. He said he wanted to get me away from people I was leaning on for help. If I accomplished this with his help and let him do things for me, we could be friends again. He was pacing to my right. He said he wouldn't hurt my kid. I became angry. I stood up and grabbed him. I told him I didn't like him. I punched him, he broke free. I ran after and reached to grab him and he just disappeared. I felt an easy cool breeze, slowly it turned warm. And that's when I woke up. That's—Larry came to the window and told me breakfast was—"

"And that was very real?"

"Yeah, that was—that was as real as my dreams used to be with my dad."

"What do you make of it?"

Bianchi paused, thinking. Then he replied. "I would say that I met the foe, the person I've been struggling with. I—I mentioned to you before that this, this person, that I talked to you in my second dream, that the note I wrote is—is that I think that it seems much like the person in the first dream and the person in the second dream were the same people, only older in the second dream. And, this is—this is the first dream that I've ever had the feeling it wasn't a constant violent confrontation."

The discussion Dr. Ralph Allison was having with Ken Bianchi was typical of the types of things Allison had heard in his practice when treating multiple personality. The information was further confirmation of that diagnosis. However, when the tapes were played by the police in Los Angeles, the homicide detectives were immediately intrigued by Bianchi's using the full name of Steve Walker. They knew that most people create aliases based on real life and usually from their own experience. Many people use family names or a variation of their own names. If "Steve Walker" could be found to be a real person somehow directly connected with Ken Bianchi's life, then in their eyes, Ken Bianchi was a fraud. He would most likely not be a multiple personality, but rather an extremely clever confidence man. The detectives already suspected that Bianchi had studied hysteric dissociation or multiple personality in the psychology books he owned, then created an act to convince everyone that that was why he had killed.

Several weeks elapsed before the detectives had evidence to counter what Dr. Allison had concluded from his interviews. The break came with the discovery of the real Steve Walker. He was a young man with a master's degree in psychology who worked at the Farmer's Market because he was unable to find a job in his field. Walker had answered an advertisement Ken Bianchi had placed in the newspaper requesting psychologists interested in working in a clinic.

The detectives were able to piece together a story of Ken Bianchi, advertising himself as a doctor, requesting applications from psychologists interested in using clinic space. One of the applications came from Steve Walker, a legitimate psychologist, who enclosed a transcript of his college records. The transcript was complete enough so that it was easy for Bianchi to contact the college, identifying himself as Steve Walker.

According to investigators, Bianchi told the college that he ("Steve Walker") had survived a horrible fire in his home. He had escaped unhurt but, tragically, his college diploma was destroyed. He asked for a duplicate diploma, requesting that it be sent blank. He said that since the original was the only one with personal meaning, he would do something special with the "replacement" by having a lettering expert put his name on. The request was not particularly unusual since graduates frequently requested duplicate diplomas—usually for display purposes. Accordingly, the desire for custom lettering did not seem unusual. The duplicate was sent without question.

Bianchi took the diploma and had his real name added to it. Then he hung it on the wall of his counseling office.

This story seemed to the homicide detectives to belie what Bianchi was telling Allison. To many of the detectives, additional proof was deduced from the titles of the psychology books found in Bianchi's Bellingham home. These included *Handbook of General Psychology, Psychoanalysis and Behavior Therapy, Modern Clinical Psychology, Diagnostic Psychological Testing,* and *Treatment of a Young Male Schizophrenic,* among others.

However, many observers didn't believe that Bianchi could have studied these books in order to "learn" how to be a multiple personality. No actor, no matter how skilled, could have maintained such a pretense twenty-four hours a day. Bianchi's reactions to different stress situations over the past several years were being documented as much as possible and it was highly unlikely that anyone could successfully fake the consistent pattern of his relationships.

The psychological experts interviewing Bianchi also had their doubts. Dr. Watkins had written a chapter in one of the books and he found that Bianchi had no comprehension of the text. Moreover, Bianchi's tested IQ score was approximately 116, a score equated with "bright normal" intelligence. According to studies of college psychology students, Bianchi's IQ was considerably lower than the minimum score necessary for those students who compete successfully in college psychology programs.

Perhaps most damaging to the "textbook theory" was Kelli Boyd's statement concerning Bianchi's reading habits at home where the books were kept. She reported that during the entire time that she lived with the man, he had never opened a book of any type. She assumed that they were just old textbooks from courses he had taken before he knew her. Since the killings did not start in Los Angeles until after he lived with Kelli, it seems logical to assume that if he were going to try to create an insanity or multiple-personality alibi, he would have studied the books up until the time he began committing murder.

Many reporters felt that the one truly damaging book was a volume on schizophrenia, the disorder which many people call split personality. The truth is that schizophrenia is a chemical imbalance which causes an individual to react inappropriately in various circumstances. The schizophrenic might hear voices and assume that they are coming from Mars rather than inside his or her head, or show other manifestations. These symptoms often disappear after drug therapy, which can counter an abnormal body chemistry balance. Bianchi's behavior differed sharply from the symptoms described in the schizophrenic text. However, the reporters mistakenly identified schizophrenia with multiple personality.

Ralph Allison knew nothing about a real Steve Walker as he interviewed Bianchi. He also was not thinking of the legal case and its future. He felt compassion for the obviously disturbed young man in front of him. He wanted Ken Bianchi to have a chance to lead a normal life, even if that life had to be led behind bars. As a result, he made a therapeutic move which would also prevent all future examiners from seeing the same man who had originally been arrested. Bianchi's mental state would be entirely different and any diagnosis made after Allison's visit would vary accordingly.

The only way to cure a multiple-personality patient is to break down the wall between the normal ego states which have become rigid abnormal personalities during the perceived horrors of childhood. One technique is to teach the patient to, in effect, talk with himself. Ken could talk with Steve, something Dr. Allison had decided to teach him to do. He also chose to impart some explanation of multiple personality, so that other doctors were later tempted to say he reinforced the concept in Bianchi's mind even if it had been inaccurate as a diagnosis. Whatever the reality, Dr. Allison did what was therapeutically best, despite the potential legal problems.

"You have to realize the basic principle is that, okay, you created him [Steve] as an imaginary playmate," said Dr. Allison. "I got that in the interview yesterday. That's why you're concerned about that particular house, that particular age [nine], 'cause that's when it happened. And very clearly, you got a perfect description of how this would have come about. Hiding under your bed, your mother screaming at you, beating you, and you couldn't cope with it. No place to run except inside your head. And suddenly you had a friend to help out. He was, therefore, your buddy, your friend, your protector, who had different ideas about how to cope with your mother. You couldn't do any of these things, however. Physically, you know, it was just an impossibility. At least from your point of view."

Allison continued, "He became a companion in your mind that could give you ideas, but none of them you could act out on. And that's when he was a young friend. No problem. Your mother wouldn't notice anything unusual."

"No, she wouldn't," said Bianchi.

"You know, it didn't interfere in your life. It was a companion for you which, in a way, was very healthy, and a lot of kids do this and it disappears when they, you know, get over whatever the problem area is. In this case, your mother didn't change."

"She stayed the same."

"And you didn't change. Then when your father died, which is when you next gave finger signals [part of the hypnosis], at thirteen. And your mother and you, you know, got into a different relationship because of that, which was even more smothering. And he, then, became nasty toward [your] mother, at that point, but you wouldn't have anything to do with it. I can't speak for recent events, because I didn't go into details of recent events as to why he should be strong now. You could pick that up, you know, at any time later. But he continues to be—from being your imaginary playmate into being all those things you didn't dare do."

"It's like a Jekyll and Hyde."

The homicide detectives were angry when they heard the tape of this interview. Dr. Allison had just given Ken Bianchi a short course in appearing insane, a legitimate excuse for his murdering actions. Maybe Bianchi truly was a multiple personality. They doubted it but accepted the possibility. However, they felt that by the time Dr. Allison left Bianchi that day, true evaluation would be impossible. If Ken was faking, he had learned more tricks of the trade than ever before. And if Ken was legitimately a multiple personality, it would now be extremely difficult to prove that fact in a court of law.

Allison continued, "There's one thing you must remember. Since you created him, you are stronger than he is. The creator is always stronger than his creation. It's only if you let him off the hook that he operates. Now, he knows that, even though he might not care to accept the reality of it."

"He knows I'm stronger. That's why he—he sat down and talked to me."

"He can't beat you unless you let him. You can throw the fight. He can't win because innately he is weaker than— You supply all his energy. If you didn't supply his energy and you withdraw the energy from him, he would be like a deflated balloon. You're the source of all his power. You pull the plug, he's got no—no charge."

"You know, when we started to get into this, I never realized that I could have created him. 'Course, then I had no—"

"Thousands of kids create 'em. Most of them dissipate them within a year or so. But if the family situation continued to be bad, you need that kind of assistance, then he can stick around."

The interview continued with Ken learning how to talk directly with Steve. It was a further breakdown of the rigid ego states.

Finally that first interview was over. Whether or not what happened was proper, it would forever change the case.

On April 20, Dr. John Watkins returned to Bellingham. Bianchi had gained greater self-understanding and was given a

Rorschach test, the familiar inkblot association test. Though a professional Rorschach interpretation requires lengthy analysis, even the lay person could deduce key elements in Bianchi's response. Steve and Ken—who, through hypnosis, were tested separately—responded quite differently. The multiple-personality theory was supported. In response to two particular cards, for example, Steve saw "broads lying side by side" and "a cat hit by a car."

Ken, on the other hand, saw two people dancing in a discotheque, "two dogs fighting over the same bone," and similar images.

The other interesting aspect of the interview included Steve looking at pictures of a number of women including the victims. He began identifying them by specific information which only the killer would know. He mentioned one woman who had shaved her pubic hair, a woman identified as Yolanda Washington. Then he went on to describe which girls he killed and which Angelo allegedly killed. He marked the pictures differently so that Watkins would have the complete rundown of death. It was further evidence of multiple personality, yet so many questions remained.

CHAPTER 10

The detectives in Los Angeles had been working constantly since the arrest of Ken Bianchi. Now that there was more information available to the detectives, the picture of the life Bianchi led in Los Angeles could be developed more fully. Among other things, he turned out to have been involved in alleged prostitution and extortion.

The investigators had located two teenagers, Becky and Sabra, who told of having gone to work for Ken and, allegedly, Angelo. At least one of the girls was supposedly in love with Angelo, and they agreed to work for him as prostitutes. Ken allegedly established working arrangements for the girls; the primary clients were a number of present and past officials and business leaders in the Glendale area.

As the detectives spoke with people who knew Angelo Buono, several bizarre claims about him emerged. His one son was the product of a marriage that was annulled the same day it took place. His divorce in 1963 was on grounds of extreme physical cruelty. His current wife, whom he had married on March 29, 1978, was twenty-one at the time, Buono forty-three. She was a Hong Kong exchange student who moved in with her parents after Angelo's alleged activities became public.

Buono was described as a master craftsman and meticulous worker by those who knew his shop. He also maintained a totally clean home in which there was no kitchen and no doors. He took all his meals in a restaurant and engaged in such pranks as showing pornographic pictures of women he dated to chance visitors. There were always young girls hanging around his house, and some apparently lived there on and off.

The county seal that Bianchi had obtained for his car was allegedly provided by a county official. The official claimed that Bianchi had requested the seal for use on an antique car to be displayed at a bank. The seal would allow the car to be parked illegally without being given a ticket. However, other witnesses claimed that it was given after the official attended parties "serviced" by the two prostitutes.

In one unusual case, Bianchi and, allegedly, Buono supplied a sixteen-year-old prostitute to a lawyer, then tried to blackmail the man. Instead of paying, the lawyer had several extremely powerful, tall, heavyset motorcycle gang members threaten the two men. The bikers were so frightening that the blackmail attempt was stopped.

Bianchi himself kept providing details during his interviews with the psychiatrists and psychologists handling the case. In May 1979, one of the psychiatrists he had to see was Dr. Martin Orne of the University of Pennsylvania's Department of Psychiatry, a well-known expert in hypnosis who had testified at the Patty Hearst trial among other cases. He had been hired by the prosecution to act in this case.

During the interview with Orne, Bianchi began talking about some of the California murders. He mentioned one girl who came to the shop to buy something. "Some seat covers or something made for her car, 'cause her car was fairly new. It was . . . orange or red, a small car, I think Datsun. It was late in the day. Steve came over, late, this was like after dinner. And Angelo was in the house talking to the girl. Apparently she'd been looking for a job and he says he can help her . . . I came in . . . I grabbed her . . . I came in and grabbed . . . but there's nothing said . . . there . . . there . . . grabbed her around the throat . . . Angelo got up . . . went and got some rope . . . tied her, gagged her . . ." His voice became softer, his words slower. "This is really hard for me." He sighed. "Do I, do I have to—"

"Can you just try to. . . ?"

There was a long sigh, then Bianchi continued: "After she was gagged and blindfolded, her hands were untied and she was—she was told to get undressed, which she did. It was done with all the girls, all the clothes, all their clothes and possessions were gathered together. They were put into a bag and dumped in Angelo's trash bin. All the girls were, with the exception of the first girl, all the girls were—were raped"

"When you say raped, wasn't a girl cooperative after she was blindfolded and gagged?"

"Only two girls."

"Well, this girl. I mean, she got undressed when you told her."

"Yeah. I wonder why she didn't run? It—it could've been because, well like, if you close your eyes, you don't know what's going on. I say rape—this is the terminology the police used. Intercourse was had with her . . ."

"But I mean . . . that's what I was really asking . . ."

"Oh, I—you know, I'd remem—I'd remember a struggle, and it doesn't seem like there was a great struggle, no."

"It would be surprising, I mean, if—"

"But it was—it was a spare, spare bedroom . . . just between the bathroom and Angelo's room . . . After—after both Steve and Angelo, myself and Angelo—my body and Angelo—got through having intercourse with her, she was then . . . her hands had previously been untied, and her hands were tied and—and her—her legs were tied . . . There was a—a rope put around her neck and she was—she was strangled. Then she was untied . . ."

"Untied . . ."

Then Ken, talking quietly to himself, almost whispered. "What a cruel thing to do."

"Then she was untied? You had a totally nude body, then?"

"Yes, and she was carried out . . . not the back seat . . . she—she was carried out to the trunk of the car and put in the trunk of her car . . . with me driving the car . . . Angelo following behind in another car. The car was taken up to Angeles Crest and . . . [she was] pushed off the side of the hill."

"How about the body?"

"What about the body?"

"Did you leave it in the trunk?"

"The body was in the trunk, yes. I don't recall taking the body out, so I—you know, I know the body went into the trunk . . . It's still there."

"That wasn't the—the one where the girl was laid out kind of like against a hill?"

Bianchi went on to discuss how the personal items were discarded. He claimed that nothing was saved despite the fact that similar jewelry had been confiscated during the searches of his home with Kelli. However, the police had already linked one ring with Yolanda Washington.

The interview with Dr. Orne was to prove unusual in that, though Dr. Orne was convinced that Ken Bianchi was not a multiple personality, he uncovered two other aspects of the murderer's mind. One was Billy and the other, appearing only briefly, was a frightened nine-year-old child.

Once again the transformation was startling. At first the doctor was talking with Steve. This violent aspect of Bianchi's mind was his usual charming self. Speaking of Ken, Steve commented:

"He's just too easy with broads, you know. He—he just—you gotta treat 'em rough."

"Yeah. And Ken didn't treat 'em rough?"

"That's right."

"Now was there some girl that you were going with for some time ever?"

"Me? Fuck no, man!"

"You like only one-night stands?"

"That's right."

Later Steve commented that he had changed over the years. "Long time ago, man, when I was a nice guy, I enjoyed being a nice guy . . . it was different. It was different because it was both of us together, friends. Until he started fighting me."

"Ken didn't even know you existed."

"When we were kids, I was his best friend. He wasn't smart enough to realize that I was his best friend. I was. He didn't realize it. I could have helped him. I could have helped him shake his old lady."

"He had a tough life."

"That's right. That's right."

"By the way. When you were a kid—not Ken, when you were a kid—did you ever kill any cats?"

"Yeah, man. Down in David Mason's basement. Yeah, I did. That was great. Put it on some old lady's porch for Halloween."

"How—what did you use to kill it?"

"A knife. Just took a knife and . . . that's it."

"Where? In the heart or in the throat or—"

"No, man, what you do is, you just, you slit the cat right between their legs, man, and just rip on up. The cat'll die."

"What other animals?"

"Used to kill a lot of rats. Killed a dog once."

"With a knife, too?"

"No, man. With a fuckin' stick. Hit the mother—hit that motherfucker and hit that motherfucker and hit it and hit it and hit it . . . until it was dead. The fucker was gonna bite me . . . you, you gotta . . ."

Orne caused Ken to relax. Suddenly there seemed to be a change. The doctor said, "Tell me about yourself. Are you Steve? Do you know about Steve? Do you know about Ken? Tell me about yourself. What's your name?"

The man sitting before Dr. Orne seemed to crumble like a scared child trying to draw into himself. "I don't know," he said softly.

"It's all right. Tell me. Things are a mess right now, but you can tell me. It's important that you do."

The man started to cry. "You're not gonna hit me, are you?"

"No, I'm not going to hit you. It's all right. I'm not your mother. She hit you a lot?"

"Yes."

"You're afraid of everything, aren't you?"

"Yes."

"And you have been living with both Ken and Steve? And you've seen this all happen. I know you're frightened. I'll get you some Kleenex. It's all right to be afraid. You can tell me about it. How old are you?"

"I'm nine."

Dr. Orne would later state in his psychiatric evaluation that Ken was not a multiple personality and had not been under hypnosis at this time. He was prepared to testify in court that he had tried the tests for the simulation of hypnosis on Bianchi. He explained to Chief Mangan that it was his professional opinion, from viewing the tapes and from the tests he himself had conducted, that Bianchi had been faking the state of hypnosis. He felt that Bianchi had fooled Dr. Watkins and the others who used hypnosis.

Dr. Orne's statements have been greatly disputed by Dr. Watkins and the other psychiatrists who used hypnosis. They feel that their evaluation of the same videotapes, plus their own knowledge of hypnosis, indicated that Bianchi was, indeed, hypnotized. However, Dr. Watkins took the issue a step further and questioned the concern Dr. Orne may have had over the relationship between hypnosis and multiple personality.

A multiple personality will change personalities as the result of stress. The individual switches without hypnosis. The hypnosis only helps the psychiatrist have a little more control over the tapping of the person's memory. Since hypnosis is unnecessary for the diagnosis of a multiple-personality patient, Dr. Watkins and others felt that Dr. Orne's stressing of the issue was academic and unrelated to the realities of the case.

Bianchi was known for his deception, however. The discovery of the real Steve Walker and Bianchi's use of Steve Walker's employment application transcript to gain a psychology diploma were examples of this. However, the basic question of multiple personality was not resolved through the hypnosis dispute.

The videotapes show that Dr. Orne was obviously surprised when he encountered what seemed to be a small, frightened child. He talked with Bianchi as though he were the age he claimed to be. Acting in that manner seemed the only way to ease the terror of the nine-year-old who appeared not to know where he was or why he was there."

"Nine? And you've never gotten older?" he said to the man before him. Then, to Dean Brett, "I'd like some Kleenex, please." He turned back to Ken. "You've never gotten older? Here you are. It's all right. Here's something to dry your eyes with. It's all right. It's all right, now. Tell me, what is your name?"

"Ken," said the voice. Bianchi had not been age-regressed as in Dr. Allison's interview. The person who had come out appeared to be yet another personality.

"Your name is Ken? You're frightened now, but it's all right. You're safe at the moment. It's all right. Nobody's going to hit you, I promise you. No one is going to hit you. No one is going to hit you. What is your name?"

"Ken. My name's Ken."

"Your name is Ken. And what is your last name?"

"I don't know."

Hypnosis was again induced, this time to calm the frightened child. However, instead of the adult Ken or Steve returning, someone new appeared. His name was Billy.

The history of Billy that eventually emerged is somewhat confused. One explanation is that he first appeared at the age of thirteen when Ken's father died and Ken could not handle the idea of going to the funeral. Billy was created to endure the trauma.

Other explanations place Billy's creation earlier, perhaps at age nine. Mrs. Bianchi felt that Ken frequently lied as a child and some doctors feel that Billy might have been the liar who appeared, a fact that would place his first appearance in preadolescence. Billy was always aware of Steve and Ken, though Ken did not know about Billy. The question remains unresolved even after many months of both therapy and questioning.

"All right Billy, tell me, what do you know about Ken?"

"Ken? I don't know Ken."

"Okay. And what is your last name?"

"I don't know."

"And how about Steve?"

"I know Steve."

"Do you like Steve?"

"He's a bad egg."

"He is? Well, how do you cope with him?"

"He doesn't get in my way and I don't get in his."

"Does Ken know about you?"

The doctor asked when Billy normally comes out. "Usually when Steve's out," was the reply.

"When Steve's out. What do you do? What's your function?"

"I just like having fun."

"Do you get into trouble like Steve?"

"No, I don't stick around long enough."

"Okay."

Billy began talking about how he had trouble understanding Steve.

"You know, he—he just won't understand that . . . that a woman is not like a piece of garbage, you know, he—he's forever screwing up with women, and what he does, instead of just backing off and trying to do something right, he just takes out all his anger and frustrations on whoever is present with him."

"And he doesn't back off. He just gets more pissed off."

"Yes."

"But still, has he trouble making it with women?"

"Yeah, he does."

"Because he doesn't know how to treat them well?"

"Yeah, it's—it's not so much that. It—it seems like he has trouble . . . sexually, you know."

"You mean he can't get it up?"

"Yeah, it's really hard for him, you know, when it comes to women. And he—he does all kinds of weird things, to—to get to the point of satisfaction."

"Like what? What does he do to get excited?"

"Well, like all those girls that he killed. You know, he—the only way he could get off is by killing them afterwards or knowing he was gonna kill 'em, and the only other way he could, you know, get it up was by tying them down, you know, restricting them, or holding them down."

"Well, couldn't he find a girl who liked that sort of thing?"

"If you knew Steve, what girl would go for him?"

"Now how about Ken? Did he have less trouble with women?"

"Ken . . . Ken . . . "

"You know, the other . . . one who lives in the same . . . body. Well, tell me about yourself. Never mind that. Just . . . you've told me something important about Steve. Tell me something important about yourself, Do you make out okay with girls?"

"No, I don't bother with girls."

"You don't like them too well?"

"No. I like girls all right. I just, you know, I just don't bother. I just mind my own business and nobody bothers me and I don't bother them."

"Yeah, but how do you get your kicks?"

"Oh, I get my kicks stealing. You know . . . the problem is that there's so much . . . you know, the rich get richer and the poor get poorer."

"Yeah."

"And problem is that, you know, when the rich are richer they just have more than they need. So why not take a little?"

"Right. And you kind of try and equalize things."

"Right."

Billy talked about how he used the money he stole, then mentioned that he was created at the same time as Steve. He talked about his earlier days, then Dr. Orne brought up Ken's mother. "How was your mother? Do you remember her?"

"I remember a lady—you know, that— Wait a minute . . . you know when I—I started coming around . . . I wondered who that man was. I started coming around when Ken's father died."

At the end of June, Ralph Allison returned to Bellingham to question Bianchi again. He had studied the interview tapes made during Dr. Martin Orne's visit and was determined to find answers to the questions which remained about Ken. One way was to tap that portion of Ken's mind which told the absolute truth.

Bianchi was not unusual in this way. There is a portion of everyone's mind—call it conscience, inner-self helper, or any other term—which has an honest understanding of what we have experienced in life. Theoretically, when this part of the mind is tapped, the person asking questions learns the absolute truth. Unfortunately, there is never any definite certainty that the way the questions are answered truly comes from this part of the mind. Dr. Allison used hypnosis to reach this part and the following conversation occurred:

"Is there really another personality called Steve?"

"Yes."

"Why was he made?"

"To get away from Frances Bianchi—who's now Frances [he gave her name after remarriage] not my mom."

"What age was he made?"

"Around nine or ten years old. He was just an imaginary friend. He broke away at the time that my dad . . . died."

"What kind of activities was he involved in Los Angeles?"

"The killings of the girls."

"Why?"

"Their prostitution. The killings of the girls to get not only sexual gratification, but also it gave a personal sense of stimulation or excitement. The killings basically because the killings were somewhat necessary."

"And they just happened to get hurt and killed because that was the only way he could feel he had them in his power?"

"Right. I don't think he really enjoyed hurting the girls. But I don't think it really bothered him either."

The subject switched to the two teenage prostitutes. The doctors had all been briefed concerning Ken's background and were aware of the prostitution charges against Bianchi. ". . . by the way, who was working the two girls when he was—when, you know, the body was in Los Angeles?"

"Steve."

"Now he used to beat them then?"

"I know. I wish I could have done something about it at the time."

"Tell me what he used to do?"

"Well, he'd just work 'em, you know, he'd send 'em out to all calls or . . . set up appointments for 'em. And he'd always make sure they'd go to their appointments and . . . when they did something wrong . . . you know, that's the strange thing. He only hit one girl once . . ."

"Yeah."

"That's strange for him, if you know him. He—he never slept with any of 'em, though."

"He never slept with any of 'em? How about Ken?"

"NO!"

"How about you?"

"Not me. It's not my thing."

Billy went on to talk about how Steve had beaten Sabra with a knotted towel once. He hit her several times, frightening her.

Billy discussed the counseling service, saying that it involved primarily himself and Steve. Steve had had the courage to send for the diplomas, then get the names faked. Steve apparently handled all the necessary work to get everything started, even though Billy was the mastermind and the person who would have handled the counseling had anyone actually shown up for help.

Later Billy asked if the doctor knew how he, Billy, got his name. "Steve was going to a store one day," said Billy. "And I decided to come out. And when I did, some guy was passing by and, and mistook me for somebody else and called me Billy. And I liked that. It's, you know, it's a nice name . . . Billy."

"And henceforth you were Billy?"

"So I decided to keep it. Yeah, it's a nice name. It's got a nice ring to it. Billy."

"If he'd have called you Billy Jones, you'd be Billy Jones?"

"Yeah. I just like Billy, though."

The interview continued for a few minutes, though no new ground was covered. The important part was the introduction of Billy and the new information he had provided.

To the detectives reviewing the tapes, the entire situation was a possible fraud. They felt there was a good chance that an obviously disturbed man wanted a way to confess to his crimes, then establish an alibi which would protect him from serious penalties. Bianchi would thus be using the multiple-personality ruse to avoid the death penalty, and the doctors who gave him information on multiple personality were just strengthening his knowledge.

CHAPTER 11

While most of the psychiatrists were attempting to learn as much as possible about the Los Angeles case, one doctor had an intense interest in the Bellingham killings. This was Dr. Charles Moffett of Bellingham, an adviser to Judge Kurtz. He had seen Ken Bianchi at the end of April and had sent the judge his findings approximately three weeks later.

Most of Moffett's discussion with Bianchi went over familiar material. However, two new areas were explored in some depth. The first was child abuse, for Ken was claiming to remember incidents in his past which added impact to his claim of experiencing fear when his mother would punish him.

"My mother was—was putting my hands over a gas burner," said Bianchi, recalling what he wasn't certain was a dream or a memory. "There were things that—that I dream of once in a while—things that really stick with me and I—I try to figure them out and I was thinking about this dream, and I recall it just like it happened yesterday—could happen with my mom. I can— I can see her dragging me through the dining room into the kitchen—both hands, she had already beaten me with a wooden spoon, and I had done something wrong and she—she was gonna—she had the burners on and she was gonna put my hands over the burner and I was afraid of the fire. And, I'm not afraid of fire now. For some reason when I was small I was really afraid of fire. And even though she didn't actually burn me, she did put my hands over the fire, and she did come close to doing it several times before that . . . And I—she may have done it because I either took something of hers out of the house or I broke something of hers, I don't know. I can't remember. But I remember her vividly. I can see her drag me across the dining room; I can tell you the furniture in the dining room, the picture that was up on the wall. And getting back to this other person . . . I went over my notes and I—the flashes I've been having, the dreams, they stay in my head. The name Steve being so familiar to me. Familiar to me, but foreign. As I mentioned before. And I really feel that there's another person inside me . . ."

Later Bianchi said, "The thing about my mother putting my hands on the flame and whipping me with this broom before that? There was something, I was thinking about things that happened on Villa Street, 'cause I'm—I'm trying to keep chronological even though it's not in exact order. I keep trying to pick my brain [about] different events. And I remember the back room on Villa Street, and there was something . . . I remember one time, my mother breaking dishes, throwing them at my father. We had stairs there . . . They had an argument and I remember he got a bloody nose from so much happening and he was up on the bed. But there was something that involved me. There was a confrontation in that house that involved me. I know it. I knew it. I felt it, but I didn't know exactly what it was. And through a series of things happening. That dream, my trying to recall, all these different things happening, I've been able to grab hold of what that thing was that I was trying to remember. And that's exactly what it was. She had beat, me, I'm sure for the exact specific reason— that's a generality, the reason—and I can see her dragging me through the dining room into the kitchen and, you know, the stove. And I couldn't do this before. There was—I felt what I thought of Villa Street that there was some reason that I—there was a confrontation in that house that really just sort of sat there. It's like having, knowing a word and you say it's on the tip of my tongue. You don't have a full grasp of it."

"But you remember your father intervening on your behalf in this particular . . . and then her wrath turned on him with the dishes and so on?"

"No, he wasn't home. My father—"

"Oh, were two different episodes—"

"There were different episodes. My father was gambler—he liked to gamble on horses. Take him to a horse track and he's happy forever, you know. Matter of fact when he was buried, we put a—a horse inside his casket, yeah, and, a bookie sheet and the whole nine yards. He and her—he gambled too much sometimes. He meant well, he just wanted to make extra money, you know, and he was always on the losing end, usually. And he—I guess they had gotten into an argument over gambling and I remember him coming down the stairs and the dishes flying. I was between the living room and the dining room. I backed off and moved back into the living room when it happened. And I remember after it was all over and quiet I went upstairs, and he was lying in bed, he was on his back, and he had cotton stuffed up his nose 'cause he had had a nosebleed. I don't know if it was from being hit, from the excitement, something he did—I don't know."

"Speaking of anger, your mother apparently had no problem venting hers."

"Yeah, I—if you're familiar with some of the interviews I've had when this whole thing began, somebody asked me for a description of my mother, I gave a true and honest, frank description of her. I've experienced a lot as far as reading things that people have observed of her, recalling things that she's done. She can be a very irrational, very hot-tempered person. Yes, very much so. You know, more than I ever realized. Perhaps I didn't want to realize."

"How could you not realize it, Ken?"

"You know, it's like a parent being aware . . . It's like a reversal of roles. It's like a parent being aware that their son just knocked that bird's nest out of the tree 'cause they saw it with their own eyes, but their son would never do anything like that. You know, it's—I never felt my mother could be that mean. My mother be that mean? Never. I never saw my mother as a person.

I always saw my mother as Mom. Now that I'm starting to see her as a friend and as a person—as a real human being the same as all of us, I'm starting to see her faults. I'm starting to see a lot clearer that what she did was wrong and irrational at times."

Ken later talked about his attitude toward his father's death and his own desire to leave school. "Yeah, I wanted to do something else. Something other than school. Yeah, especially after my dad passed away.

"Freedom had more meaning than anything else to me, and sitting in a classroom was not my idea of—of passing time. When my dad died, we were just starting to know each other as father and son. It was like coming out of a cocoon for the first time. As a matter of fact, my mom stayed behind and worked and my dad and myself and my aunt and uncle and cousin went to Old Orchard Beach, Maine, just a couple months before my dad died. My dad died in July, and we'd just got back the beginning of June. We went away for about a week or two. Up there. And it was the first time I've ever been alone with my dad. And it was a really great experience. I was just starting to get in touch. And then, we came back and he just—he suddenly died.

"You know, it's a funny thing about that. My dad died at work. And two—two police officers came over to the house. They had been trying to get ahold of us and I guess my mother was gabbing on the phone, they couldn't get through on the phone so they came over to tell us. And they walked into the house and I was on the porch playing cards with some friends. And I heard my mother crying and I knew something was wrong and I went into the house and they told me what had happened and I can—I remember the upset and I—I remember how lost I felt, and how hurt I felt. My mother says—my mother says that I stood there and screamed and screamed and screamed. I don't remember screaming and screaming and screaming. I remember going in, going into my room and, crying my eyes out for a little while, and then I didn't shed a tear for the longest time, throughout the whole funeral, for the longest time. I didn't even shed a tear after that. As many times as I even saw other people crying. For a couple of years after that I just, I stuck right to home, I didn't go out and do the things you know at the school, but was home.

"After school, home, into the room, just locked myself in there. It just—I took it really hard, you know. He was, poor guy, he was still very special to me. Matter of fact, he is still talked about after all these years with respect for the things he's done for other people—unselfishly. And this makes me feel good. You know, he's still remembered in that way. And, a matter of fact, before I went to California, I remember it was, was like, waist-deep in snow. And by hook and by crook there wasn't anything that was gonna stop me. The cemetery where he's at is large. It's probably about eighty-ninety acres. It's huge. It's called Holy Sepulcher. The land where my dad is buried are all flat markers. I took my mom's car, told her I was gonna go someplace. Drove down as far as I could drive towards the cemetery, parked on a side street and I walked about, little less than half a mile to the cemetery, hopped over the cement fence, it was maybe about yay high, and all you can see is just a pure white blanket of snow. And don't ask me how I did it, I just walked straight ahead until I thought I'd walked far enough, turned right, kicked around a little bit and—bingo I found his headstone, cleaned it off—and, and, I knelt down and said a prayer and talked to him, you know, and, and left. For a couple of years, I had dreams."

Bianchi continued, talking about the dreams of his father. "And it was always a friendly type of situation, you know, he'd be sitting in a chair and I'd come in and sit down next to him and nothing would be said but I would feel like we were talking, you know, and I'd feel very close to him. And he'd tell me everything's gonna be okay. And they'd last, it lasted for about three years and then they stopped."

Bianchi talked with the doctor about his life before the arrest, then turned to the thought of murder. He first spoke of his sense of wonderment at the charges, then, without seeming to change personalities, was able to remember the deaths rather vividly. His easiest comments began:

"If you knew the times that I've said why, why me, you know? Why am I in here? Why? You know, what did I do to deserve this? I can look at police reports, which I've got 'em all. Facts in the case and things like that and I'm just in total disbelief, you know. Dean and I went around and around for weeks and weeks and weeks and weeks because whenever they'd come up with something it's—that's impossible. It—there must be another reason for it. There must be another reason for it, you know. I— You know, there —is a possibility now, that I may have had more to do with these girls dying than I realize. I can't imagine taking a life, you know, but it's something I've gotta face up to as a possibility. I can't imagine being with these girls. I can't imagine killing them, but there are so many things that point in this direction that I've gotta realize that it's a possibility. You know, I had so much going for me. My family, my son, good job. I can't believe I could do anything as—as disgusting as take a life. You know, life is too precious. I don't know. I—I just—I still can't believe I'm in here. I used to wake up nights thinking I was home. And then it, you know, it hits you that, God, I'm in here. What'd I ever do to deserve getting in here?"

Denial. That was the one consistent observation of both the medical people and the law-enforcement officers reviewing the tapes. Ken Bianchi did not want to admit any possible involvement in the killings, even though the same mouth which uttered denials also could speak of memories of the killings. Before Dr. Moffett had finished, Ken was able to tell of the deaths in Bellingham. He stated:

"I remember myself leaving the house. I had planned not to go to my [Sheriff's Reserves] meeting. I just wanted to go and get away."

"You were supposed to go to a meeting?"

"Right. I left the house, I went for a drive, went to the office. The next—"

"How were you feeling?"

"Good. I was feeling tired. I'd—I'd put in a pretty long week. And I just felt like I wanted to be alone, you know. I just wanted to go; I used to go for a lotta walks and things like that, and do some jogging. And it was just one of those times I wanted to get out to be alone. I was feeling pretty good, just kinda tired. Drained. The next thing I knew I was on Willow Road over there by the cul-de-sac. This is the way it was before. So now what happened was I went for the drive, stopped off at the office. I drove over to the Catlow's house, the girls were there. From the reports and everything I've put together, and what I—the call, the arrangement that was made—I'm pretty sure of it taking place. Basically from what I've read, and little bits and pieces and from what I remember. That's one part of that whole thing that's still not crystal clear."

"Try to restrict yourself *just* to what you remember thinking, feeling, and doing. Now, I don't care whether it's easier for you to think as Steve, or Ken, or whatever."

"I—I can't think as Steve."

"Okay. I want you to if you can. Replicate how Steve felt."

Dr. Moffett was letting Bianchi express himself in whatever way would be most effective for him. Moffett was not asking to talk with Steve. He was not trying to reinforce or deny the multiple-personality concept. He wanted to know what Ken could remember and there was a chance that Ken's denial mechanism would be such that he would only talk of death in terms of Steve, not himself. This was not the case, though. Ken tapped a fairly complete memory, though it is unclear whether this was because of the breakdown in the walls of the different ego states started by Watkins and Allison.

"I went over to Catlow's house [the murder scene]."

"Yeah."

"The girls were there out in front sitting in the car. And I waved 'em in, into the driveway, and they parked their car. And we went into the house. And I showed 'em around the house, showed 'em the downstairs. Pardon me, you have—you have to understand, you know, my body went downstairs. It's there, uh, one part, now we're downstairs. One part I can't quite put together because I remember my pistol being in my holster being in my closet. I still would swear up and down it would be. Yeah, but the memory I have is that I had a gun and held a gun on them. They were told to get onto the floor. Both of them were tied. This is so hard. Karen Mandic was taken in, there was, downstairs in a living area, bedroom, bathroom, basement . . . Diane Wilder was, was put in the bathroom and, to sit on the floor. Karen Mandic was, was put in the bedroom on the bed. Something was taken from her pocket. What was taken from her pocket? A can of Mace was taken from her pocket?"

"A can of Mace?"

"Yep. This is hard. I don't understand why. Both girls were untied one at a time and told to take their clothes off, tied back up again. Both girls were sexually assaulted. And the reason why they didn't find any trace of that is because a prophylactic was used."

"Condom."

"Yeah. Both girls got dressed the same way they did before. One was untied, she got dressed, tied up again. The other one— you know there's—there's—I don't get any feeling of sexual stimulation."

"In recalling this?"

"Yeah, yeah. I should have."

"Yeah."

"Once both girls were dressed with face down, Diane Wilder was—was strangled first. And then Karen Mandic."

"With what?"

"Some kind of a white cord or white string. I keep thinking clothesline cord, but I don't think so. It seems bigger than clothesline cord."

"Nothing you usually carry around with you?"

"It doesn't look familiar. I don't know where it came from."

"Are you seeing it in your mind's eye?"

"That's what I'm trying to do, to give you detail. Both girls were carried upstairs one by one."

"After they were dead?"

"Put into the back of the—car. For some reason, Steve, my body, me—whatever—got into the truck and drove the truck to a—there's a school a ways away from there—got out of the truck and walked back to the Catlows'. There's no reason for that, either. That's really a strange thing to do."

"While they were in the car outside."

"They were still in the back of the car. Walked back to the Catlows', got into their car, drove it to this cul-de-sac, parked it . . . Before all this happened, when the girls were first carried up, before I got into the truck when they were, once they were in the car, their books, purse, and everything were put into some kind of bag. I keep thinking plastic bag. Seems like a yellow plastic bag."

"Why was that done?"

"I don't know. I don't know even where the bag is. I—I can't—I don't know where the bag is. It's—it's got their books—"

"Never been found?"

"No, it's never been found."

"Did those items seem to be of some personal value?"

"I don't think so, um, it, it could have been, it, it seems to me from, from what I've put together and everything, and from what's been told, what's been told to me, it seems very true, that Steve is very clever."

"He must be."

"Because I've thought of why, I've been trying to think of where the books and where the purses and everything, and why the bag. When—when I remember Angelo's back in Los Angeles, I remembered that after the girls were killed, all their belongings were put into bags and put in a trash bin—his trash bin. And it may be evidence, you know; books and purses, evidence."

Bianchi then talked about driving the girls to the cul-de-sac. "I got out of the car, walked down the cul-de-sac, made a left, walked down to Willow Road, that's when Steve left and that's where I was."

"That's when you came to as you? How'd you feel when you came to?"

"Really like I'd just been in a battle, you know. Just really, I mean, more tired than I was to start off with. Confused, a little scared, didn't know what I was doing there. The first thing I—I saw is I turned like this and there was a park there—Fairhaven Park? Is it? And the first thing I saw was—was the park and the archway, and everything. And that's—I was, I was actually—my—it's a strange thing because my—it wasn't like I was just standing there, my feet were in motion, walking, and I just sort of took a glance around after I first glanced at the archway to the park, and just kept walking trying to figure out what I was doing there, how I got there, just had no idea. It really bothered me a lot from that point on. And I came across my truck. I didn't remember putting it there. My pants were ripped, I remember that 'cause I felt a cold draft, I felt a sudden cold draft and I looked down and my seam of my pants were ripped on the inside."

"How did you rip your pants?"

"I don't know. They—if it's the pair I think I had on that night, they had a small rip anyway to start off with. They were very poorly sewn in the crotch. So it may have been picking up the bodies. The motion I can see is of going through and picking up the bodies, it may have been from bending down and doing that. The—the strain just tightened on the material and the material gave way. That's speculative, also."

"The seam had parted, rather than a tear in the material?"

"Yeah, it was just a seam that came apart. That also is somewhat speculative, 'cause I don't remember them, actually hearing them tear and rip when all this was going on. Got back in my truck and drove home."

"You said, in speaking of sexually assaulting the girls, that you should find it sexually exciting in the recall, but you don't. Why do you say you should find it sexually exciting to recall?"

"'Cause I—I never—I've never engaged in—uh, every sexual act I've engaged in has been a mutual thing and I—I get sexually aroused. I get something out of it, you know."

"With a cooperative partner."

"Really, it's—you know, it's really nice. Even—even one time when I had sexual relations with a prostitute—which was once— even though I didn't feel all the same things, the emotional, the physical drive and everything was just really outstanding, you know, it it's just a human thing, you know, it's . . . and I can't feel this when thinking about those two girls being killed."

Details. Bianchi was confirming what the police had been discovering with their investigation. He was stating the situation as he recalled it, not in the form of Steve. But what did it mean?

Dr. Moffett questioned the theory of multiple personality, in part because of the way both Steve and Ken seemed superficial caricatures of good and evil rather than real personalities. He also talked of Steve giving commands to Ken, including urging Ken to commit suicide. The doctor felt the problem was far more serious and that Ken might be a delusional psychotic.

The formal comment was "Bianchi should be diagnosed as psychotic, probably Schizophrenia, undifferentiated type." He also said that Bianchi "should be considered insane under the law.

Though he intellectually knows right from wrong, the combination of his grandiose alter ego and his dissociation and lack of awareness of violent aspects of his own being would not permit him to effectively control and govern his own actions."

The summation read: "In essence, what I am saying about this most unique psychiatric case is that one cannot be half a killer and half insane. In this man, he is a killer and insane."

The problem is that others disagree. Bianchi was alone with himself most of the day. He had visitors—police examiners, his lawyer, and John Johnson—yet he spent more time with his own thoughts than a free man normally is able to do. Dr. Watkins had triggered an awareness of the full memory within and Dr. Allison had asked him to share a dialogue with Steve, which he had done. The symptoms of multiple-personality disorder were fairly well gone by the time Dr. Moffett saw the man. He was not the same person he had been when arrested. What that meant in terms of the accuracy of the diagnosis is unknown. What mattered was that the Bellingham police had additional information for the conviction.

CHAPTER 12

On June 1, Dr. Saul Faerstein of Beverly Hills talked with Ken Bianchi on behalf of the judge. Dr. Faerstein was hostile to the multiple-personality concept and felt that Bianchi was competent to stand trial. His interview, like Dr. Moffett's, explored the murder of the two women in Bellingham as well as Ken's experiences growing up.

Bianchi told the same stories of fearing his mother, loving his father, and the times of abuse. He also discussed his early sexual relations. He told of losing his virginity at age sixteen to a high school tramp.

"She was real skinny, like a toothpick, and she had big knockers, you know, she just . . . She had a big set, and she slept with just about . . . It's a wonder she wasn't a walking disease carrier, you know. I never got anything from her, but she was the first person . . . who was it who fixed me up with her?"

What was the first time like? "It was—it was neat," Bianchi said, laughing. "It was neat, everybody was standing in line. You know, there was—it was either over at her house where her parents weren't home, or it was . . . in the—in this clubhouse that was built where I used to live on Courtright Lane. When we first moved in there across the street and down the street was all the woods. Now it's all homes. But it was all woods. And there was a tree house built into the woods by everybody. All the guys. And she used to go up there. But she was—she was the freebie."

"It was a pleasurable experience for you?"

"Yeah."

"You said you were, you wondered how you never got anything from her—the clap. Did you use a rubber with her the first time?"

"Oh, yeah, that's why. What a stupid thing for me to say. Yeah, I always used a—a rubber was always used with her."

"That was such a stupid thing to say?"

"Well, before when I said, I never got anything from—You can't get anything from—from a girl if you use a rubber. Right?"

"So you always used a rubber?"

"Yeah. Everybody always used a— She even had her own supply."

"Very considerate"

"She, yeah. She was good about that. She was. You know, she just loved to do it, and that's . . . she . . . lousy in school, great in bed. You know, just one of those things."

Bianchi continued talking about his other experiences. He said that most of his sex education came from the street and was rather conservative. He also mentioned looking at magazine pictures at home.

"Did you look at pictures or buy magazines or go to movies?"

"You bet, and used to get horny. My parents had magazines around that I—I literally would accidentally come across them. They'd just put 'em in the wrong places and I'd come across them from time to time. And it excited me. You know, it—it got me horny. I never did anything about it. I was, you have to understand that, that wet dream I had when I was a kid . . . was scary for me. You know it wasn't that I had—had some people that I could turn to and say, hey, look, this happened, you know, what is going on, you know? Honest to God, I remember that night and when I first woke up I thought something was wrong. It scared me. It was new to me. I didn't know what was going on."

The only major addition to the information was the greater detail Bianchi provided concerning the Bellingham killings. He supplied the information without hypnosis. He started with the cord he used to bind the victims. "I think it may have been some cord—white cord, that I had at my house—that's used in, in traction. In hospitals, when people are put in traction. It's really strong. It's—it's good for, you know, it's good for almost anything. But I think that's what was used. I'm almost positive."

"Did you take that when you—at the same time you were taking the gun from the house?"

"No; there was a yellow bag and it was under the seat of the truck. And that's something that's not . . . that I—I'm not sure of how it got there. Everything was in this bag and it was—there was Ace bandages . . . that rope, rubbers . . . condoms . . . that's it. They were inside, a yellow bag."

He spoke of the violent details, the rapes, the use of separate condoms dropped down the toilet. He described the rooms where each girl was placed while he had sex with the other. He mentioned that he was on the carpeted floor of the bathroom when raping Diane Wilder. Once again the police would check the fiber samples from that bathroom floor.

He told of taking a long cord and cutting pieces specifically for the strangulations. The murders took place in the unfinished basement.

Bianchi talked of the anger he felt at the time of the deaths. It wasn't a feeling directed toward the girls. It was just an uncontrolled, brutal violence.

"Brutal because both my hands were just—I mean, shaking and—it seems like I—I can see my knuckles getting whiter and whiter and, you know, I had the cord wrapped around my hand, and it was just pulling tighter and tighter."

"You were behind them?"

"Yeah. The cord was sort of to the side. They were lying face-down."

"You were sort of over their bodies behind 'em?"

"Right. Yes."

Then Bianchi finished adding the missing details concerning the items used for the killings. He spoke of gathering everything together in the plastic bag. Then he drove his truck to the school and dumped the bag in the trash.

"Do you remember what you put in the plastic bag?"

"Yeah, it was the Ace bandage material, used on the girls. It was the cords used to strangle them with. The cords used to tie them up with, hands and feet, when I went back downstairs to get the bag. I also got the gun."

"And what did you do with the gun?"

"Put it in the truck."

"So just the cords and the Ace bandages were in that yellow bag?"

"And some books the girls had and Karen Mandic's purse. Oh, and the—the silver foil from the—the condom packages."

"Why did you put all those things in the yellow bag to take with you?"

"To get rid of everything, rather than leave it there."

"Why not leave it there? Would anyone know what it was, or. . . ?"

"Well, yeah. I—I would imagine since it was Karen's purse that was in the bag."

"That would identify Karen."

"Right."

"What would identify you?"

"Nothing. Nothing."

"Do you remember why you would've gathered up everything to take with you?"

"No, all I—all I have is is the feeling, you know, that . . . feeling, it was just like a second nature, you know . . . just get rid of everything, leave nothing behind, you know, leave the place as— as I had come into it."

Bianchi told of straightening the top of the bed, flushing the toilet, and checking to see if anything had been disturbed. Dr. Faerstein asked: "Was there any other clothes or any other materials that the girls had left behind in the house or had with them besides the books and the purse?"

". . . I know now that . . . I think before I took off . . . This is another thing where I—I—I'm not sure of the timing, the sequence. Before I took off . . . in the truck with the bag I made another trip into the house and there was Diane Wilder's coat and scarf. And I put it behind the seat of the truck. The seat drops—drops back. I put it behind the seat in the truck."

"Why behind the seat, rather than in the yellow plastic bag?"

"It was—it wouldn't have fit."

"It wasn't that big of a bag?"

"Right. Next question . . . When I dumped the yellow plastic bag in that container, which I did, for some reason, I didn't grab the coat and the scarf. But instead, what happened was . . . Friday . . . what I remembered before was going to South Terminal, and I remember pulling up in front of South Terminal, and I remember being just about at the guard shack. There was a little spot in there, which I, you know, had—had been like the missing link in my—my thinking of what had happened that Friday that I was picked up. I know now that the coat and the scarf were put by one of the brick buildings. I think behind some pipes or by some pipes."

"By the guard shack?"

"Yeah. I don't understand why that was done Friday and why not Thursday night. That's, you know, in the dumpster with everything else."

"Do you remember putting the coat and scarf by the pipes? By the brick—"

"I do now, yeah. Absolutely. Just like it was yesterday."

"Tell me what you remember about putting them there, what you were thinking."

"Just devoid of all thought . . . I—I can see myself turning around, the physical action. See myself getting out of the truck, reaching behind the seat, grabbing the coat, putting the coat behind the pipe, walking away and into the compound. What I was thinking, I don't know."

Details. The case was sealed with the various confessions. There was no question of Bianchi's guilt in the Bellingham murders. Adequate physical evidence would have resulted in a conviction without his confessions, the details he provided so perfectly matched what only the killer could be expected to know that even Dean Brett was certain of his client's guilt.

The one lingering question was the state of Bianchi's mind. Dr. Faerstein concluded:

"No one single psychiatric diagnosis can accurately describe the defendant. He manifests symptoms and behavior consistent with several categories of mental disorders. Kenneth Bianchi is diagnosed as having a Personality Disorder with features of sociopathy, explosiveness and narcissism. He also can be characterized as having a Sexual Deviation Disorder with features of sexual sadism and violence. The use of the psychological defenses of repression and denial since early childhood has manifested in isolation and splitting of affect, somatization, and what is described by Mr. Bianchi as amnesia."

At the end of the report, Dr. Faerstein made reference to a number of points relating to Bianchi's motivation and his longstanding interest in the police. When he was tested as a child, some of the tests included having him draw pictures. Ken, as a boy, almost always liked to draw police officers.

"I would like to add one note of speculation which may shed some light on the motivation for these crimes. From his earliest years, Kenneth Bianchi admired and dreamed of becoming a law-enforcement officer. He drew the figure of a policeman in a childhood Draw-A-Person test. He studied police science at junior college. He applied to law-enforcement agencies for jobs in New York, California and Washington, but he was always rejected. Perhaps he saw this goal as the achievement of some victory over his mother whom he saw as another authority figure. All these rejections by law-enforcement agencies made him bitter. In the long string of murders he committed, he demonstrated that he *had* mastered the science of law enforcement and that he was a better policeman than any policeman on the force. He left no clues. He went undetected for over a year. So in the process of achieving his victory over the female authority figure by killing her surrogates, he also vanquished the male authority figure by eluding the police, sheriffs, and detectives."

CHAPTER 13

The Bellingham case was closed. All that remained was a hearing on Bianchi's sanity which would take place in October. However, the decision to have six psychiatrists officially speak to Ken and analyze his mental state meant that, in July, he still had to meet with Dr. Donald Lunde. Dr. Lunde was an expert in the field of murder and madness who works at Stanford University in California. He did the same type of preliminary investigation conducted by the others, then concentrated on getting the details of the California crimes. Bianchi would be extradited after his Bellingham trial and the material brought out now would be of great help to everyone involved with the Los Angeles case.

The first shock came after a fairly lengthy interview. Bianchi admitted that his first intended victim was not a prostitute but rather the daughter of the famous movie actor Peter Lorre. Ironically, Peter Lorre played monstrous madmen in numerous movies. Lunde asked if any other victims had been rejected before the violence had actually begun.

"Peter Lorre's daughter was going to be a victim. It's a strange thing—I was talking to Dean about that—I think I wrote him about that. Peter Lorre's daughter was—was—could have been a victim, I don't know how—but somehow the notoriety—the fact that who she was—you know, Peter Lorre's daughter—somehow stifled whatever was going—I don't know why—it's the only connection—it's something that stands out in my mind as being somehow important, I don't know why. But I can remember her showing—showing the pictures of her sitting on her father's lap. She looks just like him, too."

"Where did you meet her?"

"This is in downtown Los Angeles—just on a side street."

"What was the situation? I mean, how did you—did you pick her up?"

"No, the—the thing was, the thing was the Hillside killings was the . . . pretending to be police officers and that sort of thing, and . . . she was stopped for that reason. There were other girls, too."

"And so . . . she was actually driving, you mean?"

"No, she was walking."

"All the girls were walking."

"All the—"

"That's something I never thought of that I just—all the girls were walking, none of the girls were ever driving."

"—and, okay—"

"Wow, that's really strange. I'm sorry, go ahead. That never occurred to me . . . before."

"Did you and Angelo both say that you were police officers?"

"No, we took turns . . . It was never—never both. Naturally at one—naturally when one says that he is, people just take it for granted that the other person with him is also."

"So that other person would be visible—not hiding in the back seat or something?"

"Right."

"What was the car? I mean, it wasn't a police car, obviously. Was there any—was there any [attempt] to make it look as if it were?"

"There were several cars used. See, in Los Angeles, what you have to remember is unmarked—there are unmarked cars. I mean, they're—they're not like here—unmarked cars with little spotlights on the sides and everything. Unmarked cars down there could be anything from 'fifty-seven Chevys to—to . . . station wagons to almost anything—any vehicle whatsoever."

"So the idea was that you were undercover kind of?"

"Plainclothes."

"With her—okay, you go up to her and I sup—you show her a badge?"

"Yes..."

"And what do you say?"

"Hi, we're police officers. Would you step over to the car, please?' And she stepped over to the car. And ah, 'Do you have any identification on you?' And when she showed the identification along with that picture of her father."

"Okay, and what happened next?"

"Just the conversation about 'Oh, no kidding—so that's really your father.' 'Oh, well, you take it easy and you know you shouldn't be on the street at night, out walking alone.' She was going to get her husband. Walking to where he was working."

"Was the time of night, you know, within a fairly narrow range or could it have been most any time of night?"

"That's another thing—with all the girls, the time was usually between eleven and two, I don't think it was ever—"

"And they would be usually walking—alone?"

"Right."

"Now in that case, for instance, would both you and Angelo talk to her or just one of you?"

"For that one—that one girl?"

"Let's just take that one."

"Both. It wasn't always both—"

"And then—how would the decision be made as to whether—you know, the decision was made—that she would not be a—was that because, I mean, you—did—the two of you talk it over or did you know, and did you discuss it in such a way that the girl couldn't overhear your conversation—or how did that work—or did you have some kind of signals worked out between the two of you—or—"

"With that incident—with that incident I can see Angelo tugging on my arm, and [I] got in the car, and he said, you know, forget it. Leave it alone. He ended the conversation telling her to be careful and you know, just, just to be careful and tugged on my arm. We got in the car and he said no, forget it, and we took off."

"Now the fact that you were out to begin with, would that be a decision that was made, you know, as a result of a discussion that . . . you know, 'well tonight, let's do it' or was it looser than that?"

"I don't know. . . . For the—for the first girl, the black girl, it started with a conversation about did he ever kill anybody. It started on a conversation about killing people.

"Then it was—I'm not totally a hundred per cent clear on whose idea it was about the acting like a police officer, but that's actually how it started."

Bianchi talked about how a variation of the police ruse was used to pick up every woman they murdered. For example, actress Jane King:

"The police really did a terrible job on that . . . Jane King was waiting for a bus. The police ruse was used again. Only it was used differently . . . I know what took place at the bus stop— I don't—I'm really not clear on what conversation took place prior to that. what took place at the bus stop was—she was offered a ride. Angelo came along—I was at the bus stop, when I was dropped off there—what was discussed before that—I don't know. But . . . she was offered a ride and she was a little hesitant and she was told that—that . . . we were police officers and she felt very confident and off we went. She got in the car and off we went and . . . part of the conversation that I can remember that happened after that was Angelo said something about, excuse me, he had to get home. And would she mind very much if we dropped him off first and then I would drop her off home, and she said no. And home was over at Angelo's. When we got to Angelo's . . . naturally she was sitting in the middle of the two of us . . . and . . . I grabbed one arm and Angelo grabbed the other and she was handcuffed and told not to say a word and she was escorted out of the car and into the house."

Bianchi then explained how the women were handled when an "arrest" was made. Most of the girls were arrested for a crime when the police ruse was used. As Bianchi explained, "Washington it was for prostitution; Miller it was for prostitution; Kastin it was for . . . a burglary that had occurred somewhere in the neighborhood, which was just made up for questioning; Weckler it was for the party; King, it was for a ride home; Wagner was . . . for questioning, I can't remember what kind; Hudspeth it was . . . the ruse for a job; Martin was . . . for prostitution; and Johnson and Cepeda was—I'm not sure—was . . . being out late at night."

The most horrible of the crimes Bianchi discussed was that of Kristina Weckler. She was the only victim who was tortured, and Bianchi had difficulty discussing the case.

"Kristina Weckler, okay . . . Why the police ruse wasn't used, I don't know. How it got into the discussion to go over to her house, I don't know. She—she was invited to a—seems like she was invited to a party; I can remember going to the door and I can remember her—her getting her coat and things and leaving and coming out and getting in the car with Angelo and . . . it doesn't make sense to me because she and I were never—hardly even talking friends—I didn't know the girl—hardly—really hardly—just enough to say hi to her—all the time that I lived at the apartments. That doesn't make sense to me. I wasn't familiar with her enough to—"

"Do you remember picking her up?"

"Yeah . . ."

"To—like she was going to go out with you?"

"Yeah, it, it doesn't make sense."

"Did she live nearby? Or how did you meet her?"

"No, she—she lived in an apartment complex that I used to live in."

Bianchi continued, "She wasn't—I wasn't living there when she was—"

"This isn't Tamarind, was it?"

"—she was killed. No, this is, this is—"

"That's different?"

"This is on—"

"This is in Glendale."

"In Glendale."

"Okay, and so you picked her up but Angelo was with you?"

"Yes, he was waiting in the car."

"Did she—when she saw him, did she—what did she say?"

"I can't figure out that—there's—there's part of that that's like a puzzle. I can't figure out, number one, why she went with me and, number two, why she didn't say anything when she recognized Angelo. I can't remember—any real distinct conversation. . . . When she got in the car, we immediately went over to Angelo's house and...she went in and when she got in . . . I grabbed one arm and Angelo grabbed the other and we escorted her to—to the chair and told her to keep her mouth shut and she was gagged and blindfolded."

"Had she been . . . handcuffed in the car?"

"No, she wasn't handcuffed at all—until she got to Angelo's."

The subject moved on to other victims, then returned to Weckler because of the extreme horror she had been forced to endure. "They said that they—didn't make any sense at the time, so I thought I'd really think about it," said Bianchi. "They found needle marks on her. That was—there was a variation. What happened was Angelo had an idea to kill her other than strangling. So what he did was, he came out of nowhere with a needle—a syringe. He—"

"What was in it?"

"He—I—I think he mentioned . . . his mother was in the hospital at the time and I think he may have robbed it from—stolen it from the hospital. And I'm not ever really sure what he filled it with . . . I could just see fluid in it and—"

"Didn't work?"

"No."

"Well, that explains the needle marks."

"And, also, I think it was her—I'm not sure—exactly sure who—I think it was her that that she really didn't die of strangulation. She didn't die—die of—of manual strangulation. She died of gas asphyxiation."

"How? How so? How did that happen?"

"Oh God, do I have to? She—she was brought out to the kitchen and put on the floor and her head was covered with a bag and the—the pipe from the newly installed stove, which wasn't fully installed yet, was disconnected, put into the bag and then turned on. A—there may have been marks on her neck because there was a cord put around her neck with a bag and tied to make more complete sealing."

"I wonder, how long did that take then, I mean maybe—"

"I don't—"

"Hours?"

"Quite a while, probably—probably about an hour, hour and a half."

The violence was interspersed— with reminiscences of a normal life with Kelli: playing with Sean, feeding the boy and carrying him through the streets of Bellingham, sharing the kind of adventures every father enjoys with a growing baby. Bianchi spoke of his relations with Kelli, going to movies, to parties, spending evenings with her family. The only time his voice grew angry was when he was talking of the venereal disease and the rape she tried to keep from him.

The obvious joy in Ken's voice when speaking of his daily activities added to the horror of the situation with which the police were involved. Here was a man who might have been anybody's father, anybody's husband. Yet this was also a man who could periodically be overcome by a rage so great that someone had to die before he could relax. He would go out at night, strangle and rape, then go home to Kelli as gentle and loving as ever.

The litany of death in Los Angeles continued. It was a story of terror and violence, of cruel brutality. The detectives who listened, who had been tracking Bianchi for months, who had seen the young women after their deaths, hated the accused murderer even more now. They heard such statements as:

"When she was dead, her body was put aside. And the other girl was brought in blindfolded asking for her girl friend. And she was told that she would be seeing her girl friend pretty soon."

"In regards to the killings, there was never any—socializing. It was just go over and let's go out tonight and try to pick somebody up and he'd say, okay, and he'd go get his stuff and change his shirt and out we'd go."

"Miller was handcuffed as soon as she got in the back seat of the car."

The gag "Would be on . . . until Angelo . . . until Angelo— you know, had oral sex with her."

The killings that allegedly occurred at Angelo's house always took place in the same room. "Always in the spare bedroom. Always on the floor."

"I was—I was doing an awful lot of thinking, trying to feel—trying to get a feel for what exactly was going on what the reasons were for everything taking place . . . basically—what the motivation was—or the emotions that were being felt. I've always felt a great anger—I mean, a really intense, horrifying, just cut-loose anger . . . It seems to me I've—I've put the reasons for the killings and what took place prior to and during . . . as falling into three categories. One category is—is to get me—the second category is because there was a—a sexual arousal with a—having sex, knowing that the end product is going to be the killing itself—that being an arousal also; and . . . thirdly, along with that . . . which came to me just a little while back, the third major reason is—is because—this is terrible—this is in no disrespect for the girls—dead people tell no tales. No witnesses.

"But that was the very—it doesn't seem to me when I get that feeling—that's a very strong . . . reason for it. There was a more stronger, personal, emotional rage arousal from that."

Bianchi discussed the first two killings, which were of greatest interest to the press: Yolanda Washington and Judy Miller. One went almost unreported and the other intrigued the newsmen because of the position of the corpse. Bianchi mentioned the Yolanda Washington killing and how Angelo had picked her up when he was alone in the car. He said:

"She was picked up by Angelo, Angelo had sex with her first . . . and then took her to a—a spot where I had been dropped off, by a gas station. He pulled up and I—she was in the—the front seat. He pulled up and . . . I walked up to the car and opened the door and got in and used—used—we used the police officer ruse. I'm not sure—there's a part missing in there. I know that—that she and I ended up in the back seat but I'm not sure exactly when she got in the back seat if it was there or if it was someplace else . . .

"I had sex with her," he continued. "And—and then after that, while driving on the—the freeway, she was strangled on the floor of the car . . . Once this was done, all her jewelry was taken off and . . . we were at some apartment complex, by a freeway . . . Nobody in particular lived there—the jewelry was thrown into the bushes there. It seems like it might have been a stop-off or a pull-off point on the freeway—an exit; and . . . from there all her clothes were—were taken off and . . . brought into the front seat. I got into the front seat of the car—her body was taken to— you know, this is—I'm relating this to you and . . . this is—the only one that was done outside of Angelo's house."

He continued: "Her body was taken over by Forest Lawn and—on Forest Lawn Drive—and dropped there."

Bianchi also discussed Judy Miller, whose death was oddly upsetting for him as well as for others who saw her body later. He started explaining: "Miller and Washington were the only— were the two where . . . I was not in the car . . . at the time of the pickup."

"Where were you at—Miller—you were at Angelo's house?"

"No, Miller—I was on a street corner on Sunset Boulevard. I know it was Sunset because I can see—I can see all the build-ings."

Dr. Lunde said, "Okay . . . Miller was picked up by Angelo and then you were picked up on a street corner. And . . . was she immediately gagged, handcuffed—anything like that?"

Bianchi answered: "Miller was handcuffed as soon as she got in the back seat of the car."

"Who would usually—I don't know if there was a usual pat-tern—was there one of you who was usually the driver and—"

"No,"

"You alternated? Okay, in this case, who put the handcuffs on her?"

"I did."

"And what else? Any gag? Blindfold?"

"No—no, there was never any further—anything further than handcuffs until Angelo's house—at all."

"Okay, what was said to her at the time you—"

"Just that that . . . it had something to do with the prosti-tution—I would imagine that, you know, prostitution is against the law."

"This was still a part of the police-ruse thing?"

"The police-ruse thing was used in almost all of them."

"Okay, so the handcuffs were—"

"Part of that."

"Explained and then so—they would have the impression that they were being taken to a police station, right?"

"Right."

Bianchi explained that Judy Miller was gagged, then the handcuffs removed long enough for her to take off her clothing. She was made helpless again as soon as she was naked. He then told what happened to her after that:

"Angelo had sex with her. Just plain ordinary intercourse. There was also some—some oral intercourse between him and her . . . I'd had s—regular intercourse with her, and then she was allowed to get dressed. She went to the—to the—she went to the bathroom right after that, before she got dressed."

Dr. Lunde asked how Judy Miller responded during the rape.

"I don't remember any struggling—passive, it seems like; not real cooperation, but just lying there."

Judy Miller was allowed to go to the bathroom. She remained gagged but was not handcuffed. When she returned, they got rope—"some kind of white rope. I can't tell you exactly what kind, I don't know. It seems like it came from Angelo's shop."

"Was that sometimes used to tie the wrists around handcuffs and also legs?"

"Yes."

"What would be the purpose of tying the legs?"

"I have—let me add my own—as best I can figure, the only purpose that that would serve is so that the person wouldn't run—so that the girl wouldn't run. If she—if it seemed like, you know, she would have to be left alone for a little bit—you know, getting everything together; put it in bags; make sure nothing was left behind and everything and her legs would be tied."

Judy Miller was left on her back, watching as Bianchi prepared to kill her. The terror in her eyes upset him. He told of seeing drawings made during electrocutions which were shown on television—sketches of prisoners strapped to the electric chair, knowing they were about to die. He mentioned how he saw the same type of fear with Judy Miller.

"She saw that what was coming—and when I saw the sketches of this guy and his eyes were like this big, because he knew it was going to be the end . . . it—it happened, you know, it looked almost identical to her and that—I saw that and that clicked some-thing in my head, and it just really—left a really bad—effect on me on top of everything else. I couldn't put my finger on it, you know, I searched myself and I knew what I was feeling about the general—the whole general thing but there was something more I couldn't touch on—and that's what it was. It was . . . Miller . . ."

The words came haltingly. Ken Bianchi's mind was over-whelmed by his memories. He did not want to face the reality of what he had forced himself to forget. He did not believe in mur-der. He did not want to take a life. He had left the Sheriff's Re-serve when he realized that his gun was not for show but to cause death when the situation warranted. Yet he had violated his ex-pressed moral code. He had taken a life, not once but over and over again.

There were times when Bianchi would weep in his cell, then feel guilty for shedding tears. Twice he tried to commit suicide: one time, in Bellingham, he went so far as to fashion a noose from clothing and try to strangle himself on the bars. Both times the hypnotic suggestion of Dr. Watkins took control and he stopped himself, then called for help so he could talk through his extreme depression.

The more Bianchi was questioned, the more he became re-volted by what he was saying. Eventually his mind would rebel entirely. When he went to Los Angeles several months later, he began to remember the crimes in a way he could deny. His mind became like a videotape player, showing him killing the girls as if he were seeing it on television. He could see himself commit-ting the acts of which he did not morally approve, but he did not participate in the actual killing.

A normal person remembers the actual experience. If you pick up a rose, carefully hold the stem so as not to stick yourself, then bring it to your nose to enjoy the fragrance, you also recall your hand position, the appearance of the flower, the fragrance, and the joy of the experience. Your memory is subjective. You relive the event in the same way you enjoyed the circumstances the first time around.

According to the psychiatrists, Bianchi had an "objective" memory of the murders. He could remember an incident only by seeing what amounted to a videotape showing his entire body approaching the flower, picking it up, and smelling it. At such times, he would not relive the feelings, the smells, the other sensations. To Bianchi, the fact that he had a normal, subjective memory about every part of his life and an objective memory only of the murders made him feel less responsible. He did not feel emotionally involved. He thought that somehow information might have been subconsciously implanted. In this way his troubled mind handled the difference between his moral code and his actions.

Yet always there was a part of Ken Bianchi that knew the truth. Part of him suppressed the sensory memories that would have enabled him to again feel the terrified bound and gagged bodies pressed under his flesh as he raped his victims. There was a part of him which remembered his muscles tightening as he pulled a garrote about the necks of the women, which remembered handling the naked, unmoving, stiffening corpses. And when that part of him released even fragmentary memories to his conscious mind, he recoiled in horror from himself.

During those moments of relived horror, when Bianchi was able, if only briefly, to recognize the full reality of what he did, he also thought of Kelli and Sean. Kelli might change her name, marry someone else, and never tell Sean about his real father, for all he knew. She said otherwise, but he just wanted her to disappear—to be dead or gone from his life forever. He wanted Sean and the freedom to raise him, with or without Kelli. And it was all too late. Part of him had to go on and part of him longed to die, to escape the disgrace and the sense of moral responsibility. He was living an ongoing nightmare which he realized might never end.

Because there was still speculation about the honesty of Bianchi's implication of his cousin, Dr. Lunde gratefully retreated from the horror stories of torture and death. He had built the police case considerably for the Los Angeles authorities. He decided to take things a step further and have Bianchi explain the layout of Buono's home. This would help establish the credibility of the charges leveled against his cousin and also show whether or not it was physically possible for the murders to take place there. Naturally the detectives would check the place to see if it conformed to what was described. Bianchi began drawing a floor plan, saying:

"This was the bathroom, this was the spare bedroom . . . this was what is now the den here. This was the living room. This was the dining room. This was Angelo's bedroom . . . this here is a—is a kind of a—you just walk into a little foyer like a washing machine and dryer here—you walk out here and there were steps down and whatever car was used was usually parked right in front of the steps or pulled back further—his shop is in the back here—pulled back further; further back you go the darker it is and there's a big awning over the shop that extends on a ways."

"Is this—are there—is there a big fence or trees or something that blocks this?" asked Dr. Lunde.

"Yeah, this is just a—there's a fence there—now there's a wrought-iron fence and . . . there's a wrought-iron there and there's steps here. What blocks it is that there's a glass company next door here which is up close—it's closer to the street than his house. His house sits back a ways . . .

"For example, if this is the street and this is the sidewalk. His house sits back, whereas the glass company sits next door right out further."

"This is the front door, is it?"

"Right. See, the thing is that there's a—a car wash next door. There's a car wash next door; there's the glass company next door on this side . . . so it's all pretty well—you know, there's—there's really no—"

"Would somebody be looking out through for passersby while the body was being put in the car or—"

"Yes, Angelo would go to the front—he would go to the front door or to a—a front window to see if there's any cars coming on the street. Usually at the times that all this was occurring, was late at night and the traffic was very little."

"And like, what he'd say, 'It's all clear,' or something like that?"

"Yeah," said Bianchi. He then added: "Nobody ever walked by at the time and there were no cars driving by."

Eventually the psychiatric examination ended. Dr. Lunde had gone a long way toward helping build the Los Angeles case against

Bianchi as well as adding information concerning the defendant's mental state for the Bellingham authorities. As he said, in part, in his report to the judge:

"It is my opinion that Kenneth Bianchi is suffering from a Dissociative Reaction, extremely severe, bordering on psychosis. This condition has been present since at least age nine and is manifested by periods during which the defendant acts without awareness of his actions and for which he subsequently has amnesia. During some of these periods the incredible amount of unconscious (repressed) hostility toward women present in this disturbed man surfaces. The best demonstration of what I have just described is seen in some of the videotapes which were made while Bianchi was under hypnosis and emerged as a quite different personality calling himself 'Steve.' whether or not Bianchi represents a true case of multiple personality is debatable, in my opinion, but certainly the psychological dynamics of his very disturbed personality structure are similar to those which have been described with respect to multiple personality, which is simply a sub-type of Dissociative Reaction. The question of whether or not the defendant is malingering or faking these symptoms of a Dissociative Reaction (e.g. amnesia) is one which I have considered in some detail over the past month."

Dr. Lunde then went on to discuss Bianchi's attempts to pass himself off as a psychologist. "My own examination indicates that Bianchi is not psychologically sophisticated enough nor is he intelligent enough to have constructed such an elaborate history which might afford him a mental defense if he were subsequently charged with a crime. Furthermore, one would have to assume that Bianchi began plotting his strategy for these crimes and his defense at about age nine, since this is when the first documented symptoms of his mental disturbance occurred. Bianchi does not simply suffer from 'convenient lapses of memory.' He appears to have genuine amnesia for various events which have been documented over the years and which have no bearing on present criminal charges or any other conceivable criminal charges."

And then it was over. The next major event would be Bianchi's court appearance and the many ramifications for family, friends, and the entire legal system.

Only Kelli had to constantly endure the nightmare of confusion. Ken wrote frequently and the letters were those of a gentle human being, not a madman.

"Ken told me of his sensitivity and of his realization that I could be so emotionally vulnerable as well," said Kelli. "He said he felt that his heart was breaking, that each day was harder than the last. His cell seemed to be shrinking in on him, the confinement overwhelming all but the love he had for me and Sean.

"He also wrote to Sean, though it would be years before our son could read the letter. He spoke of his tremendous shame and great love for our baby. He told Sean that he thinks of him constantly. He spoke of dreaming that he will once again hold Sean and be a real fatherly presence, not just a memory. It was a letter so filled with love and anguish that I still cannot read it without crying."

PART 4

"I Confess"

CHAPTER 14

On Friday, October 19, 1979, a sanity hearing for Ken Bianchi was scheduled for the Whatcom County Court House. It was to be the largest hearing of its type ever held in Bellingham, and public interest was intense. Approximately fifty people showed up by 8:30 A.M., including several high school psychology class students and one couple who were there on a lark. As the police and sheriff's department used metal detectors to run security checks on everyone, the couple began kissing and fondling each other in line. It was a different kind of date for them, a little like going to see a monster movie on a Friday night, only this time the "monster" was an emotionally troubled man named Ken Bianchi.

The press corps was admitted first. A single photographer from the *Bellingham Herald* would take pictures, which would be wired to newspapers and magazines throughout the country. A radio-station reporter was equipped with both a portable police radio and a broadcast radio so he could transmit live over the air whenever that might be allowed. Both audio and videotape recordings were made, though direct broadcasting of the hearing was not permitted.

The press corps was placed in the jury box since the hearing would only be before Judge Jack Kurtz. One observer noted that the news media seemed to be sitting in judgment on both the accused and the spectators.

Members of Bianchi's family, including Kelli Boyd and a priest who was a close friend of them both, sat in the front. The families of the victims were also represented, though no hostility toward either Kelli or Ken was evident. However, Bianchi had been asked to wear a bulletproof vest under his three-piece suit, and members of the Special Weapons and Tactics Unit stood around the perimeter of the courtroom. The entire area was sealed and no one was allowed in or out during the proceedings.

The *Bellingham Herald* is the only daily newspaper serving the area, and its deadline was simultaneous with the end of the hearing. Two advance stories had been written, one if Bianchi pleaded guilty and one in case he pleaded innocent. Under Washington law, Bianchi could plead guilty at the hearing and receive a sentence for his crimes without a formal trial. The police agreed to relay Bianchi's decision so that the paper would have the correct headlines and story. The reporter who was to notify his paper stood outside the courtroom. Had he been inside, watching the proceedings, he would not have been allowed to go out to make the call.

Kelli Boyd sat nervously on the bench, occasionally looking at the reporters. She was determined not to show emotion. She wanted the world to know that no matter what Ken Bianchi had done, she was a woman to be respected. She had loved the good in the man and still did. She also feared the unknown part of him that had allowed him to kill and kill again. She had avoided reporters and publicity as much as possible since his arrest, but today she felt it was important to be in the courtroom.

Dean Brett had worked out an arrangement with the Los Angeles and Bellingham court authorities concerning his client. Ken Bianchi would plead guilty and agree to testify against his cousin in exchange for a prison sentence instead of the death penalty. He would receive a life term for each murder count, which would effectively keep him in jail until his death. He would also openly name Angelo Buono as his accomplice, at which time an arrest warrant would be served on Buono in Los Angeles. The police were ready to move in the moment they received word from

Bellingham that Bianchi had named his cousin in open court. Without that statement, they could not be certain that Bianchi would later testify against his cousin.

Ken Bianchi had been having great difficulty accepting the idea of a guilty plea and had not discussed the matter very much with Kelli. Until the day of the hearing, she had no idea what he would plead. Dean Brett was almost in the same position because Bianchi was having great difficulty adjusting to the idea of his own guilt.

"These hands killed," Bianchi was told to say as he stared at his hands before entering the courtroom. It was an exercise John Johnson had devised to help Bianchi face the actions he had committed. "These hands killed." He said it every day, never wanting to believe the reality of that statement.

Bianchi and his attorney had worked until late Thursday night, discussing the hearing. Bianchi wanted to fight the case. He felt that he was innocent, a victim of circumstances, that the real murderer had to be someone else no matter what the physical evidence at the crime scene might reveal.

Brett went over the evidence. There was no question of the guilt. Pubic hairs, carpet fibers, numerous other evidence all had been analyzed and linked with Bianchi. In fact, it was this overwhelming proof of guilt which made the situation so rough for him. He wanted to deny and deny and deny, yet that was impossible. He was guilty. There was no way of avoiding that reality. By 11 P.M. that Thursday night, even Ken had to admit that confessing his guilt and taking his punishment was the proper thing to do.

Bianchi had to sit and listen to the police report of his crimes. The report detailed the charges against him and how the case unfolded. As the murders were discussed, Ken frequently wept, overwhelmed by emotion.

Then, still sobbing from time to time, Bianchi commented: "I can't find the words to express the sorrow for what I have done. In no way can I take away the pain I have given to others, and in no way can I expect forgiveness from others."

To those who were empathetic toward the man because of his tortured mind, Ken Bianchi had become his own victim as he was ordered to serve two life sentences in Washington state. To others, the tears Bianchi shed did not represent remorse. Instead they seemed to be tears of frustration: he had been caught before he could kill again. In any case, Bianchi would never again walk the streets a free man. Within twenty-four hours of the hearing, he was on his way to Los Angeles, where, on Monday of the following week, he was sentenced to additional life terms as part of the agreement to testify against Buono. He would spend up to thirty-five years in California prisons, then he would be transferred to Washington state to serve terms there.

Angelo Buono's arrest came within an hour of his being implicated in Bellingham. The cousin claimed innocence, though the police were satisfied that they had taken the proper second man to jail. Proof of innocence or guilt would have to be established in the courts. What was important was that two men had committed the crimes, Bianchi had named Buono, all other suspects had been investigated and cleared, and the murders had stopped. There seemed to be no question that the proper actions had been taken. The trial would establish Buono's guilt or innocence.

The police in Bellingham had been extremely understanding about Ken Bianchi's mental state. Everything possible was done to keep him living in reality. He was encouraged to confess, encouraged to feel that by admitting his actions and the actions of everyone else involved, he had a new chance at life. No one told him he might be released. It was obvious that he would serve his sentence for the rest of his life, but they were careful not to play upon his sense of guilt.

Los Angeles authorities did not have the time to get to know Bianchi. Those who did know him at all thought of him in terms of the murders. They saw the violence he had cold-bloodedly committed and they were appalled. Some hated the man. Others felt be was not worthy of their contempt. He was a nonentity, a bug to be squashed or preserved forever in a tightly sealed jar, ignored by everyone because he wasn't important now that he was caught. They did not see him as a warm, loving, flesh-and-blood individual whose troubled mind had caused horrible violence.

Because of their hostile perception of Bianchi, the Los Angeles authorities would make little effort to fully understand what sort of emotional support he would need. They could accept his willingness to deny reality but they chose to make him face the enormity of his crimes by going over them repeatedly. They would discuss them again and again, pressing him for the details he was finally able to remember. They even went so far as to take him from the jail at night, heavily guarded, and drive from location to location as he physically relived the crimes he had committed.

Gradually Ken felt he had to deny the reality of his actions. He had to blame someone else. He could not have killed anyone. He was innocent. Someone else did it.

The first obvious breakdown occurred in October when Bianchi, in the Los Angeles County Jail, reached a point where he felt compelled to deny the Bellingham case. He wanted to believe that his crime, if any, was in being present at the deaths of the two women. He developed a "second man" theory which he reported in a letter.

The letter discussed Ken's "memory" that he was not alone the night Karen and Diane were killed. He said that he walked into the room and saw the two young women hanging from the rafters. He was horrified by what he saw and enraged by the action of the man who was with him.

Bianchi was equally concerned about the way he reacted when witnessing the killings. He spoke of another person inside himself who was a "voyeur." He was shocked to find himself enjoying the sight of death, and the memory of that pleasure continued to haunt him.

It was a dramatic statement: the revelation of a second man, a different killer. Ken's guilt was only in watching without trying to stop the crimes. And it wasn't true. The strangulation marks indicated that the girls could not have been hanged because the marks were not deep enough to indicate that their full body weight was suspended. There also were no beams to allow this action.

A second problem with the two-men concept was the matter of the pubic hair evidence. If Bianchi was not naked with the women, how did his pubic hair become entangled with theirs? It was all a fabrication, a created fantasy with no basis in fact.

The letter continued, talking of innocence in Los Angeles. The innocent Ken, desperate for the approval of the police officers investigating the case, had confessed to murders actually committed by Angelo.

Bianchi told of having the same problem with Los Angeles. He claimed that after studying the police in that city, he felt that if he told them the truth about what happened, they would laugh at him. He claimed that a part of him enjoyed watching other people kill, even though he would never do it.

Bianchi claimed that he had altered the facts in his confession. His letter stated, in effect, that Angelo had done everything and he had been an observer. He said that, at times, he made a mistake in his testimony, describing the fact that "they were killed," meaning "by Angelo." However, he related that he then corrected himself and stated that *he* killed the victims. He knew they would believe such an admission over what he claimed to be the truth, that he had done nothing but observe.

Bianchi felt that his guilt was in not stopping the killings. He claimed to have a part of himself that enjoyed them. The actual acts had to have been committed by someone else.

On December 11, Bianchi went so far as to name a second man for the Bellingham killings. In his letter concerning the story he explained the sexual approach known as "Bondage & Discipline" (B&D), a type of sadomasochism in which a person gets sexual pleasure with a partner who is handcuffed, tied, or otherwise made helpless, then spanked, beaten, whipped, or hurt in some other way. Physical pain is an important part of the relationship, and deaths occasionally occur when this is "enjoyed." Ken talked of being curious about it and then spoke of the Bellingham case.

This time Ken wrote of a man named "Greg." The person was known to the police in Bellingham and was later investigated intensely after Bianchi's letter became known. The investigation positively cleared Greg of being anywhere near the crime scene the night of the murder. There was conclusive evidence that he could not have been involved with the deaths, and that the story about him was a total fabrication.

Bianchi said that he, as "Steve," used to talk with Greg about B&D. He said he had thought that Greg's interest was just fantasy. However, when Greg supposedly met him at the Catlow house, Greg, according to Bianchi, planned to suggest that he, Greg, and the two women engage in B&D.

Ken said that he left the house right after Greg started talking with the girls. He said that when he returned, the girls had told Greg he was being foolish to suggest it and that they would report both men to the police for bringing up the idea. Bianchi said that apparently Greg lost his head, fearing that the publicity would embarrass his family. Greg then killed the girls, disappearing from the area after the crime was over.

The "second man" was obviously a convenient choice: Greg truly was dead; he had been in a motorcycle crash near the general area where the bodies were found. It was possible that when Bianchi was desperately trying to find a way to deny his actions, the combination of the man's death and the fact that he knew him led to that particular false alibi.

Bianchi continued with his letter. He expressed concern with the fact that the evidence did not always coincide with what he was certain was the truth. He said that when the police in Los Angeles took him to where the Hillside Strangler victims were killed, he had trouble remembering anything when he knew that Angelo had been the driver of the car. He could remember details from the nights he drove, but not when Angelo was allegedly at the wheel. Everything seemed vague.

Then Bianchi returned to his story about Greg. He said that he had given the bag with the Ace bandages and rope to his friend before he left the Catlow house. At that time he thought the items would be used to bind and gag the women for mutually enjoyable sex. He felt they were not part of a murder kit as the police would later theorize.

Bianchi said that, upon reflection, Greg must have seen his family and personal freedom as being important to protect. It must have been that fear, according to Bianchi, which led Greg to take the lives of the women when they threatened to report the men for suggesting B&D.

The letters Bianchi wrote about these incidents with Greg kept changing. Earlier, on November 10, Ken had written of Greg in a different way. At that time Ken spoke of the Billy personality who, claiming to be Ken, called Karen and Diane about the job. He was not really trying to hire them for a job, though. He was actually trying to arrange a surprise blind date for both Greg and himself. Ken would never date, and apparently Billy wanted to see women other than Kelli. He felt that he, as Billy, could arrange the date and enjoy the women.

In this letter Billy was the person who met Greg at the house, then left to go to the store. When Ken/Billy returned, the girls were supposedly bound and gagged, sitting on chairs, with ropes around their necks. Greg allegedly claimed to have done this because he was angry with the girls for refusing to have sex with him. When Greg pulled the chairs out from under the girls, the nooses became taut and the girls were strangled.

Steve supposedly came out when Billy went into shock. Steve said that he would dispose of the bodies once Greg gave him a hand carrying the women to the car. Steve allegedly told Greg to leave while he stayed to dispose of the bodies. He knew Greg was in trouble and Steve wanted to help. This letter stated that the rest of the police information, concerning the body disposal afterward, was correct. But he was innocent of the killings.

The remainder of the letter related the confusion in Bianchi's mind. He could not understand the sperm on the outside of the clothes, though he thought it came from Greg, who climbed on top of one of the girls after she was bound. He also mentioned that he later learned Greg was killed in a freak motorcycle accident after Ken's arrest. The accident occurred in the area of the crimes and eliminated the chance for Greg to prove the "truth."

During the next few months, Bianchi continued to react adversely to pressure. He continued having doubts and asked a writer who spoke with him in jail to explore what he felt were discrepancies in the case against him in Bellingham. Because he had been allowed to read police reports on the cases before being interrogated by police, he assumed that he had remembered the information on the paper as though it were a personal memory. This would be possible, but it didn't happen in Bianchi's case. The information he supplied during interrogation was far more complex than anything he had read. He provided details that theoretically only the killer could have known.

Another question related to the pubic hair, which provided a conclusive link.

Third, a witness saw a truck owned by the security agency for which Ken worked eighty-five miles from the scene of the crime at the time of the crime. This occurred on a different night, a fact Ken did not mention. Ken could account for the other two trucks being used the night of the murders and assumed that the third was his. He had not really been near the home where the deaths took place. What he failed to accept was the fact that the truck reported eighty-five miles away was located there on a different night, not the night of the crimes. Even Bianchi's own leads led to the conclusion that he had to be the murderer.

The pressures increased. Ken talked frequently with his mother, whose approval he has always sought. She wanted desperately to believe in his innocence and was deeply hurt by the statements being made concerning his violent childhood. She and her new husband relocated to California just to be closer and to avoid the newspaper reports that were appearing in Rochester. She told him of her financial problems and he felt guilty about not being able to help. It was another reason for him to refuse to face even the possibility that he could be responsible for the murders.

Another reason for Ken to deny the reality of his crimes was Sean. Ken adores Sean. The boy is the one joy in an otherwise troubled existence and Ken feared the loss of the child's love. Kelli was working with him, showing the baby pictures of his father, to keep the memory of the man alive for her son. Yet Sean had only known Ken as an infant. He was growing rapidly and he was losing an understanding of what "father" really meant. Ken sensed this and also recognized that in the years ahead, Sean would read about him and possibly be filled with loathing. He wanted his son's love and he felt that his son could not love a mass murderer.

The arrest of Angelo Buono did not help. Angelo had been something of a father figure for Ken. Regardless of what Angelo had done, Ken's testimony would be a major factor in gaining a conviction. That knowledge hurt and Ken felt guilty for turning against him.

Kelli had begun dating again and Ken knew it. He knew she would one day have relations with another man, and he hated the idea that she would not move back to Los Angeles to be near him, then relocate near whatever prison would be his final living quarters after the trials were completed. He wanted her to "disappear" and have the memory stop hurting. He wanted to deny the love and eliminate the guilt of hating her for making him want her so badly.

Even the public seemed a source of pain when they cared. One young woman, a beautiful former Playboy employee who was living with a television reporter, corresponded and visited with Bianchi. She seemed to sincerely care about his troubled existence, even though she used only her first and middle names, hiding her last name from him. However, she appeared to be a plant to gain his confidence and put information on the air.

Investigations into the woman's motivations were never completed. She was denied further access to him. However, she did tell a story of Ken's mother visiting him at the jail, when Ken became so irate that he had to be put in restraints for a while. This story was told to a writer and later appeared on a news broadcast from the television station where her boyfriend was employed. The problem was that none of the guards at the time remember any of that event. Bianchi was never violent after the visits of his mother, despite what the woman said.

Trial delays and a number of firings of Buono's lawyers also added pressure. Ken might be ready to testify one week, only to have the hearing date changed to a different week. He called his mother and talked about the case, citing "facts" which were not true. He asked Kelli why she wouldn't believe what he said even though his statements were consistently proving to be false. At times he would seem to say one thing to one guard and something different to another guard. If you talked with six visitors about what he said on the same subject on the same day, each visitor would stress that Bianchi was perfectly normal. Then each visitor would quote Bianchi and you would find that each had heard different stories.

By the middle of 1980, Bianchi seemed to break down completely. He could not face the crimes he had committed. He spoke to family and friends, telling of the "real" killer who would one day be caught. He spoke of money being spent to hire private investigators to check out discrepancies which would prove his innocence. He was denying reality so strongly that he seemed to lose his credibility as a witness. If he was brought to the stand to testify against his cousin, he would be unpredictable in his statements. The situation greatly concerned the prosecution and there was little that could be done.

At this writing, Ken Bianchi still has not faced responsibility for his own actions. He is desperately trying to find a way out. He talks of special investigators, hopes of new evidence, discrepancies in the Bellingham cases, people on the police force who are out to "get him." He cannot accept his past actions despite all the evidence against him, including his own videotaped and audio-taped confessions.

Ken's mother, the former Frances Bianchi, lives with her new husband within driving distance of her son. She loves him with full acceptance of his goodness and his failings. She is horrified by the crimes and has come to accept the probability that he did commit the murders. She has read about how interrogation under hypnosis is conducted so she can fully understand the fact that Ken was not led to say untrue comments while he was hypnotized.

What hurt Ken's mother the most is the way she is indirectly being charged with his murders. In the tapes, she has been accused of child abuse by her own son. The reports from the DePaul Clinic, which were made public, also speak against her. Yet the child abuse was never truly documented. All that is certain is that the doctors and social workers seemed to resent Mrs. Bianchi's concern for her child and the way she expressed herself. When she acted normally, seeking a life centered around church, child, and a home in a more expensive neighborhood, she was called irrational. In reality, she was simply pursuing that which other women from her cultural and ethnic background traditionally seek. Her domination of the household was normal for an Italian Catholic. The husband traditionally sits back and has no involvement until the child is a teenager. Again this is what happened between Ken and his father.

Mrs. Bianchi feels that her son might be genetically damaged. His real mother was a heavy drinker and Ken was an unwanted baby. Could that have been abuse? Could that have caused him to behave abnormally? No one knows for certain.

Months after the investigations into Ken Bianchi's mind and family history, Dr. John Watkins and others evolved a theory that may answer the question of why Ken Bianchi developed as he did. The reasoning reinforces Mrs. Bianchi's feelings that the charges made against her were wrong. It also reflects many of the current theories of abnormal child development.

Dr. Watkins stresses the fact that Ken's real mother never wanted him. He was abandoned to a neighbor who, in turn, began taking the child from door to door, leaving him with whoever would have him for the day. The infant was fed, his diapers were changed, and little more was done. There was none of the loving touching, the human contact which makes for emotional bonding. The first true love Ken was shown came after he was adopted by the Bianchis—four months after birth.

What happens to a child who is not held, caressed, and loved immediately upon birth? Studies in New York hospitals almost thirty years ago revealed that when an infant was not placed immediately with his mother, death frequently occurred. The hospitals studied had removed the babies to a sterile atmosphere rather than laying them with the mother or having pediatric nurses hold and comfort them. Several hours could pass before the infant was closely touched and loved. The infant death rate in these hospitals was shockingly high at that time, and the rate declined considerably when the babies were immediately laid next to the mother or constantly held by a nurse if the mother was sleeping.

Ken Bianchi was obviously too strong to die. Unwanted by his mother, lacking in close emotional bonding to any woman for day after day following his birth, Ken may have been emotionally damaged before adoption. Even at that age, he would come to fear the constant change in home life. To him, each new "mother" caring for him would have been a new rejection.

When Bianchi came to live with his adoptive parents, he may have been so damaged that any normal punishment would have seemed like rejection. If he was scolded for knocking over a lamp during play, he might have unconsciously feared that this woman who truly loved him was going to throw him away as so many others had done. He would have been terrified by normal discipline, the type every good mother must use with any growing child. He could have perceived these terrors as child abuse, although they were created inside his mind following the trauma of not having a normal early home life. Thus there is a good chance that the only truly loving experiences Bianchi knew were with his adopted mother, yet the damage done during the first four months made him see his childhood as filled with abuse.

Kelli Boyd lives in fear of the day when she must tell Sean about his father. She is not the type of woman to hide the truth from her son. She is also not one to let the boy hate his father. She wants Sean to understand Ken, to love him if he can, but at least to have total acceptance of his humanness.

Kelli hurts in other ways. She fears commitments to other men. She thought she knew Ken. She loved him and was certain he was normal. The problems came from his being irresponsible at times, not from violence. Yet if she could so easily misjudge a man who killed so many women, what might she do in the future? Can she become seriously involved with anyone and still feel safe? She does not know and is afraid to become very serious about anyone now. She realizes the fear and the pain will eventually subside, but for now she is torn between love and a sense of revulsion. It is a condition that only time can heal, yet time seems to be moving so slowly that the nightmare may last an eternity.

Angelo Buono sits in the Los Angeles County Jail, well separated from his young cousin. He is defiantly protesting his innocence and the state of Bianchi's mind makes the charges against him subject to question. Yet the psychiatrists all seem to agree that the stories of his involvement could easily be truth and there is no question of the physical evidence of two killers in Los Angeles. The problem is the objectivity of the jurors. Will they listen to the facts, making their decisions based on evidence and testimony, or will they vote by guess, going by "gut" emotions and Bianchi's appearance on the stand? Buono may be the second man the police are seeking. However, he may also be yet another victim of the Hillside Strangler. The sad part of all this is that whichever way the jury decides, the truth may remain uncertain.

Ken Bianchi's future will be a series of prison cells and psychiatric treatment. Yet what will the treatments be? Is he a multiple personality or is he not? Drs. Watkins and Allison are convinced that he was one at the time of the crimes. They saw him when others did not and their suggestions resulted in changes in his memory. Thus he might be curable since multiple personality is a treatable disorder.

Or is Ken a psychopathic killer who takes life without remorse? Many police officers prefer this explanation. If he is, there may be no treatment possible.

Whatever the truth might be, the city of Los Angeles no longer cares. The Hillside Strangler is safely behind bars and will be for the rest of his life. The Hollywood street scene has returned to the bizarre state which passes for normality. There are new indulgences and new bogeymen to fear. Reporters such as Jim Mitchell have moved on to promotions and new stories to cover. The police are back to their regular patrols. The trials that remain are but an anticlimax. The Hillside Strangler is now just a faded memory, a nightmare no one wants to recall.

And then Bianchi, the confessed killer, continues to sit in his cell, protesting his innocence.

The deterioration of Ken Bianchi increased dramatically as his cousin, Angelo Buono, prepared for the preliminary hearing on charges of prostitution, extortion, and related crimes. By November 1980, Bianchi was insisting on his complete innocence of all the murders, both in Los Angeles and in Bellingham. He was willing to talk about his cousin, but his statements always stressed that he was innocent and Buono was guilty.

"We think the jury will tend to disbelieve whatever Bianchi says," explained Roger Kelly, the prosecutor at the time. If Bianchi would state that both he and Buono were innocent, that statement could result in the jury's deciding that since there was overwhelming evidence against Ken, Buono must also be guilty. As long as Bianchi protested his own innocence, but asserted that Buono was guilty, he was a risk on the stand because the jury would likely assume everything he said was a lie. This would mean that they would think Buono was innocent regardless of other evidence.

The prosecution felt that the case against Buono was strong in the areas of the prostitution and extortion charges. However, Bianchi was the key to the murder case against Buono, all other evidence being circumstantial. Taken together, the evidence in the murder case against Buono seemed overwhelmingly devastating. Taken separately, much of the evidence, other than Bianchi's statements, could apply to numerous other possible suspects.

At the time of this writing, Angelo Buono's trial is still ongoing. Gerald Chaleff, Buono's attorney, refuses to comment on the murder charges against his client. He points out that his job is to defend his client until a jury decides guilt or innocence, and that any verdict might be subject to appeal.

While Bianchi was the key to the prosecution's case, Roger Kelly and his staff were running into problems. Bianchi began to deteriorate, and it was pointed out to the prosecutor that on any given day Bianchi was giving conflicting stories to different visitors. A psychiatrist had been assigned to work with Bianchi, though that effort was not proving productive. This was a case which was simply radically different from what anyone anticipated at the time of the arrest, and those involved did not know what to expect next.

Bianchi's mind could not handle the idea that he was guilty of crimes which violated his personal moral code and the way he was raised. The greatest positive evidence against him was connected with the two Bellingham murders, so he began focusing his denials on that case. His efforts came in two forms, one with reasoned logic and the other through an alleged attempt to show that the real killer was still at large. This latter effort involved Veronica Lynn Compton, a twenty-four-year-old fledgling playwright and actress who was arrested in Carson, California, on October 2,1980.

Compton was charged with the attempted murder by strangulation of a woman named Kim Breed, who lived in Bellingham and was an employee of the city's Parks and Recreation Department. What made the arrest unusual in terms of Bianchi's credibility and his potential for testifying believably against Buono was the information which began to unfold upon investigation of Veronica's recent history.

The arrest followed a number of unusual circumstances. First came the anonymous mailing of packages—containing a cassette tape recording of a male voice taking credit for the Bellingham killings. One tape went to the police, a different one to Dr. Ralph

Allison, and a third to a priest. Each contained a confession to the Bellingham murders that was personalized. For example, Allison's package asked, in part, for psychiatric help. It also contained a woman's bra, though the reasoning behind its inclusion is unclear. The bra probably was meant to imply that it was an item taken from a victim, though the clothing cannot be linked in this way. However, no reference was made indicating the bra's significance.

Bianchi had confessed in his hearing to killing the Bellingham women as they lay bound and gagged on the basement floor. The voice on the tape said he strangled the two women as they walked down the steps to the basement. That would also have been consistent with the strangulation marks found on the victims' necks, but would not have accounted for the hair and carpet-fiber links with Bianchi. Thus the man's confession, even if genuine, would not have cleared Bianchi of involvement. The physical evidence had been too damning.

The voice on the tapes sounded phony to the detectives who heard it. The men had heard numerous confessions over the years, and the voice on the tape did not ring true. The man sounded like a very bad actor reading a script, not a criminal confessing the most serious of crimes.

The tape to the priest stated: "Father, I want to ask you your forgiveness. I want to confess to you. I needed some money and I met this guy in California who, well, I was responsible for the murders of Diane Wilder and Karen Mandic.

"Hardwick, a cop out there, did it with me. I knew it was wrong when I started in California with Angelo. Those other girls did not really matter.

"I'm asking for forgiveness. I know I'll go to hell. That's where I belong. I'm really sorry. Father, please pray for me."

When the police searched Veronica Compton's trailer, they found another cassette which had the same male voice. This tape sounded like a practice tape. It was as though she had recorded the man reading from a script so they could hear how his "confession" sounded before mailing the tapes.

It was obvious that Veronica was involved in an effort to free Bianchi, but the question of why remained. Then a check of the mail Bianchi had received and the visitors he had had began to show some possibilities.

Veronica claimed to the authorities and the press that she had known Bianchi since 1977, though she knew him as Steve Walker at the time. Steve Walker was the questionable full name which emerged when Dr. Allison pressed Bianchi for a last name for the violent personality Steve. However, as has been seen, it is doubtful that the "Walker" part of the name existed before it came up in the questioning by Dr. Allison.

Veronica said that she had had an affair with Steve Walker. She claimed that he shared her bed during the nights of the Los Angeles murders for which Bianchi was convicted. She claimed to have been out of the country during the arrest and hearings involving Bianchi and came forward only when she learned what had happened. She offered various documents which, at this writing, are believed to have been prepared at some time after January 1980, not before, as she alleged.

The investigators learned that Veronica, whose attempts at writing usually involved plays with sadomasochistic themes, began corresponding with Bianchi in January. Prosecutor Kelly had helped make certain that Bianchi had great freedom in terms of both mailing privileges and visitors. Telephone calls and visits by strangers all went unmonitored. There is censorship in prisons for convicted felons, but Bianchi, though a convicted felon himself, was given great freedom within the county jail structure where he was being held until he testified against Buono. Thus an outside relationship could have developed without anyone else being aware.

In June, Veronica Compton began making regular visits both with Ken and with his mother. She had apparently obtained Ken's mother's address and telephone number from him, and she had called to talk of her love for Ken and to say that there would be new evidence found which would get Ken released in two months. She had managed to obtain a dinner invitation as well, introducing her own seven-year-old son to Ken's mother.

There are numerous questions remaining unanswered about the entire situation with Veronica during this period. One suspicion was that she was somehow linked with friends of Buono who, in effect, set her up. They encouraged her to visit Ken in the hope that something would happen which would cast further doubt on Bianchi's credibility. According to police, Veronica had written several plays in which violent sex was a dominant theme, and it was felt she might like the violent aspect of Bianchi. This is pure conjecture, however.

What is certain is that Veronica and Ken seemed to have fallen in love. Ken called Kelli's sister in July to see if she knew a lawyer to handle real estate. Ostensibly, he hoped to sell Veronica's trailer home and buy a town house where they would live once he was released—as he was certain he would be.

From the time that Bianchi became serious about Veronica, he stopped telephoning or writing Kelli Boyd. He is basically a "one woman" man who makes a total commitment to any woman he loves. Had he truly been actively involved with Compton during the time he was living with Kelli and terrorizing the streets of Los Angeles, he would have left Kelli to spend all his time with Veronica. The fact that he was intensely faithful to Kelli throughout the crime spree, then dropped contact with Kelli after Veronica began visiting him in jail, bolstered the police theory that Veronica's love trysts during the stranglings were imaginary creations.

No one is certain that Ken Bianchi knew that Veronica was planning to try to free him. If he did, then his protestations of innocence are further destroyed by the violent approach that was tried. He has not been charged as an accessory. The Bellingham authorities believe that the action was Veronica's idea.

On September 19, 1980, according to statements provided by the near-victim and the Bellingham police, Veronica allegedly attempted to commit a copycat strangulation murder. The police stated she was in Bellingham, staying in a room at a downtown motel, registered as Cindy Wasser of Dallas, Texas, and she went to a bar, where she met a twenty-six-year-old woman named Kim Breed. They talked, and "Cindy Wasser" explained that she was an actress from Dallas and that she was pregnant. She was wearing a long gray-blond wig, sunglasses, an off-white muumuu, and blue thongs.

Kim Breed knew nothing of this woman, who introduced herself as "Karen" at the time. The two women did some grocery shopping, stopped by Breed's home to feed her children, then went to the motel. "Karen" allegedly claimed that she had left something there that she needed to pick up.

Once inside, according to charges brought against Compton in Bellingham, Compton managed to tie Breed's hands, took a white cord similar to what had been used in the killings committed by Bianchi in Bellingham, and began strangling Breed. The intended victim started to lose consciousness but managed to fight off her attacker. Her work with the Parks and Recreation Department had made her unusually strong, and she was able to struggle free. Breed fled the room, rushed to get a male friend, and the two of them returned to get the attacker, who had vanished. However, enough evidence was found to require Compton's arrest the following month.

In November, Veronica Compton was extradited to Bellingham to face a grand jury indictment for attempted murder. William Johnston, Compton's attorney, was concerned about the way the press was linking Bianchi's name with his client who, at the time, had to be considered innocent.

Veronica Compton had her day in court, was convicted of attempted murder in Bellingham, and sentenced to life in prison. One of the officers who investigated the matter reported, possibly jokingly, that Veronica later told him that she had never loved Ken Bianchi. The man in whom she was seriously interested was another Los Angeles murderer whom the police nicknamed the Sunset Strip Slasher.

Bianchi, shattered by the situation with Compton and desperately trying to avoid accepting involvement in the murders, wrote to me on November 24, 1980, just before he was to testify in closed session against Buono. This was additional proof that there were going to be serious problems with him as a witness. However, the prosecution continued working with him in the same manner which eventually would force a radical change in the case.

The letter Bianchi sent me explained that he had extremely mixed feelings about all the charges against him. He was trying to go over in his mind what had happened in both Los Angeles and Bellingham, to sort out what he had done or not done and what he knew about Angelo.

Bianchi spoke of the memory problems he has had all his life. He admitted that he could search his mind for the rest of his life and still have gaps. However, he felt that his protestations of innocence over the previous nineteen months represented the reality of the case.

The letter related Bianchi's concerns about the way the case had been investigated. He felt some of the evidence might have been planted or misinterpreted. He could not offer any counter evidence and admitted to the memory loss. However, he stressed that his personal feelings convinced him that there was no way he ever could have committed murder.

Bianchi spoke of his confession, perhaps the most damning part of the evidence against him. He avoided the fact that the confession provided details completely unknown to anyone but the killer. Instead, he concentrated on the problems he was having with his memory. He said that the confession seemed the most logical thing to do since he was on trial for murder, and the statement he made saved his life. He was also a logical suspect at the time, but the logical suspect is not necessarily the guilty party.

After relating the tremendous emotional toll of the case and trying to prove his innocence so many months after the arrest, he went into points of discrepancy. One was the issue of the discovery of the pubic hairs which had been raised and countered earlier. The second involved the supposed eyewitnesses who had again been checked and discarded. Finally, he questioned the credibility of the witnesses who said Ken had called Karen.

The tone of the letter was a constant questioning of the evidence, the way the police operated, and the memories of the witnesses. He questioned the reliability of what was found and the timing of the discovery of some of the objects, including the coat belonging to one of the girls. He also mentioned an unrelated case handled by his attorney in which a search of a car conducted by the Bellingham police failed to locate a quantity of marijuana concealed in the back. The reference was an effort to show where the police had allegedly overlooked evidence in the past.

Bianchi expressed no memory of the details he had outlined during the taped interviews. The coat and other clues were credited to "Steve" during sessions with the psychiatrist. "Steve" had apparently planted the items, unbeknownst to Ken.

The questions raised were valid ones, yet they had all been answered previously, sometimes through investigation, in other instances through the interrogation of Bianchi. The physical evidence was quite specific, and included material found on Bianchi's clothing. Karen Mandic's telephone number had been found in Bianchi's home, and his business card was located in hers. The fact that Diane told no one about the job—one of the questions Bianchi raised—was not a serious consideration since she went along with Karen at what amounted to the last minute. Karen was the person officially hired.

There was also the question of all the confessions. Bianchi's letter failed to contradict the tremendously damning videotaped confessions which show him speaking voluntarily.

Dr. John Watkins, who maintains that Bianchi was a true multiple personality at the time he saw him, feels that Bianchi probably created a new personality or reactivated an old one to handle the stress in jail. He was being forced to face aspects of himself he hated, and his denial mechanism has always done this by letting a different personality take control. If this was the case, then the personality writing to me might very well be innocent. This personality did not commit the crimes. It was some other personality. The fact that they all share the same body is a bit of logic which would not necessarily be considered by a true multiple personality.

Dr. Watkins reviewed the letter Bianchi sent to me, then responded in detail to what he had seen. He wrote, in part:

"I have always said that if his (Bianchi's) dissociation were truly broken down and awareness of his crimes became 'subject' that he would probably go into psychosis." The psychosis could occur with signs that others might have taken as being normal. For example, sources within the jail system mentioned that Bianchi seemed to withdraw after learning of Veronica's arrest. Instead of withdrawing in grief for a short period, had Bianchi gone into psychosis, his withdrawal might actually have been a temporary catatonic state. That catatonic state, if it existed for a short enough period of time, could easily have gone unnoticed by those around him. It would be too close to a normal shock and grief reaction to be obvious.

Dr. Watkins continued: "He has now rescued himself from psychosis by returning to a complete dissociative reaction. He is back to where we were in February 1979 when his Ken state had no awareness of even the presence of Steve, let alone Steve's crimes. His letter makes no mention of Steve, and I wonder if he even remembers the psychiatric interviews in Bellingham, or if they have been incorporated into what he describes as his 'memory problem.' I had foreseen the possible break into a psychosis; I did not foresee the return into a complete and almost 'perfect' dissociative reaction. I have never seen a multiple personality in which the walls of dissociation are so thick and impermeable. But then the disparity between the Ken state and the Steve state makes such a massive dissociation necessary if he is to survive a complete psychotic breakdown. 'Ken' simply cannot accept, understand, remember or believe that he (the good boy) could possibly do such crimes. Hence, Steve must be massively dissociated from awareness. And apparently, for the moment, Steve is 'hiding.' Accordingly, Ken's abilities are concentrated in searching (almost paranoid-like) for some other explanation to the predicament he finds himself in. Unless the dissociation breaks down again, he may well spend his life seeking these explanations of why he who 'knows' himself to be innocent is convicted of a crime which 'he' (Ken) did not commit.

"Steve, of course, could be activated again. With hypnosis he could be brought out—although I think Ken would be very wary again of letting himself be hypnotized. However, a good practitioner could do it. Steve could probably also be reactivated with sodium amytal or sodium pentathol—and, of course, he may choose to come out spontaneously again at some time. We would know of such occasions if Ken complains of further amnesic periods. Ken will be of no value to the prosecution of Buono, because he (Ken) now knows nothing of the crimes. Steve could be a witness if he were activated but may be scared and resist emerging again. Had the prosecution accepted the dissociation diagnosis and treated Ken appropriately, they could have had a credible witness against Angelo.

"In reading Ken's letter a thought came to me. He describes two incidents in which supposedly the police searched near the truck first and didn't find the girl's coat but did so a day later. Also, the temporarily missing 'account card' about the Catlow's which was later found. It would be of interest to inquire of Steve whether he returned to put the coat beside the truck and to replace the card. Since he was motivated into getting Ken accused of the crime, it makes sense that Steve took the coat there by the truck the day after in order to point the finger at Ken.

"You know, Ted, as long as Ken, the police, the prosecution, the et cetera are all so concerned in checking all the little details like the above and the inconsistencies, they will all be confused. Once they can accept the fact that Ken is a true and very complete multiple personality, then all the confusion clears up. The inconsistencies become clear. His erratic behavior makes sense. However, legal precedent doesn't know really how to deal with such a case (as I noted in my ego-state articles, in *Psychiatry and the Law*). Ken's other personality, Steve, did commit all those crimes, and Ken is an unstable multiple personality who is a menace, especially to women, if he were free. He will require continuous incarceration, and only very sophisticated and skillful treatment can extricate him from his dissociative reaction without precipitating a complete psychotic breakdown—a treatment which I doubt society and the law would provide and which, even if provided, would be difficult because of the very few psychiatrists and psychologists in the country who understand the disorder and know how to treat it.

"Incidentally, if Ken (in his present state) testifies against Angelo Buono and states that he knows of Buono's killing he will be lying. He may do this to please the prosecution or to secure some promised benefit. But Ken now (the one who wrote that letter) is no more aware of Buono's crimes than he is of Steve's. He can be easily tangled up by opposing attorneys since he will not know the correct details."

Dr. Watkins's words proved prophetic. Months of closed hearings were held during which sources within told of inconsistencies in Bianchi's testimony. He would change his story two or more times during any given day. He consistently maintained that Angelo Buono was his accomplice when he would admit to the murders, but many times be would simply deny all knowledge. The prosecutor, Roger Kelly, was keenly aware of the problems he was facing, yet little was done to experiment with different approaches to helping Ken Bianchi become an honest, credible witness. The support system that had been established was obviously a failure.

Despite the problems with the preliminary hearing, a decision was made to hold the trial of Buono. However, on July 6, 1981, Ken Bianchi went into an open court hearing and denied killing any of the victims in Los Angeles. That same afternoon, Bianchi returned to the stand and bragged of the killings, describing each murder in detail and implicating Angelo. His statements were made calmly, very much like those heard by Dr. Donald Lunde many months earlier in Bellingham.

The dual stories on the witness stand were not unexpected, but they revealed the problem Roger Kelly had previously not made public. The lack of willingness to try a new approach was previously noted as recently as three weeks before the July 6 hearing. At that time, Dr. John Watkins sent a letter to Roger Kelly, offering to help the prosecution with the case. It was to no avail. Dr. Watkins's letter went unanswered by Kelly and his staff.

Whether or not a different approach to working with Bianchi would have resulted in greater stability is not known. All that is certain is that without changes, there was no way to succeed. Finally, just seven days after the fiasco on the witness stand, Roger Kelly asked to drop the murder charges against Angelo Buono. He said that Bianchi's testimony was critical to the case and the changes in testimony made Bianchi not credible.

Kelly quoted, in addition to what had been made public on the witness stand, the various problems first revealed publicly in this book. This information included the letters Bianchi wrote to Dr. Ralph Allison trying to blame a second individual for the Bellingham murders, denying his own active involvement. The statement that Bianchi only faked hypnosis with Dr. Watkins also was repeated, thus casting doubt on the original confession naming Angelo Buono.

At this same time, an investigation into Ken Bianchi's background in Rochester, New York, indicated that the true number of women killed by his hand may have been greater than was known. Bianchi may have been involved with three killings known as the Double Alphabet murders.

Carmen Colon was a child with everything in her favor except for a limited intelligence. She was a happy, energetic ten-year-old, trusting and well liked by students and teachers. Her intelligence was limited, around 70 on a scale where the average person is approximately 100-110, but she was able to function in a way which was of help to her family. On November 16, 1971, the Rochester, New York, child went from her home on Brown Street to the Bull's Head Plaza, two blocks away. Her mother was sick and she was going to pick up the prescription the doctor had ordered.

The medicine was handed to Carmen at approximately 4:30 that afternoon. One hour later, more than ten miles away, motorists along Interstate Route 490 saw a nearly nude child running from a car that was backing toward her. The car, whose license plate was not recorded by witnesses, was the identical color and model of one regularly driven by Ken Bianchi. However, none of the investigators or the witnesses were aware of this fact at that time or for many years later.

Almost one hundred cars passed the site by police estimates. The nude child was obviously terrified, yet no one stopped to help. Motorists talked with the police later, but none had the sense to check and see what was happening. As a result, two days later the child's body was found off Steams Road in the community of Riga. She was wearing a purple sweater, socks and tennis shoes. She had been raped, strangled, and beaten. Her skull was fractured and there were numerous other injuries as well.

The community was enraged. The child had been from the Puerto Rican section of Rochester, a fact which normally would have downplayed publicity. However, the idea that this was a child, innocent, trusting, friendly to everyone, made the story more important. The newspapers expressed their anger and concern. The public tried to make up for the fact that no one had stopped to help the frightened girl, but to no avail. Endless leg work, countless hours of overtime, and all other efforts resulted in no success. The case ended without solution.

A year and half passed when Wands Walkowicz, age eleven, went three blocks from home to buy tuna fish and bread at a delicatessen. The food she purchased for her parents totaled $8.52, and the bag of groceries (less expensive than now) was large. The child headed for home at 5:30 that Monday afternoon, struggling with her load. She never returned.

The following morning, the raped, strangled, but fully clothed body was found on a hillside off Route 104. The second of what were to be three murders had occurred.

There were only a few similarities between the first case and the second. It was raining lightly both days, the afternoon sky being overcast. Both girls were carrying packages and might have welcomed someone giving them a lift. The causes of death were identical and the girls were less than a year apart in age. However, there the similarities seemed to stop.

Wanda was considered a tough, street-wise child. She was small, just four feet tall and 65 pounds, yet she was known to be able to beat up older boys in fights at schools. It was believed that there was no way she would have gotten into a car unless she knew and trusted the person driving. Yet the people she definitely knew were ruled out as suspects. This meant that it was either a stranger, perhaps dressed in the uniform of a professional she would have felt safe with (policeman, fireman, ambulance driver), or someone she knew who had been overlooked in the investigation. The latter might be a store owner, deliveryman, or a similar individual.

Once again the search was intense. Once again there was a dead end. Even worse, this time no witnesses came forward.

On November 26, 1973, the last of the victims lost her life. This girl's name was Michelle Maenza, and suddenly there seemed to be a possible new clue. Michelle Maenza. had the initials "MM;" Wanda Walkowicz had "WW." And Carmen Colon had the initials "CC." The double alphabet murders. It may have been deliberate or it may have been coincidence.

Michelle was a fat, unpopular fifth grader. She was the class outcast, the child who is the brunt of jokes, teased in the schoolyard, and generally is miserable with kids her own age. Her disappearance made the most sense since she might have been the type to go off with anyone who was nice to her. She might easily have been encouraged to go for something to eat with a stranger, to accept a ride because it was raining, as it had been earlier, and because she also had been walking to a shopping area.

A difference between Michelle's case and the other two was that she was on her way to the supermarket, not coming home from a store. Her mother had left her purse at the supermarket on Saturday, and Michelle was on her way there when she disappeared. The last time a child dressed like Michelle had been seen that day was at 3:30 in the afternoon, but the outfit Michelle was wearing had come from a popular sale at a local department store. Many little girls were similarly dressed, and witness identification was not positive.

Two days later Michelle, fully dressed but raped and strangled, was found. This time, however, the facts were different. A wrist print of the killer was discovered on the neck of the little girl. The scientific investigation team of the Rochester police used a special method for lifting it.

The clue of the wrist print, kept secret for eight years, was a major one. According to information from FBI experts and others, a wrist print with proper points of identification is as unique as a fingerprint. Each time the wrist print is compared with the wrist print of a suspect in a recent case, it is possible to determine whether he or she is the guilty person. However, wrist prints change with age. An individual's wrist print today is expected to be different from the print the same person will have in ten years. The print will still be unique in a decade, but it will also be different from the print of the same person when younger.

The situation with the wrist print is quite different from that with fingerprints. Fingerprints do not change with age. Thus a fingerprint can be used to convict or clear a man many years after a crime. The wrist print can only be used for a relatively short period.

The investigation had many leads because the public was outraged. Rewards were offered. A secret witness line was installed to get the public to help. Anonymity was assured for anyone willing to get involved. Yet most of the callers had nothing to offer other than the fact that they had noticed the double alphabet situation.

The police did not believe that the initials had anything to do with the crimes. They felt that if the initials were a factor, then the killings were deliberate. This meant that the girls would have been stalked over a period of time by the murderer. Such an action would have been noticed by passersby because the areas were such that strangers or even local residents acting in this manner would have seemed odd. This was not the case; no such behavior was noticed.

Some of the officers even questioned whether all three cases were related. The first death was the only one where violence was obvious beyond the rape and strangulation. It was felt that the last two victims may have been lured to their deaths while the first was taken away by force. However, an equally good case could be made for the idea that the man had so much trouble with the first victim that he changed his tactics for those who came later.

The Monroe County Medical Examiner put together what he believed might be a psychological profile of the killer. Among other details, he said that the man had great fear of rejection by women. He felt that the same man was responsible for all three killings and that the deaths were well planned. He thought that perhaps the man worked in the social services department and had knowledge of the roads. Upon reflection, several years later, it is obvious to the police that such a profile fits Bianchi.

There have been many rumors of what may have happened during the Rochester investigation. The truth is that at no time was Ken Bianchi a suspect. He was an unknown, though a man whose troubled personal life and work as an ambulance driver would have allowed him to be involved. The facts known today which link him to the crime—the car, the fact that he had the time to do the killings without detection, his emotional disturbance and anger with his first wife, and possibly the wrist print were not known at the time. It was an unsolvable case on which the police wanted to close the books.

One story has it that political action within the department led to an investigator blaming a fireman whose record for sexual misconduct could have made him a suspect. However, the fire-man could not clear himself because he had died before the ac-cusation was made. The evidence was circumstantial at best and later was found to be inadequate. Today the man's name has been cleared and the investigator involved has retired.

The reality of the situation is that of all the people who might have been linked with the crime, Ken Bianchi remains the stron-gest suspect. Some of the psychiatric experts, such as Dr. John Watkins, believe that Bianchi could confess to the crimes, assum-ing he is guilty, if given the right circumstances, Watkins feels that Bianchi needs to be approached as "Steve" since it is Steve who committed the murders. Even those investigators who be-lieve Bianchi is faking the multiple personality think that talk-ing with him as Steve will get a confession. They had seen Bianchi brag when he is claiming to be Steve and feel that an interroga-tion about Rochester done in this manner will get the answers they are seeking.

The Rochester authorities have admitted privately that they are not greatly concerned with trying Bianchi, if he is guilty. They are more concerned with closing the books on the cases. So long as Bianchi can never get out of prison, assuming he is guilty, then it is not worth the great expense of a trial. However, if Bianchi is innocent, that means that there may be a child killer waiting to strike again, either in Rochester or elsewhere.

The wrist print became an issue in the Los Angeles case in August of 1981. The attorney for Buono, Gerald Chaleff, wanted to have Bianchi's wrist print checked. No one knows for certain that a change has occurred with Bianchi's wrist print, and a posi-tive link with the Rochester killings can be important to his case. The implication would then be that Bianchi acted alone for three murders in Rochester and two murders in Bellingham. It would then be logical to believe that he may have acted alone in Los Angeles. Killers often follow consistent patterns.

The police point out that two men committed some of the crimes in the Los Angeles cases. The similarities in all the kill-ings exist with the rapes and strangulations. The fact that Bianchi worked alone at times and with an accomplice at other times is not particularly important. The patterns criminals follow are seldom completely consistent. Rather, a number of factors, such as the rapes, the stranglings, the dumping on hillsides, match. But other circumstances, as for example, how the victims are chosen, the kind of car driven, and perhaps the number of killers, may vary greatly.

The lawyers for Buono have another point in their favor when attacking Bianchi's credibility. They stress that Bianchi has always stated that Yolanda Washington was his first victim. If they can prove otherwise, then there is even more reason to consider him a liar.

Again the police have a counter to this. They feel that Bianchi, or any other criminal, would be foolish to confess to any more crimes than were known. He could be positively linked to Washington's death but to nothing prior to that time. Even a man with a multiple personality can see that talking about something that is not known to the authorities could result in his being tried and possibly receiving the death sentence. Past circumstances with the various state and federal courts made the death sentence not a factor in past trials. By the time a trial could begin in Rochester, capital punishment might be a very real threat in New York State, where the new trial would be held.

Superior Court Judge Ronald M. George refused to stop the murder trial of Angelo Buono when all the problems became apparent in July of 1981. Roger Kelly put together a lengthy memo to District Attorney John Van de Kamp, Kelly's superior. This memo showed numerous discrepancies in Bianchi's testimony during the various interrogations in Bellingham and Los Angeles. These included such details as exactly who was driving the car used to pick up the two schoolgirls at the Eagle Rock Shopping Center. Bianchi also reportedly told one of the prosecutors that he had faked the multiple-personality story. He said he never killed anyone and was never present at the deaths. However, the judge felt there was a need for the issue of Buono's guilt or innocence to be decided in a court of law.

The conflict within Los Angeles was resolved when the California attorney general's office stepped in to study the case in August of 1981. After reviewing the entire matter, including the objections by Kelly, Attorney General George Deukmejian said that there was enough apparently valid evidence to warrant a trial. It was announced that the state would prosecute Buono for murder despite the reluctance of the county of Los Angeles.

The true final chapter of the Hillside Strangler story will never be written for Ken Bianchi and Angelo Buono. As the trial unfolds in Los Angeles, it is doubtful that a satisfactory solution will ever take place. Angelo Buono may be guilty. Angelo Buono may be innocent. He cannot account for his time during the periods when the victims were killed, nor can hundreds of thousands of other men. There were witnesses to Buono's capacity for criminal behavior whose testimony can be countered by those who feel he is a hard worker, a skilled upholsterer, and a good citizen. The testimony by Ken Bianchi is damning, but also ever-changing. All that is consistent is that he always blames Buono for being an accomplice. Thus the jailing or freedom of Angelo Buono will not prove conclusively what has happened. A jury may risk sending an innocent man to jail on the chance that he was a killer and could kill again. Or the jury may risk freeing a guilty man on the assumption that there is reasonable doubt in the case. Either way the answer will fail to satisfy anyone.

The Double Alphabet murders will likewise not have a satisfactory solution unless the killer—be it Bianchi or someone else— confesses with details known only to the murderer. Ken Bianchi, if guilty, is not likely to confess. The evidence available at this time is not adequate for a conviction and may not be adequate for an arrest. As each new day passes, the chance of finding more conclusive evidence fades even further.

Kelli Boyd has found more inner strength than she had imagined possible. She and Sean were on welfare for a while, but Kelli hated receiving charity. She went to work for a hospital, even though it meant that her income was reduced and she could not afford day care. The care of preschooler Sean has become a communal effort among Kelli and several of her friends who have children, jobs, and different hours at work.

Kelli is also planning to return to school as soon as this is possible. She has been working as a secretary but wants to become a fully registered nurse.

Any love or compassion Kelli might have once felt for Ken Bianchi is in the past. She hates the man for what he did and his refusal to either admit his guilt or try to seek psychiatric help in prison. The Veronica Compton case was the final shock for her, and she will never let Bianchi see his child. She hopes to one day change her identity and relocate so that she can raise her son in a normal environment.

Personal relationships with men have been difficult for Kelli. She continues to fear the unknown. She made a mistake once. Could she make the same mistake again? Ken Bianchi was a gentle lover, a wonderful father—and a man who raped and strangled other women. Would she see a potential problem? Could she differentiate a man's immaturity from psychotic behavior? Those who know her realize that she can. She is older, more mature, slightly hardened, yet willing to risk her heart to find happiness.

Kelli is dating again. She wants marriage, a normal existence, a father for Sean. She knows that she could spot a problem before she could be victimized by it, yet the nervousness remains. Life is moving forward and it will get better. For now, though, she is still struggling to get through each day.

Ken's mother remains hurt by every story concerning her son. She loves him, no matter what he may have done. He tells her he is innocent and she wants to believe him. She worries about attacks against herself caused by the reports related to his childhood.

Yet the truth of Ken Bianchi is that no matter what pressures may have made him the man he became, he acted as an adult. He knew he was troubled, different, yet he did not seriously seek psychiatric counseling. He has had options as an adult and the knowledge that murder is wrong. Even if he is a multiple personality, the condition is not considered insanity by psychiatrists, but the coping mechanism which begins with a troubled child.

The evidence against Ken Bianchi is overwhelming. The questions which have arisen concerning the identity of an accomplice do not relate to his personal actions. The physical proof of his guilt cannot be diminished because of his anguished pleas or angry outbursts against those who refuse to become a part of his delusional system.

The biggest question remaining concerns the future of other men and women whose childhood perceptions of life may be creating the mass murderers of tomorrow. Ken Bianchi was a deeply troubled child. Doctors and social workers have documented their concerns for this growing boy. They put his name in their reports. They talked of their theories concerning why his actions may have been abnormal for a child. Yet there was no effort to reach him, no attempt to help the problem child obtain a better grasp of the world. The authorities made their reports, filed them, and went on about their more important work. The troubled child became a disturbed adult, a man who could kill over and over again.

One possible answer is to find a way to help children spotted by specially trained teachers and others. There is fear that parents may bring lawsuits against such individuals. It is often assumed that all such troubled children are being abused, yet the reality is that disturbed children can come from good homes. The perceptions of reality a child may have can differ from the facts, yet this will not be known without counseling. Had anyone taken the time to truly involve himself or herself with the developing Ken Bianchi, as many as seventeen people might be alive today.

A troubled child can find a way out of the problems which beset him. Many abused children grow up to be healthy adults who do not perpetuate the abuse with their own offspring. Many disturbed young people come to analyze their own actions, then change so they can lead normal lives. But many troubled children do not have these inner strengths and resources. They need an occasional outside helping hand, no matter how good their family life. Such help was not given to Ken Bianchi. There is no record of anyone reaching out, even though professionals recognized that the child is father to the man.

Ken Bianchi was allowed to grow up without any effort to help him perceive life in a healthier manner. Now his life is over and he will spend the rest of his days behind bars. How many other children face this same fate because we have yet to hold out our hands while they are small? The answers may only come when we are again shocked by another outbreak of senseless violence and death.

THE REST OF THE STORY
The View With Twenty Years' Perspective

I was racing through the Hilton Hotel lobby, down an escalator, to the ticket counter of the adjacent Chicago O'Hare Airport. It was late morning and I had just returned from East Chicago Heights, a community I assumed would be a few minutes outside of the downtown area. Instead, as my taxi driver and I discovered, the street we needed to take did, indeed, go through the downtown area. Then it continued on into the suburbs, the exurbs, and through a region of what appeared to be small farms. Eventually we located the radio station where I spent an hour talking to the host, answering questions from callers, and then raced back to catch my flight to Los Angeles.

"Mr. Schwarz, it's good to have you with us," said the ticket agent. "I saw you on Tom Snyder's show Monday night."

A fan. I had been on the road almost three weeks, promoting the book you just read, and this was the first time anyone had recognized me. Even more surprising, since this was Wednesday afternoon, was the fact that the Snyder show, "Tomorrow," had been aired at 1 A.M. Monday. Perhaps the ticket agent needed more excitement in his life. Nevertheless, I wanted to talk. I wanted to bask in what little celebrity I could claim. However, if my watch was right, the last boarding call had probably been made for my flight. I would run for it, but most likely I would have to see if I could get a seat on a later plane.

"Don't worry about the time," the ticket agent told me, smiling. "We'll hold the flight for you."

Sure.

I grabbed my bag and raced down the corridor to the security check-in. As I lifted my bag onto the X-ray machine's conveyer belts, one of the security guards looked at me and said, "Don't worry, Mr. Schwarz. They're holding the plane for you."

I smiled, said "Thank you," then retrieved my bag and ran down the hall. For a moment I thought about hopping on one of the electric carts, but I was already running faster than the cart drivers could move through the crowds. The drivers had to watch out for passengers blocking the way. I could simply run like a crazed football player, moving in and out of lovers sharing a last minute kiss, bored children sitting on the floor with toys guaranteed to trip the unwary, old men and women using walkers or wheel chairs, and college students bearing backpacks. I figured the plane was already starting to taxi away from the gate, but I wanted to arrive breathless, hoping the airline personnel would take pity on me and place me on the next flight to L.A.

Finally I reached the gate; the door to the ramp was, indeed, closed and the seating area empty of passengers. Before I could ask where to go to book a later flight, an attendant smiled and said, "Don't worry, Mr. Schwarz. We held the plane for you."

I handed the woman my boarding pass, then stared in amazement. First the gate door opened. Then, as I went down the passageway, there was the sealed, wide-bodied DC-9. The door swung open and I stepped into the plane. It was filled almost to capacity with more than two hundred passengers. Some people were glaring and pointedly looking at their watches, obviously concerned about Los Angeles appointments or the short time they would have to make connecting flights. Others leaned forward, either putting on or taking off their glasses, depending upon whether they had myopia or hyperopia, trying to decide if they had seen me before.

I made my way to my coach seat two-thirds of the way back— peasant class—the airline equivalent of steerage. Its single luxury was its location on the aisle. Only one person's elbow could jam me in the ribs during the flight. Hardly the place for someone important enough for the crew to delay the plane, yet delay it they had, and as I settled into my seat, one of the flight attendants asked for my autograph and offered a complimentary drink.

The men and women seated around me glared. Either I was one of them—unable to afford First Class—or a rich and famous person whose name should have been on the tips of their tongues, and who was trying to make a social comment by hanging out with the "little people." Either way, I was a damned nuisance. But…for the moment, I was a celebrity—sort of.

* * *

Celebrity. After thousands of hours of investigation and millions of dollars for investigator's overtime, serial murder came to mean celebrity. The horrors of what the victims endured meant little to strangers who once followed the case in newspapers, magazines, on radio, and on television.

Parents, siblings, lovers, and friends of Bianchi and Buono's victims were left to grieve alone as the dead became statistics after a troubled year in review, their humanity, hopes, and dreams long forgotten. The families of the law enforcement officers who worked seemingly endless hours to solve the murders grew tired of hearing the stories of what the men and women had seen when they went from corpse to corpse, hillside to hillside. The post-traumatic stress that sent some to therapy and others to alcohol was not mentioned by the news media.

What mattered now was celebrity.

Some of the celebrity issues involved journalists like myself. I had the three-week "tour" of the nation, moving from city to city, talk show to talk show, news show to news show. I learned how fast I could get a suit dry-cleaned. I learned when to use a commercial laundry and when to wash undergarments in the sinks of hotel rooms. And, I learned what it was like to flick on a television set and hear my name being spoken.

A detective who gained the interest of both a writer and of television executives claimed that he had used his wife to gather information about Angelo Buono's shop, where several of the murders occurred. There were dramatic stories about the couple acting on their own to gain information that would link the cousin. The problem was that there were transcripts available from wiretaps used to gather evidence between the time Bianchi was arrested and the time Angelo Buono was taken into custody. These appeared to be the sole source of information and matched the material allegedly "overheard" by the daring couple.

Reporters began looking for hindsight stories so they could keep making appearances on nightly news shows. A single murder was usually not an important event in Los Angeles County. Entry level reporters and reporters making the switch from radio to the better paying, higher profile jobs in television often were assigned these routine killings. Sometimes they gained a few seconds of airtime and a tragic shake of the head by the studio anchor. Sometimes the footage was tossed because more important stories developed closer to airtime. However, once the Hillside Strangler appeared, these same reporters suddenly had expertise the station "stars" did not. They rode the murders to what they hoped would be fame and fortune, gaining ever greater air time until the L.A. killings stopped and they could only do weekly wrap-ups—that is, until the Washington state arrests.

Some got a second chance at fame when the trial finally began; others were bumped from the story by the station's more experienced personnel. A handful did move to better jobs, and a few, unable to respect the often superficial, highly competitive business they were in, worked desperately to retain "face time."

The face time efforts were often deliberately misleading. One evening while I was in Los Angeles, watching a television news program, a reporter made a "shocking revelation" that the Los Angeles Police Department had had reason to investigate Ken Bianchi months before his arrest. The reporter showed a computer printout proving that Bianchi was known in the police files to have had reported contacts with four of the twelve victims. Had they done their job, the reporter falsely railed, other girls would still be alive.

I called the reporter after the newscast. "I'm familiar with the report you showed," I said. "But you're doing the police an injustice. They handled the investigation flawlessly. They used computers to determine how many known contacts various area men had with the victims. Some had one or two. Bianchi had four. There were some with eight or more, and some of those also had criminal records, something Bianchi did not. They were eliminating them one at a time, but they started with those who had the most contacts. By the time they were getting close to Bianchi, he had left the city for Bellingham. It was only after Chief Mangan learned more about Bianchi's past that he was linked in a meaningful way. The Los Angeles cops would have been derelict to start with a guy who only had four contacts when other men, including one guy who was an ex-con who had done time for violence against women, had more known contacts."

"I know that," the reporter told me. "But I have to earn brownie points with my boss at the station."

"You're needlessly hurting police officers who did a great job," I said. "And you're probably scaring the public about the future."

The reporter did not care. He had extra face time. He had a chance to move to a higher paying job. He had celebrity.

Then there were the hangers-on, the women who came calling at the jailhouse door once Ken and Angelo were safely locked away. There were writers like myself who became familiar faces on news and talk shows throughout the United States. There were ministers who filled the pews of their churches by relating Ken Bianchi and Angelo Buono to Armageddon, the apocalypse, and whatever sin was their pet hate of the moment. There were television investigative reporters who had become so adept at showing the five basic facial configurations of their profession—shock, sadness, concern, hope, and relief—all the time keeping their hair flawlessly in place while standing on a hillside, overlooking a crime scene, that they were promoted to positions as news anchors in higher paying markets. Newspaper reporters gained the prestige of columns. And police officers in administration—men and women who had not pounded a beat since their rookie year—were given raises, promotions, or retired and financed for a run at political office.

One way or another, too many of us benefited from celebrity.

In my case, the Chicago flight seemed the defining moment, but it was not my only encounter with what celebrity could mean. A floor director for one Los Angeles television program approached me to tell me how much she had been looking forward to meeting me. The beautiful young woman with a British accent explained that she was a fan of my writing. She said she had read all my books, then both named and discussed them knowledgeably.

"The Hillside Strangler scared me," she said. "I live alone, so there was no one there when I read it."

"I live alone," she repeated, giving me her address. And that's when I realized she was trying to pick me up. She had read my book, met me in person, and she was coming on to me.

I don't know what I would have done had I not been a relative newlywed in a second marriage, which I didn't want to destroy. In one fantasy, I went to dinner with her, returned to either her apartment or my hotel room, and made mad, passionate love until she had to go to work or I had to make another appearance somewhere. Eventually we would tearfully part, though only long enough for me to pack my possessions and move to Los Angeles to be with her.

In another fantasy, the nightmare one, the romance began in much the same way. Then, some time between the first kiss and adjourning to the bedroom, she would talk about the murder technique *she* used for *her* victims. She would talk about wanting me to write her story. She would want to sacrifice her next victim with me present so I could capture every subtle nuance of her technique.

Since the affair was only happening in my mind, I did not have to consider the reality of sexually transmitted diseases or the lack of our compatibility in every way, except with the subjects I wrote about in the books she had read. I did not have to remember that I hate the idea of living in Los Angeles, a city so earthquake prone that some kindergarten staff personnel once asked parents to supply appropriately sized body bags in addition to pencils, crayons, and tissues.

As I fantasized, the floor director and I would either enjoy the start of a great romance (and a messy divorce) or I would be in the midst of a living, breathing Stephen King horror novel.

Using better judgment than I wanted to exercise, I thanked her, went on the show, and returned to my hotel room—alone. Celebrity.

*   *   *

Yet through it all, the story of the Hillside Strangler brought out emotions and stories I never expected to hear, and frequently did not want to know.

For example, while I was working on the book, Veronica Compton was going through her own personal hell. A series of personal traumas, coupled with a job and social position that gave her access to alcohol, drugs, and any other destructive vice she wanted to try, were slowly destroying her. Eventually she entered Good Samaritan Hospital suffering from sleep psychosis, panic attacks, and other biochemical reactions that exaggerated the emotional problems for which she had yet to seek counseling. She began to think of herself as potentially insane, and when she spent time working with Ken Bianchi, she thought of him as the one person who understood her.

"Ken calmed me," she wrote later. "Promised me he'd keep me connected to reality and protect me from the monsters: the creeping terror that panicked me with a real fear that the Boogie Man was after me. I couldn't escape the delusion that I was being stalked. The Boogie Man was real, hiding under my car seat, in my closet, under my bed, outside the shower. He was out to kill me and no one could save me but Ken. Ken was strong. He had powers. I could let him control my life and then the Boogie Man couldn't touch me. Just do as Ken commanded. He told me I needed more cocaine, more pills, more scotch [sic]. Just do it, he said. Just do a little more and think of him, how he could protect me."

Veronica was falling apart emotionally. She was a beautiful woman, brilliant, from a highly respected family and, if there were any dirty little secrets, they were well hidden. She was not someone who would seek counseling. She was someone who would be strong, who would handle her problems herself or with the help of her husband at the time. Except that she couldn't. No one could. Instead she habitually listened to a Walkman cassette with earphones so that she could create external sound to try and block the voices that filled her head.

"As the surrealist world fused with the disorganized voices, their combined power found higher ground where energies were under their control. My own mind became more and more vacant as the thoughts of others were gathered. Life was purposeless; all was magic. There were no choices in life, only the passive sleep of an abducted consciousness. With weak eyes and a soul battered to complete helplessness, I was carried from one visual and audial [sic] horror to the next. I had no power whatsoever to halt the taking of the familiar world. It was being torn from my eyes, ears and body, and nobody had answers to what was wrong...no one but Ken. Pills, injections, more pills, cocaine and alcohol. Talk. The visits became confessionals. In the Name of the Father, the Son, and the Holy Ghost gave no consolation. In the name of the Hillside, the Strangler and Ken, there was at least a man, a voice, and direction."

By July of 1980, Veronica had reached bottom. She was emotionally disturbed and used drugs to avoid the nightmare inside her mind. She had reached the state of drug-induced psychosis, but no one noticed. No one reached out. She could no longer relate to the real world. She wrote, "Ken is everywhere; he knows my every move. He follows me. On the company yacht at sea, the radio transports his voice. At the Beverly Hills Hotel Polo Lounge, the phone is brought to my table. At the office up the road on Robertson Boulevard, the phone rings as I enter the reception room. At my father's home, he meets me; then later driving home in the limousine, he's on the car phone. Says he'll call me at home in half an hour. More booze, more cocaine, more pills. There is nowhere to get away to and to what end anyway. To meet my lunacy alone? More pills, more cocaine, more booze.

"My husband will do nothing; I must be all right. When I begged him to commit me before I start killing people, he cried and said he couldn't. Maybe there is nothing so wrong that I should worry. What more can I do? The doctors know that I'm losing control but they haven't locked me up. What's happening? What is right, what is wrong? What is good or bad? I don't know.

I don't know anything but Ken and Ken is God. Ken is my savior and salvation. He knows that nothing is so real that we can't overcome it. More pills, more cocaine, more booze."

Veronica might be called both a willing participant in the aftermath of the murders and, in a sense, the last victim of the Hillside Strangler. She attempted murder on Bianchi's behalf, then was either physically unable to overpower her victim or thought differently and fled—there would eventually be two stories. Either way, Veronica, in her moments of madness, wanted to free Ken.

According to the alleged plan, Veronica would bind and strangle a randomly selected victim, then set the scene so it would appear obvious the Hillside Strangler had killed again. She willingly accepted a secreted container of Ken's sperm. The sperm, placed on the vagina of the next victim, would "prove" that he was innocent because everyone knew Ken was locked away in maximum security. Her guilt concerning the effort is without question, yet in her descent to madness, so is her innocence.

Veronica's appearance on the witness stand in her own trial worked against her. She came across as arrogant and deceitful as the transcript shows.

Veronica's defense attorney was Bill Johnston, and the prosecutor was David McEchran. The following testimony is from when she took the witness stand in her defense on March 18, 1981.

Johnston: Could you tell us a little bit about your education?

Compton: Well for the past six years—it's been almost seven years now—I have been with Lee Strasberg's Theatrical Institute, and I was just accepted two years ago to study directly under Lee in his Master's Class. Dustin Hoffman was in it, Marlo Thomas, those kind of people were in the Master Class. With Lee Strasberg.

Johnston: And have you written plays and books?

Compton: Ah, yes I have. I have written plays and three screenplays. Some of those were musicals....

Johnston: What are some of the subjects that were covered in the books and plays?

Compton: Political, political issues, love, musical, comedy types of things, period prose, which takes place in the seventeenth century...murder, history, suspense type of things, psychological dramas—I am very much into psychology and psychological dramas…And as for the books I have written, I am completing an autobiographical work right now. And, ah, one of short story fiction. They are all murder stories.

Johnston: Can you tell us a little bit about your background until now?

Compton: Well, I grew up around television sound stages, art openings, nightclub performers, judges' chambers, because my family has been very interested in politics, those are my father's best friends—politicians and judge— and a lot of college campuses.

Johnston: Can you tell us about the writing business in Los Angeles and what a person must do to gain some notoriety there?

Compton: Well, there's an axiom that is used among people in the business, and that is there is no such thing as bad publicity. All publicity is good publicity. There is no such thing as a bad review—as long as you get into those papers, then that's what gets you off. That's how you make the money; that's how you get the notoriety. That's how you get the acclaim. That's one of the ways that you are taught.

Johnston: Okay, thank you. I have no further questions.

*   *   *

McEachran: You met Kenneth Bianchi on a daily basis?

Compton: Yes, sir.

McEachran: Also, you've indicated to numerous people, including a writer for the *Bellingham Herald*, that you love Kenneth Bianchi and that you would even go to jail for him. Did you mention that?

Compton: Ah, yes but there was a premise upon which it was made.

McEachran: You don't deny making the statement.

Compton: It was an exploitive statement.

McEachran: …Didn't you do this to show that Kenneth Bianchi was innocent of the Hillside Strangling murders here?

Compton: No, sir.

McEachran: Didn't you feel that if a body was discovered here, strangled, same MO as the killings that have happened here for which Kenneth Bianchi was convicted, that would show that Kenneth Bianchi was not guilty of the crimes that were committed here?

Compton: Sir, I never anticipated a body being found here.

Among the stories Veronica told on the stand was one that she was visiting Ken Bianchi and interviewing him for a story she was writing. She stressed she had also talked with homicide detectives, naming some, such as Ed Henderson who had worked on the Hillside Strangler task force. "Since I am an unknown writer, I embraced an idea for publicity. In that idea I grasped the most sensationalistic murder case I could because I had just completed a murder play, which I believe is very explosive, very dynamic. And I want it sold.

"I thought the best way to do it was to get the homicide people involved, make a big scandal, and then have them say, 'Oh, see, it's not really someone on the loose strangling people. It's just a writer out doing something dumb.'"

At another point in the trial, Veronica explained that she never loved Ken Bianchi. She made up the story for publicity. She soon began screaming at the prosecutor, "I tried to tell you guys I was innocent, but you didn't believe me. So my idea was to exploit the situation…. I figured, what the heck. Take the game all the way."

Kim Breed's character was also attacked during the trial. Among the stories Veronica told was that Breed was bribed with cocaine to tell the police that a man who looked like Bianchi, along with a man who looked like Buono, tried to strangle her in the motel. But when Veronica tried to put a noose around Kim's neck, using the knot Ken had taught her, Breed was too drunk to realize Veronica would only pull it tight enough to leave some marks that would remain until the police arrived. Eventually, she said that she was actually planning to do three look-alike attacks, the one in Bellingham, one in Oregon, and another in Texas.

The jury came to several conclusions. They recognized that the victim was probably intoxicated and in shock, the reason the attempted murder had not been reported the moment Breed was free from Compton. They also felt, based on expert testimony, that the abrasions found on Kim Breed's neck when the police arrived were far too deep to be anything other than a murder attempt.

Later, when interviewed by Bill Johnson of the *Bellingham Herald*, Veronica was quoted as saying, "I wasn't fooling around with Kim Breed's life any more than the people who put on "Candid Camera" fool with their subjects' lives. They are constantly blowing people's minds.

"When I set this thing up, all I wanted was the publicity. I was never trying to play myself off as a murderer. I didn't know I could be liable for obstruction of justice charges if Kim had filed the police report. Had I known what I know now, I wouldn't have done it."

Johnson said that Veronica talked of wanting to become rich and famous through her actions. He also quoted her saying, "I am [a] very good writer, I am very into myself, very much so. I love myself immensely—I am very narcissistic. Believe me, I had to have an enormous ego to do what I did."

In truth, Veronica's ego was shattered. She was a disturbed young woman who had become the willing pawn of an even more disturbed young man.

The conviction proved to be of value to Veronica. Serving time helped her change. Away from easy access to drugs and alcohol, her body was able to detoxify. No one cared that she came from a background of wealth and privilege when she put on the prison uniform and had to adjust to the regimen demanded by the warden and the guards. The only part of her history that mattered was her education. She was able to work with many of the inmates who had no hope upon release unless they could learn to read, write, and master the other skills needed to hold a job that would assure independent living. As her mind cleared, she entered counseling—both alone and in groups—that helped her heal. Yet while she was learning about herself and gradually finding ways to change, she was able to use her insight to counsel others. She found meaningful purpose and success in prison in ways that eluded her in what the inmates call the "free world."

Not that Veronica was a model prisoner. She was rebellious even in her healing, and when she saw the opportunity, she managed a short-lived escape.

Veronica also had the good fortune to meet a man through his prison work. He was well educated, honest, and hard working, and he was respected in the world of academia. He saw the woman inside the hardened shell, the one she had kept locked in a box sealed with drugs and psychosis. They fell in love, married, and eventually earned conjugal visits that resulted in a child they both adore and whom he raised alone until her release.

Ironically, the happiness and success Veronica achieved might not have happened had Ken Bianchi not become involved with her. He became a piece of her madness, bringing her to a point where others had to take notice. It would have been easier if her first husband would have committed her. It would have been easier if a forced intervention would have helped her stop the drugs and alcohol, then seek counseling. But neither friends, nor family, nor coworkers fully understood what was happening. And, Veronica was too far gone to be able to recognize she had a problem, much less to consider doing anything about it.

*   *   *

Veronica was Ken Bianchi's last victim. Ironically, he was also the person whose involvement in her life assured that the world she inhabits today is nurturing, loving, and truly happy.

Veronica's story, as horrendous as it was for everyone involved, was the story of just one woman involved with men who commit serial violence. What was more shocking for me was the range of women I discovered who were part of a culture of friends and fantasy lovers of one or another of the men whose rapes and/or murders terrified communities and made headlines in small towns and major cities throughout the United States. Some of these women were lonely, yet they were either unable to establish a relationship or feared the repeat of a previous love that had gone bad. Others felt themselves lost. A few were desperate for celebrity of their own, to become "somebody," by being connected with "fame." They did not seem to understand or care about the difference between fame and infamy, between earned accolades and notoriety. They fed on the egos of the emotionally disturbed and the violent, who, in turn, took advantage of them.

My first introduction to the women who sought "lifers" rather than freely living males came via the sister of a serial rapist who is serving life in maximum security in a California state penitentiary. The sister was neither violent nor a groupie. She worked in the music business. I met her when I went to her office to interview her boss for a magazine article. She learned of my conversations with Ken Bianchi and some of the women who were standing in line at the county jail to see him. She told me that my shock at discovering killers had groupies was surprising. She had seen such women trying to make contact with her brother, who was serving a life sentence for serial rape.

The crimes this man committed began in ways that made his future unpredictable. He was dating a coworker at a fast food restaurant and claimed she agreed to sex, then changed her mind. The attorney convinced the jury that the girl had gone too far, that the man's reaction, while technically rape, was the result of normal adolescence and immaturity on both their parts. "She was a virgin working her way through community college and teaching youth Sunday school at her church," the sister told me. "I knew my brother was guilty of deliberately raping her, and the situation just made me sick. The defense attorney tried to picture her as some experienced 'cock tease' who got what was coming to her."

There was no question the second time. He hit the woman, breaking her jaw. This time he spent a few months in jail, getting out early for good behavior.

"I don't know if harder time would have changed things," said the man's sister. "Probably not. It's just that nobody looked at the fact that there were very few women working in the prison where he was sent. There was little opportunity for his anger.

"Our parents were killed in a car crash when he was seven and I was four. None of our relatives wanted us, so we were placed in group homes. These were like orphanages, but they included kids who were taken from their parents because of abuse of one kind or another as well as whose parents were too sick or hurt to take care of them. My brother's group home was brutal. There were beatings and eventually word got out about problems there. The place was closed down though I doubt anyone did any follow-up on the kids who were placed there. I do know my brother was raped and beaten. He's a big man now, but he grew late. He was nearly sixteen before he began to grow, so he looked like a boy no older than one in fourth grade.

"Mine wasn't easy, but it wasn't like his. The couple who mostly took care of us were religious fanatics who thought that children suffered only if they were sinful. The woman said we must have done something bad for God to take our parents, and if we hadn't, then our parents were paying for their sins. The couple was convinced that hard work and harsh discipline would save us from a life of I don't know what.

"I married while in high school, just to get out of that place. Thank God I didn't have any children. The marriage lasted about as long as you'd expect for a couple of kids, but I eventually made it on my own, got through school, married a great guy, and have a family I care about. My brother…. There was no talking with him and I had little contact over the years unless he was in jail. Now he'll never get out, and I'm sorry to say it's the best place for him. That's why I can't understand the women."

The brother's crimes began during his teen years and grew increasingly violent. He picked up a hitchhiker, took her into the woods, and eventually left her naked and bleeding, with her hands tied behind her back. She made her way to the highway where a motorist found her and took her to the hospital. The defense attorney tried to make it a case of rough sex that got out of hand, but the police found that the pickup truck he was driving had the passenger side door rigged so it wouldn't open from the inside. Still, he did relatively short time before his release.

Before the brother was finally put away for life, there were victims who ranged from sales clerks, kidnapped on their way home, to at least one forced entry into an apartment near a county hospital complex. Usually the violence was brutal but fairly quick, and the man fled before anyone became aware that his victims were in trouble. However, he eventually decided to prolong the torture of two victims he kidnapped and took into a wooded area near a small college community. They were bound, gagged, and tied to separate trees. The initial attack had apparently been unplanned, and once he had them helpless, he went to get the tools he decided to use to torture them.

Before the man returned, a retired professor who routinely walked his dog in the same wooded area discovered the victims. He freed them, called the authorities, and sheriff's deputies were waiting when the rapist returned. In his car they found lengths of rope, screwdrivers, box cutters, and a small butane powered, portable soldering gun that could be used to apply intense heat to a small surface. This time he admitted what he planned to do, and he received a sentence that would keep him in jail the rest of his life.

The trial received extensive local publicity. The man had roamed a multi-county area. Women working and living there had no idea who he was, what he looked like, or if they might be targeted as victims. Everyone was frightened, and many women carried guns or knives, or carried makeshift weapons, like miniature baseball bats or spray bottles filled with ammonia, wherever they went.

The jailing should have been the end of the story. The news media lost interest, and it wasn't the kind of serial rape spree that captures the imagination of true-crime book publishers. The man's sister made contact with him, knowing she, her husband, and their children were the only family he had. She decided to show him she cared even though she hated what he had done and was relieved that he would never again know a day of freedom. It was during one of his collect telephone calls to his sister that the man began talking about the letters coming to him at the maximum-security state penitentiary.

"My brother sent them to me," said the woman, sharing the writings from several different women. The letters were written on inexpensive stationary, on lined notebook paper, and on letterhead that looked as though it had been taken from one or another of the senders' places of work. Some were written in pencil, some in pen, and some were typed. Some were printed and some were in an almost spidery cursive. There were letters that showed the writer to be semi-literate and those that indicated a woman who probably had an advanced education. All of them asked for help with either their relationships with men, sexual relations, or their daughters who were going through adolescence.

One of the letters told of a teenage daughter who was becoming promiscuous with her boyfriend. The writer wanted the convicted rapist to help set her straight. "My husband left us a few years ago," she said. "A firm man would keep her out of trouble."

There were letters wanting the rapist to teach early adolescents about sex. There were questions about romance and marriage. Many of the women explained that they were unmarried— single, widowed, or divorced—and needed a knowledgeable man to help them guide their children.

Many of the questions reminded me of special family programs held for parents both in my church and in the public and parochial schools my children have attended. They were appropriate questions for parents whose children were going from childhood into puberty. They dealt with menstruation, dating, curfews, rebellious language and attitudes, and the like. They were all questions any parent might have, yet for which more appropriate resources were readily available, including in any local library. School counselors, clergy, organizations such as Family Service Agencies and Planned Parenthood, and numerous other resources exist in almost every community. A violent rapist who had been convicted of such crimes as kidnapping two young women he planned to viciously torture was an inappropriate resource. Yet to most of the women writing, this rapist was a strong male figure they wished to consult for advise. The advice columnist from Hell.

With the assistance of his sister, I approached the rapist and asked permission to contact the women who had written to him. I mentioned that I had written this book, among others, and he became livid. He told me I was a shameless name-dropper. He was horrified that I had so little self esteem that I had to mention the Hillside Strangler in order to impress him. He told me that not only could I not write the women or talk to him, I should get a life instead of trying to find my importance through such celebrities as Ken Bianchi and himself. He held me in disdain, like a rock star dismissing a fawning groupie who mistakenly thought the rock star having sex with her had anything to do with love, commitment, or his bothering to remember her name.

*   *   *

I asked corrections officials about the disturbed communication between inmates and adults on the outside. It would seem that such mail should not be allowed, yet the reality of the corrections field is that, so long as an inmate is not committing a crime from within prison, he or she has fairly free use of the mail.

"There are limits to what we can do to protect society from the inmates," one Florida corrections official explained. "Prison is a closed society where the inmates greatly outnumber the staff. We have old men who just want to be left alone to get through each day and die in peace. We have young punks who are viciously violent and determined to prove that they're as tough in here as they were on the streets. We have men who are mentally ill, though we're not allowed to call them that. They knew the difference between right and wrong, that's the reason they're in jail instead of some nut ward somewhere, but that's a technicality of the law. These guys are whacko and have been known to suddenly freak out, tearing at their bodies, attacking other inmates, attacking the guards.

"We're always walking a fine line here. Most of these guys are going to return to the streets. We've got to be sure they have a GED and some training because if they can't get a job, they go back to crime. The public doesn't want to hear that, though. They don't want them getting a free education. They want them punished, so we're always having to explain ourselves, especially when we need technical supplies like computers. We limit Internet access to people we trust, and some prisons do not allow inmates to have access to any machine that can go on the Web. But like everything else, knowing the basics of using a computer is a skill as important for these men and women as being able to write a correct sentence, use math for cashier work or the building trades, and even how to talk to a potential employer.

"It's the same thing with letters and telephone calls. We screen them, but if they're not doing anything illegal, what are we going to do? Some of the jailhouse ministers we let in are frauds or part of nut groups, but if they're straight with the inmates, running legitimate Bible studies and holding services with licensed clergy, we let them do their thing because it keeps things calm, and some of the men are turned around. The same with letters and phone calls. They have their romances. Some of them ask to get married. Some of them get visitors who are screened before they come. Most of the women would run screaming from these guys if they met them on the streets, and most prison romances don't last more than a week or two after the guys get out. Again, it's a matter of risk assessment.

"Would I want my daughter corresponding with an inmate? Of course not. Would I want to stop all of it unless the women can prove some prior connection to the men they contact? Not unless I wanted to have a riot on my hands."

When I talked with one woman involved with a serial killer whom she contacted after reading about his trial and conviction, I mentioned that the man had a pattern to all his crimes. First he would securely bind and gag each victim. Then he would rape them over a period of hours, always finding justification for beating them. If the woman resisted in any way, he told the police, "The bitch thought she was too good for me and had to be taught a lesson." If she thought that cooperating would save her life, he said, "She was nothing more than a whore trying to come on like she was scared when she really wanted it. The cunt had no right to tell me she didn't want me when she couldn't get enough of me." No matter what his justification, the woman was going to be rendered helpless and beaten.

The girlfriend giggled when I explained this, and then said, "I wouldn't mind his tying me up and having his way with me."

"But several of the women were killed," I reminded her. "And others ended up in the hospital with broken bones."

At this point, she became angry, threatening me with a lawsuit if I identified her or told "lies" about her "lover." She refused to believe the brutality. "That's what the police say," she said. "He told me the ones who died were accidents, and he's been honest with me about everything else, so I don't see why I shouldn't believe him."

"What about the ones in the hospital?"

"Rough sex," she said. "It's not my style, but I've had some friends who tried it. He wouldn't do that with me. He was just trying to please them. He's really a very gentle man. That's why things got out of hand. Men who beat women know how far to go so they won't leave marks and get in trouble. He is so loving, he did what they asked for and didn't know how to do it right. That's why they accidentally went to the hospital. I like my sex gentler so that would never happen to me."

*   *   *

The socio-economic backgrounds of the women who fall in love with men convicted of serial violence do not follow any consistent pattern. Alicia, a schoolteacher, ignored the reality of the killer she befriended by saying, "I personally wouldn't want to dig up all the details from my past." She described herself as living "an average middle-class life—I'm in my 40s, married with kids." She wrote to the killer because she was impressed that he "actually confessed to what you did and expressed a little remorse about it." This was despite the fact that in the previous 25 years, each time he had been paroled, he committed violent acts against women. He also made clear that if released again, he would return to such violence.

The denial of reality by the women writing to psychopathic male prisoners can be shocking. One woman wrote that when thinking about the crimes that sent her correspondant to jail, "It has a tendency to jolt me out of the warm & safe place that I have reserved for you & I in my mind."

Another, Amy, ignored the reality of the man with whom she was corresponding and fantasized him in a more comfortable way. "I can't picture you doing any of those things [rapes and murders]. It's not a picture of a person that I've gotten to know."

Linda exaggerated her past while underplaying the horrors of a prisoner's crimes by writing, "There are things that I've done that I will never be able to be honest with you or anyone about. But who the hell cares anyway. I just feel so lucky that we are getting to know one another & are finding many similarities."

Connie took matters a step further. When writing a serial rapist who had stated that if he got out he would kill his next victim because he didn't want to return to jail, she said, "From what you have described of your girlfriends, you have trouble making good choices in women because you're trying very hard to be accepted and loved."

Another woman apparently analyzed the man she knew from his letters and came to the conclusion, "I continue to think of you as a little boy (not that I'm speaking of immaturity, but a small, lonely & perhaps, lost, little child). I pray that you may connect the child within & find a very special man."

Amy, the woman who did not let the serial killer's reality interfere with her mental image, had a rude awakening after she corresponded with two such men for several months. One of the two serial killers was facing a parole hearing, and she told the other killer, who had no chance of ever walking free, that if the parole were granted, she would marry the man. However, before she knew that the parole hearing was a formality and the turndown the man received was a foregone conclusion, Amy took stock of her life. She was a single parent who had been forced to go onto welfare after a hurtful divorce. She had a series of low-level jobs, each educating her for the next level in one or another company until her hard work brought her into management at the same time the parole hearing was scheduled. She realized that if the killer were paroled and she married him, she would be ridiculed. She would either be fired or put under intense scrutiny and pressure. She also realized that the man would expect a physical relationship with her and she was not ready to have sex with him.

Amy wrote to both men. She broke off with the one who had a chance of being released, and she told the other he was her true love. She had gotten along for years without sex and could live quite well without it. She would be faithful to the serial killer who had no chance for parole.

The lack of a sense of self-worth among the women who are part of the "entourage" of serial killers can be shocking. One woman wrote, "I felt anger & rage to the point of self abuse while stuck living with my mother, who sadistically & totally enjoyed raging & screaming at me—& at times enjoyed physically abusing me."

The most chilling story I heard was one involving a woman who had contact with Ken Bianchi and two or three other serial killers. She was well educated, beautiful, and had been a rising Hollywood area business professional.

"It started with telephone sex," she told me. "He told me where he wanted to touch me and had me do it for him while I held a picture of him in my mind. I touched my breasts and my nipples. Then I pulled down my panties and started stroking myself between my legs. It was pleasant at first. I had masturbated occasionally as a teenager and this was something more. I was listening to a man's voice, my eyes closed, my hand between my legs where his hand would have been if we were on a real date. I just didn't think about the fact that he was calling me from the county jail and I was in my apartment. I listened to his words and touched myself.

"Then he told me to do it harder and I did. The friction was becoming unpleasant, but it was as though I could not stop without his permission. He told me to rub, to work my hand as deep inside as I could, to go harder and harder.

"I remember tears coming to my eyes. It began to hurt. I wanted him to stop. He kept telling me to rub harder and I did. I was battering myself. It was as though he were raping me using my hand. I thought I could never stop. I never thought I could say whatever he wanted to hear, make whatever sounds he expected, and not touch myself. I never thought about the fact that he was in jail and I was in the living room of my apartment. I did what he told me to do. It was as though I had no will of my own.

"I know I did. I've had years of counseling. I understand my low self-esteem and the problems I had because of sexual abuse by my uncle. I'm not the person I was then, and I have to take responsibility for what happened. I was in control then and I'm in control now. Ken was in jail, with no way to touch me. Yet I let him rape me by doing whatever he said."

The one consistent factor among the majority of the women interviewed, or whose writing was obtained, was their obvious safety. The serial killer was whoever and whatever they wanted him to be. "I always know where my man is going to be sleeping each night," one woman said proudly. She was looking at an incarcerated deviant as being faithful so long as he was behind bars. It was as though the man had betrothed himself to her, then voluntarily entered a monastery to avoid the temptation of any other woman. The love was chaste, yet "forever."

Ken Bianchi was among those who eventually married a woman who corresponded with him, starting in 1986 when he was confined in the Walla Walla Penitentiary. Shirlee Joyce Book was 36-years old and the mother of a teenaged son when Ken Bianchi, then 38, proposed marriage to her. They had corresponded for two years, exchanged taped messages, and enjoyed numerous telephone calls—collect, as required by most prisons—to her home. Eventually he arranged for a ring to be sent to her.

The marriage occurred on September 21, 1989. His parents, an attendant, and two convict friends of Bianchi were all present for the fifteen-minute ceremony. They planned to eventually honeymoon in a trailer on the prison grounds that was available as a reward for married inmates who were allowed conjugal visits with their wives. However, though the couple was legitimately married, the publicity over Bianchi— a man who was involved with as many as seventeen murders, the majority of which involved rape—overcame any good time he may have earned.

One unusual part of the day occurred before the ceremony. The groom, in a rented tux, and the bride, dressed in a traditional gown, were given thirty minutes to be alone together. It was the first time they had ever met.

Shirlee Bianchi moved to Washington State to be near her new husband. Later, reporter Diane Albright interviewed her, not because of Bianchi but because of her first love—the late serial killer Ted Bundy, who had been executed by the state of Florida. Bundy had confessed in detail to many of the killings for which he was accused, but that did not matter to Shirlee. "They killed him, an innocent man," she told the reporter. "They weren't Christians who done that to him."

Shirlee added, "I would still be with him if they hadn't fried him." What she did not mention was that, unlike Bianchi, she had had no contact whatever from Bundy; all efforts to reach him had been rebuffed by the state of Florida, the prison system, or Bundy himself.

There were also the religious idealists, like the women who believed that if a man spoke about God in the same manner that they believed, he had been healed. "He told me he spoke in tongues for the first time," said an ecstatic Arizona woman. She was attractive, well educated, and a communication specialist who had experienced difficult personal times. Her mentally ill sister committed murder. She had committed adultery, and then entered into a series of promiscuous affairs. Unhappy with her life and feeling lost, she turned to religion. She found a Pentecostal Church whose complete acceptance changed her life.

"These people don't care who you've been or what you've done. The world may not forgive you, but God will. Paul was struck blind on the road to Damascus. He went from one of the early Christians' most zealous persecutors to being the founder of the church and the spreader of Jesus' teachings, praise the Lord."

Her contact with the man was part of a prison outreach run by her church. The inmate was a multiple murderer, rather than a serial killer. Several people died during a weekend of robberies where witnesses were not allowed to live. There was never any question of guilt, and both he and his partner accepted responsibility in court. They were sentenced to death, though there was a chance the sentences could be changed to life with no chance for parole.

The woman felt a special friendship with the killer, who welcomed the outreach missionaries. The murder spree had been brief, the motives clear. There was no insanity issue, and the man was extremely articulate. He was also not viewed by prison officials as a con artist like another death row inmate in the same prison who had developed a side business with his sister on the outside, as related below.

*   *   *

The con artist, comfortable with his lawyer's handling of his appeals, passed his time with a combination of what he, his sister, and his lawyer wanted to be viewed as good works and commercial ventures. Neither violated prison rules at the time.

The "good works" consisted of tape recordings made to influence children to stay away from a life of crime. He would talk from his cell, sometimes pacing off the tiny space that comprised his world for most of each day as he described the furnishings (bunk, sink, seatless toilet, etc.). Sometimes he told of his life in confinement, the type of food he had to eat, the limited exercise, and the loneliness and pain. He encouraged the listeners to obey their mothers, to avoid drugs, smoking, and alcohol. Sometimes his sister would record children on the outside promising to be good. Then the voices of the children would be added to the tapes. None of it was particularly convincing.

Next there were the relationship tapes. The prisoner talked about how people could become better husbands and wives. He also made suggestions concerning sex that might save a marriage or strengthen a couple's commitment. Apparently, the information was gleaned from the limited time he had to talk with other prisoners, utilizing their collective "wisdom."

The third type of tapes was pure pornography. These were sold for "amusement purposes only" and meant strictly for adults.

The sister's business was apparently conducted by mail order and through whatever outlets she could find. It was not known how well she did or what plans were made for when this con-man inmate was put to death, if the full sentence were carried out.

The prisoner the church adopted had only disdain for such scams. He was an honest man who had always tried to make an honest living except when he slipped, and then robbed and murdered. He read whatever tracts he was sent, and eventually he began using a tape recorder. His recordings were in response to questions from members of the church. He discussed his prayer life, his Bible reading, and whatever else they desired to know about. He considered them good people, yet when he talked with individuals outside the church, he admitted that he had not become the type of man they fantasized.

Eventually the inmate developed terminal cancer. He knew he was going to die in jail, but his one wish being to go into the main population so he could enjoy the larger facilities and spend more time in the open yard. He also felt guilty about using the church people, gently explaining that they read more into him than they should. Given the same circumstances, he said he would kill again. He appreciated their caring, but despite what he had told them, he was not a healing miracle.

For the woman who had been writing to him, the confession that he had not changed was proof that he *had* changed. She could not conceive of such honesty from an unrepentant murderer. She felt that God had touched his heart, turned his life around, and blessed him with whatever peace he enjoyed during his final days.

Was she right? It is impossible to tell. Such a spiritual change is rarely seen with certainty in prison because too many men become whatever someone trying to help them wants them to be. Certainly there are repentant sinners. The highly respected Chuck Colson Ministries is absolute proof of that fact. And perhaps the women who reach out to these men are what are sometimes called the "unlikely vessels of God."

At the same time, many of the women who utilize faith or the trappings of religion when "helping" serial killers have certain similarities. Often they belong to a group that engages in ecstatic worship. There is singing, spontaneous dancing, praise, and the speaking in tongues—a language they do not know, such as the language of angels, which is often spontaneously translated by another parishioner who is likewise touched by God. It is a physical as well as emotional experience.

These women have invariably had bad marriages or relationships that turned sour. All were battered emotionally and/or physically, and often they had abusive childhoods as well. They have never sought counseling, or they have been counseled within religious groups where prayer is the only answer. Sometimes they are told that their marriages should not have ended, that God joined them together and there must have been a reason they were abused. Sometimes they belong to a church following the prosperity theology concept quite popular in wealthy communities a few years back. Prosperity theology says that God always rewards people based on their goodness. An individual who is wealthy is right with God. A person who is poor, sick, disabled, or otherwise troubled is wrong with God. It is a vicious, destructive concept, yet the believers reinforce it with their praise or condemnation of fellow parishioners.

Always the criminal is a vehicle of God's work. His "love" may be their reward for changing. He may be their second (or third or whatever) chance for happiness. He may be a miracle in their lives. Whatever the case, the prison workers who know the man often see a very different individual day to day than the woman on the outside professing her love.

* * *

Richard Ramirez, a man who entered the criminal history books as the Los Angeles Night Stalker, was born in the Ledo barrio of El Paso, Texas. He was always a loner, interested in martial arts, yet practicing in his backyard instead of trying to go to a school or work out with friends. He was an avid reader of horror stories and articles about rock musicians, and he loved listening to rock music. He also began using drugs.

Ramirez moved to Los Angeles, and in 1984 began a series of burglaries of occupied dwellings. These were seen as random crimes until the throat slashing murder of Jennie Vincow, a 79-year-old woman. For the first time, there was adequate evidence to link the still unknown killer to previous murders.

Ramirez's pattern was to burglarize homes in Arcadia, Burbank, Diamond Bar, Glendale, Monrovia, Northridge, and Sun Valley. He seemed to deliberately choose locations where a husband or boyfriend was present. The man would be murdered, the woman brutalized, usually bound with rope or handcuffs. The women were also forced to swear they loved Satan, a situation originally leading investigators to think that Ramirez was part of an occult group. Instead, he used the trappings of Satan worship to justify his violence.

Burglary always seemed to be secondary to the desire for violence, and as the number of similar crimes increased, certain consistencies became obvious. The crimes were apparently planned in advance, with escape route known to the burglar/rapist/killer. While the victims seemed to have been studied and stalked, they also seemed to have been first chosen at random from the various locations involved.

Eventually a combination of factors, including DNA evidence and fingerprints, led to the identification of Ramirez. Newspapers identified him and ran whatever photographs could be located.

On August 31, 1985 Ramirez returned to Los Angeles from a drug-buying trip to Phoenix, Arizona. He entered a store and saw his picture.

Fleeing, Ramirez was spotted again and again. He desperately ran from neighborhood to neighborhood, chased by a growing number of people who either thought his behavior suspicious or who recognized him as the suspected murderer. Finally he reached the heavily Hispanic area of Hubbard Street, where he leaped a fence and landed in the backyard of Luis Munoz who was grilling ribs and hamburgers. Munoz demanded to know what Ramirez was doing, but Ramirez refused to tell him. Fearing that he was being attacked, Munoz stabbed Ramirez with the long barbecue tongs.

Ramirez fled to the house of Munoz's neighbor, Faustino Pinon, and tried to steal the man's car. Instead, he smashed it into the fence and then backed into the garage wall. Pinon grabbed him from the driver's seat, but Ramirez was able to run again.

Within moments, neighbors came onto the streets and gave chase to Ramirez. Finally, Manuel de la Torres, armed with an iron bar, dropped the Night Stalker with a blow to the head. The killer was not seriously hurt but the chase was over. Sheriff's deputy Andres Ramirez (no relation) arrived and took Richard to jail.

Once again the women came forward. Teenage girls and young women regularly attended the trial. They heard the facts. They learned of the brutality of the man. However, most of them did not care or did not believe the truth of what they were hearing. Instead, they indulged their fantasies.

Richard Ramirez became like a "Ken doll". Women looked at his picture, then used their imaginations to dress him and give him the type of daily life they thought he should have had if all their lives had been different. For example, when talking with an Associated Press reporter during the trial, Bernadette Brazal commented, "I feel such compassion for him. When I look at him, I see a real handsome guy who just messed up his life because he never had anyone to guide him."

This young woman claimed to be a 23-year-old student at California State University in Los Angeles. She felt that Ramirez reminded her of a movie star. She also said she sent him 50 letters and photographs prior to the trial. He did not answer any of them.

Still, Brazal understood. She was quoted as saying that his major problem had been his listening to bad rock music.

The most unusual woman who was a follower of Ramirez was Cindy Haden, who relocated to be near the prison so she could visit Ramirez twice a week. She appeared on Phil Donahue's television talk show, then one of the most popular on the air, in order to declare her love. She also claimed that she felt improper evidence was used against the killer, and that he may have been innocent of some of the charges. So why was she unusual? Cindy Haden was one of the jurors who convicted Ramirez.

Then there was Christine Lee, a delightful young woman who claimed to be engaged to marry the Night Stalker, though privately she admitted the statement was a sham. She had been making contact with the killer, but she was actually dating a sheriff's deputy.

"My parents have a lot of money, right? He [her father] gave me black eyes a lot, and I'd go to school…like then…then it wasn't reported, you know what I mean? My aunt has home videos of when I was six and I had two black eyes, and I told her, and she just goes, 'Oh, shut up, liar.' You know what I mean? I don't even talk to them anymore. I just stopped a few months ago."

Christine did not feel that a father should avoid violence when disciplining children. She believed that what was done to her would have been all right if she had been his son. However, a daughter should be treated differently. She had come to the conclusion that "family" meant pain and that the father was the primary cause.

"I felt like something was wrong [when her father allegedly abused her]. Like when I was 13 and I told my aunt, and she just like... 'Yeah, yeah, yeah. You're a liar.' And she told my father. And then I got in trouble for telling her. He punched me in the face.

"And then right after that I dropped out of high school, and had a baby, and I was like, I've got to get away from these people. I was like an 'A' student.

"And now by being near Richard it's like I feel like I'm embarrassing them [her parents], and I love it! You know what I mean?

"And I love embarrassing them. Like they've got really good jobs and they've got a lot of money, so this is like embarrassing them to death, and I love it.

"Like I've been on every talk show except *Oprah*, and some I've been on three times, like two or three times. *A Current Affair* like three times. *Inside Edition*...."

Christine had no illusion about Ramirez. She was comfortable admitting that the man was a violent individual. She also laughed that if he were to hit her, the guards would grab him and kill him.

Oddly, as objective and honest as Christine could be, part of her seemed to have trouble admitting that she was using a man so potentially deadly. "Another thing, I think serial killers are disgusting and I never think of him as one. At the same time I think of him as a weapon, and I stick him in my parents' face and laugh. So, you know what I mean?

"I don't believe this is happening to me, though.

"The first time I saw him was four years ago [1989]. My husband was...like...he was an animal. And I left him and I moved out to California with my cousin." Christine had been married a year, and just had had a baby when she left her husband.

"The day after we got married, he totally changed. Right before, he was all nice, this and that...As soon as we got married, the next day he changed into a different person. Just an animal. He hit me a lot, like he threw an ash tray at me and it hit me right in the face and it split open my head, and I couldn't believe it. I was like a month pregnant then, but the whole time I was pregnant, he hit me. The whole time.

"He was just an animal. We got married in November. I got pregnant in December. And I had the baby in August. And then from September through…what was it…December or November…the next three months I had to save up the money to move back out to California and get away from him. And then I went right near Richard, and for four years I've stayed with Richard. And that's what everyone's telling me now—'oh, you're just looking for safety.'

"He [Ramirez] was really nice, like when I first met him, like the first year. When I first seen him on TV, I just felt he looked…I don't know…he looked familiar to me for some reason. I don't know why.

"Like you know when you meet someone and you feel you've known them a long time even though you haven't. That's what I felt like with him. I don't know why.

"I saw on the news he was in San Quentin, and that was like an hour from where me and my cousin lived. And then I met my friend, my friend from New Jersey. She came up, too. And then one day we just went up there. But I thought it would be like a one time thing, and I just been going up for four years.

"He was just really nice, and then I felt sorry for him. Then I met his attorneys and his attorney told me, 'He's innocent. He didn't do anything. I want you to visit him.'"

The truth was that the attorneys knew Ramirez was guilty. He left too many witnesses alive. The only possible problem for the defense attorneys would have been if the prosecutor tried to clear other cases by blaming them on the Night Stalker. So far as is known, that never happened nor was it a consideration.

Many defense attorneys like to have either a female lawyer working with a sex offender or they like to have a woman connected with the man in the courtroom each day. Sexual violence has nothing to do with sexual desire. There are many murderers and rapists who return home to loving, gentle, normal women who have no idea what else the men are doing. And, there is a belief in courtrooms that if a man accused of violence against women is seen with a caring woman, he will be more likely perceived as innocent.

"Everybody's telling me that it looks good for him in court," Christine continued, "like I have two kids, and if he has a wife and two little kids, then he looks good. So that's what his attorneys want."

"One day a newspaper's up there and they took pictures of me, and *USA Today* put it on page 2. And this was only like a year after I met him. The day the newspaper article came out, my phone was ringing off the hook from every TV show. TV shows, magazines, everything, and since then, I've just been doing like all these TV shows. They wanted me to come on it and talk about my relationship with him.

"They all told me that because of my looks, it helps keep the interest."

Ramirez was convicted and Christine went on with her real life. But for her, the real motive in all of this was her relationship with her parents. "I feel like I'm embarrassing them, and I love it."

*　　*　　*

"There's something I realized from reading your book," a woman told me when I was signing autographs in a mall in Yuma, Arizona. "Children are not resilient. You hurt a child and that child stays hurt unless an adult gets involved to try and heal the damage."

"I hadn't thought about that," I lied. "But you're right. If the doctors or social workers had reached out to Ken when he was growing up, maybe he would not have become the violent adult he did."

"That's obvious," she told me. "I'm surprised you didn't stress that in the book."

Similar comments were made in Wooster, Ohio; Chicago, Illinois; Washington, D.C. and elsewhere. Sometimes the comments were made by a man, sometimes by a woman. Sometimes several people made the statement. Each time, I outwardly expressed surprise and inwardly expressed pleasure.

I'm not a "message" writer, whatever that is. My books have neither great themes nor deep messages that can be advertised on the cover of some philosophy publication. I am a storyteller, whether relating fiction or nonfiction. I want the latter to be factual, readable, and make the reader feel the books were worth the purchase. At the same time, the more I wrote *The Hillside Strangler*, the more Ken Bianchi's childhood bothered me. This was an infant born to a troubled teenager, given up for adoption—though not until after having a series of surrogate mothers and raised by emotionally troubled, adoptive parents. Each time the growing child was seen as needing help, help was not forthcoming.

I was concerned that people reading the book understand that Ken Bianchi was yet another victim. Yes, he murdered. Yes, he had once considered therapy, and then rejected the idea, when, seemingly, he heard things he did not want to know. Certainly, there was a conscious decision as a young adult to avoid the one recourse that might have prevented the first murders. He did not take it, and soon he was overwhelmed with rage that led to rape and murder.

But what about the other children who are hurting? What about those who have not reached the point of no return? What about those children who might be guided to a better set of choices?

It is not that love and counseling can make a person take the right paths in life. That is nonsense. No parent can create an environment where the child is going to always do right as an adult.

The parent's job is simpler than that, and also more complex. The parent has to present the positive choices so that when the child is ready, there is known good along with the bad. The parent does not fail if the child goes astray. The parent fails when the child lacks knowledge of that which is good.

I talked about this idea with my wife. She had been a schoolteacher. She loved children. She understood what can happen and had tried to intervene with the occasional troubled child she encountered in the classroom. Sometimes she succeeded. Sometimes the child moved on and she never learned one way or another what had been accomplished.

Months passed, then years. I went on to write other books, some of them truecrime and some not. Sometimes people cared and the book was highly successful. Sometimes they did not and those books sold fewer copies than I would have liked.

Periodically I revisited issues of child abuse and how it affects adults who have been victimized by psychological and/or physical violence in their youths. I talked with many adult victims and some adults who had been abusive with their own children. I met men and women who had suffered from hysteric dissociation as a result of overwhelming psychological trauma before the age of seven. These were individuals more commonly called multiple personalities, but a troubled childhood was always a component.

And always I came back to the idea that someone should intercede when possible.

Not that I wanted children of my own. My first wife, Nancy, and I had been quite comfortable being childless. She came from a large family with its own dirty little secrets about one of her grandfathers. Her childhood had often been troubled, and as the oldest of five children, she had already done her share of surrogate mothering. We led rich, full lives, ultimately moving in different directions without trying to include each other. When we parted, it was with few regrets—two friends who were no longer lovers. Certainly we never considered a child as a binding for the marriage that unraveled just short of our thirteenth wedding anniversary.

My second wife wanted children. She was a natural mother. But she also wanted me and proved it by moving in with me unexpectedly one night. However, I figured that any woman who cared that deeply, with whom I had thoroughly discussed my feelings before we had a personal relationship of any depth, would have no illusions about our remaining childless.

Several years passed, and I was certain there would be no children in our lives. Sure, she wanted them, but "obviously" everything was okay. She knew I had no interest in raising a family. That was why I did not expect the morning telephone call she placed to my office, telling me to come home. There was no emergency, but since I wasn't busy, I was to go to our apartment and into the bedroom. There I found her on the bed in a manner she knew would assure my sexual arousal. There would be no further efforts at contraception.

It took time, but eventually my wife got pregnant. The first trimester was a surreal experience, knowing about the baby only through my wife's comments, the fetus too tiny to make a meaningful difference in my wife's figure. Instead, the changes were psychological—my thinking about the impending fatherhood and what it might mean for every aspect of our lives. Then, at the end of the first trimester, when I was beginning to look forward to the experience I had once not considered, Leslie went into labor. The contractions were intensely painful, increasingly frequent, and there was no time to get her to the hospital. She needed paramedics who rushed her to the emergency room where the fetus was born dead. His body had formed the shape of a tiny boy, but the internal organs had not formed at all. Leslie's body spontaneously aborted the lifeless fetus.

Fertility testing came after the stillbirth. Ultimately my sperm was collected, an embarrassing situation no matter how private. I had heard that it had to be done in the lab, and I had friends who told of being shown sexually explicit magazines to "help." In truth, there is a 90-minute period from the time the sterile container is utilized until the sperm can no longer effectively be tested. Leslie and I stayed at home, worked together, then brought it to the lab with minutes to spare. It was still humiliating, but far less so than what others had gone through.

In the end, the tests confirmed two facts. The first was that my sperm was healthy and had more than enough quantity to father many children. Leslie, on the other hand, was probably unable to bring a child to full term. Any pregnancy, even the one that had ended so emotionally for us, was a near miracle.

"I think we should adopt," Leslie said.

And that's when I thought of the Hillside Strangler.

There are several choices when you adopt. You can go public or private, domestic or international. Although many people think that international adoption is best, they ignore the reality of what it means. Many of the children are orphans of war and political violence. All of the children are lacking in family histories adequate for learning what may be needed if a medical crisis arises in the distant future. Many are malnourished from devastated economies that prevent the orphanages from having enough quality food for each child. The prospective parents often feel that they are reducing the risk by taking an infant, and many are available. But there are endless unknowns and a cost that can range from $25,000 to well into six figures. Worse, where the bulk of international adoptions are altruistic, a handful are meant to assure the child will be of the same racial and ethnic background as the parents. The children are adopted because of bias, not reasoned choice.

Private adoption seems to offer an excellent chance for knowing what to expect in the future, as well as for getting the color, religion, possible intelligence, and any other factors that might exist on a prospective parent's checklist. Such adoption is usually arranged through an attorney, though there are agencies that provide the service. Sometimes the prospective parents meet the birth mother. At other times the prospective parents receive a complete background, detailing genetic conditions, health of the parents, and even an intelligence test score. The idea is to buy the perfect child, as defined by the adopting parents. The reality is that kids are no more predictable with such information than they are when the family is unknown. Serious genetic damage can occur with the "best" parents, and parents who have traits that are not desirable may have a child who is intellectually superior and emotionally more stable than the couple adopting him.

Leslie and I went through our local county agency. We said we would take a special needs child, the type of child rejected by most people. The only criterion was that the child should have nothing so severely wrong that he or she would predictably need special care throughout life. We were in our late forties at the time, and we felt that only a couple a generation younger than we were should be responsible for children with limited futures. Anyone else would be fine.

Going with the public agency made sense in every possible way. The cost was minimal and expenses are reimbursed when the adoption is finalized. Each child is put on Medicaid, and numerous counseling services are available to both the parents and the children. The idea is to create a nurturing, healthy, and successful environment. We would also have full information on the child's medical and family history, to whatever degree the county agency could obtain it.

We agreed to adopt up to three children, though we wanted to start with a single child. We also agreed to adopt a child nobody wanted.

Unwanted children, politely called "special needs," fall into one of several categories. Most often people read about the AIDS babies. These are infants born to an AIDS-infected mother and were infected in the womb. (Not all children born to AIDS positive mothers are infected). Sometimes the mother dies. Sometimes the mother is too ill to care for her baby. And sometimes the mother either has to give up the child because of inappropriate living conditions, or she chooses to give up the child because of the nightmare she feels she is facing. Whatever the case, it is common knowledge that an AIDS baby is born with a death sentence. No one knows how long the child will live, but it is unlikely he or she will become a teenager.

Some parents are quite comfortable adopting an infant who is known to be terminally ill or has a condition that means early death. They take joy in the life, no matter how brief. However, most want a child who is likely to outlive them.

The other type of child who is as undesirable as the one who will die young is the one who is so severely brain damaged that he or she will require institutional care. Often these are born with severe damage as a result of excessive alcohol and/or drug use by the parent.

Next are the children who are less than perfect in some way. Usually these are children who are physically deformed or have a lower than average intelligence. They are often considered unattractive and may require special care. A home may have to be modified for a wheelchair, for example. Special tutoring may be needed at school. Whatever the case, they represent a "problem" that many adopting parents will not accept.

Then come the children of trauma. These are boys and girls who have experienced sexual abuse, have suffered post-traumatic stress from witnessing the unexpected death of a parent through murder, accident, or illness, or otherwise have psychological problems caused by how they were treated. Some have a tendency to act out inappropriately with all adults while they learn how to behave in a safe environment, a fact the adopting parents need to understand and be prepared to handle. Others simply need counseling, often for many years, before they can live healthy, productive lives. All have a chance for excellent futures, but they require extra work by the adopting couple.

Ken Bianchi was one of the children who required extra effort on the part of the staff who had observed both the biological mother and the adopting mother. This is not a criticism of either parent but a comment on the reality of what the infant experienced before, during, and after the transition. The various agencies and hospitals interacting with the family in the years that followed all had staff personnel who avoided their responsibilities. Slight intervention in a positive manner might have averted the tragedies that shattered so many families.

Finally there are the children no one thinks might be special needs. These vary with the community. They are the children who face bias, either because of the complexity of their adoption or because of neighborhood hatred.

For example, when we adopted our first child, the county declared that *all* black males, including those in perfect health with excellent minds, were "special needs." This was because the bias by adopting couples in our county was such that it was presumed that *all* black males, though not black females or Hispanic children, would grow up to be gang members. In the next county, adopting parents knew such bias was nonsense. Their prejudice was against Hispanics, especially Hispanic-black males since *all* of them grew up to be gang fighters, using knives.

The prejudice in the world of adoption knows no logic. Eventually I came to joke that when I moved to Arizona, I had to learn to hate correctly. In Cleveland, before leaving, I was expected to hate blacks and like Mexicans and Indians. Then I moved to Tucson in the southern part of the state. There I had to like blacks, hate Mexicans, and like Indians. Eventually I moved north to Flagstaff where I was expected to like blacks and Mexicans, but hate Indians. Not hating put me out of step with the community cultures, but it was much easier to comprehend.

Other "special needs" children in our county included included any situation where two or more high IQ, healthy, handsome, white siblings who had to be adopted together. Also, all children older than three years of age. Also, two or more high IQ, healthy, handsome/beautiful siblings of any race.

Leslie and I agreed to take a special needs child, and then underwent a one-year background check and evaluation by a social worker to be certain we knew what we might experience and how to handle it. Finally, we were allowed to select a child.

We met Raheem through his paperwork. There are many ways families meet the children available for adoption. Some public and private agencies go so far as to have parties for the children and adults so everyone can play together and the cutest get to go home with someone. It is like the animal shelter puppy fairs in shopping malls. The hurt of those children left behind is impossible to imagine, but must be intense and potentially causes a lifelong sense of inferiority. It was also the type of hurt that, in hindsight, Ken Bianchi must have endured in those days after birth when he was shared among neighbors, not able to consistently bond to one person.

Raheem had been to at least one of those "meet the prospective parents" parties. He had also been on several afternoon and overnight visits with couples who were interested in adopting him. Sometimes the visits were frequent enough that Raheem was taught to think of the couple as Mom and Dad, Mom and Pop, Mother and Father, or some variation. Each time was supposed to be "forever."

The foster family seemed to want to separate each couple from the previous by changing the names they used as they prepared Raheem for his new life. Likewise, the adults interacting with Raheem felt "their" child should have a more familiar name. Among those we know he was called are Robin, Michael, and Matthew. Yet by any name and with any potential parents, Raheem was repeatedly rejected. He didn't pass any couple's unspoken yet very obvious "adorable" test.

The name change was especially sad. Not only should it have been the one consistent factor in his life, it spoke volumes of who he was and what he could mean. In the Islamic faith, Raheem is one of the 99 names for God. In Arabic, it also means both "mercy" and "God's Blessing."

Perhaps the rejections were caused by Raheem's history. Raheem was mixed race, though predominantly black. He was born addicted to eight different drugs. His biological mother did not want to raise him and signed off at the hospital. Within six months she had been murdered, apparently the result of a failed drug deal. His biological father died of an overdose.

It took six months before Raheem was detoxed and could safely leave the hospital, at which time he was placed in an infant foster care program run by a group of Catholic nuns. He did not speak, though he was capable of making sound. The failure to speak continued when he was placed in what was considered a permanent special needs foster home. Efforts were made to have him adopted—thirteen before he became our son—but it was presumed no one would take him. He was a former drug addict, and during a psychological exam before he was two years old, he was determined to be a semi-retarded mute. The foster family was used to handling such children, and, among others, they cared for an autistic boy who was seventeen when we met Raheem.

Raheem was destined for one of the programs that train the retarded to become productive adults working in routine tasks— minimum wage, rote work as dishwashers, cleaning personnel, and the like. There are Denny's restaurants around the country where the managers make a point of hiring such adults to help them be productive and develop long-term, reliable employees for jobs that normally have high turnover. The cleaning staff of our county hospital also employs them. Raheem was expected to one day join the ranks of honest, productive citizens who would never go to college and probably only graduate from a vocational high school, with a carefully supervised work/study program.

Our first reaction to looking at the paperwork of a black (we're white), semi-retarded mute who had been born addicted to eight different drugs was to say we would take him. His photograph showed a handsome little boy of three years of age whose eyes were alive with curiosity. The latter belied the paperwork, and we suspected that the history was wrong about his intelligence. It did not matter, though. He needed parents. We needed a child. We'd all adjust together to whatever else life threw our way.

At that moment in the social worker's office, I was certain I could not love a child, any child. However, Leslie loved him before she met him, and I understood that about her. I also knew that our son was going to be nurtured by me. He would never know I didn't love him. He would never know I was just trying to heal the brokenness and help him achieve whatever adulthood he could have. I would give him what he needed, constantly thinking of Ken Bianchi's background and how his nurturing needs had apparently so often been lacking.

And then we met Raheem. The first visit started at a McDonald's, then we went to the local children's museum where he played with giant building blocks. We were given just a couple of hours together before the social worker came and took him back to the foster family.

"Be sure to take him to the bathroom," Leslie told me when we knew the social worker was coming, and I immediately panicked. I had never taken a little child to the bathroom. I had never held a baby, changed a diaper, or tried to deal with a three-year-old, semi-retarded mute who probably had to "go and do something." I knew it would all come out the usual way, but beyond that I wasn't certain.

Fortunately Raheem was more experienced than I was. He had been out of diapers for days. I suggested he use the urinal because the children's museum had ones the perfect height for the very small. He walked over, washed his hands in the urinal, then flushed, looking proudly up at me. I carried him to the sink, washed his hands with soap, dried him, and carried him back to Leslie. I didn't tell her what happened until after he had left with the social worker. Leslie's only comment was, "I hope her car seat is washable."

The second visit, a day or two later, involved picking up Raheem at the foster family's house, visiting a shopping mall, and returning him. I suggested he go to the bathroom before we left, and the foster father agreed. End of that problem.

The third visit was an overnight. He wore Dr. Denton's, the one-piece pajamas with a drop back for emergencies. I tucked him in his bed-to-be, kissed him goodnight, and realized my world was changing. The next morning we took him to a coffee shop where he seemed to feel overwhelmed by too many changes. He started to cry, tears streaming down his cheeks, though no words came from his mouth. I put my arm around him, kissed the top of his head, and realized that I, too, was crying as I whispered, "I love you, Raheem." They were not just words. Three visits with this little boy and he was no longer a stranger to my heart. Raheem had become my son.

The adoption went through without a problem, and we soon learned that Raheem was not a mute. The psychologist who had made the diagnosis either made a mistake or was a complete idiot. Either way, he was wrong. Raheem could not only talk, he was so intelligent that when he realized people expected him to be silent and rewarded him for using grunts and reaching motions to tell what he wanted, he did what he thought they desired. Leslie and I told him he had to use words, and he quickly began speaking. He proved to be brilliant, and his intelligence tests placed him at the top of his classes.

I suppose that should have been the end of it. I watched Raheem grow and develop. He went from Barney to Power Rangers, from picture books with few words to chapter books he sometimes read and we sometimes read to him.

During this time I had a rather odd letter from Ken Bianchi. He had learned I was talking to Veronica Compton from her prison cell. She, like him, could call collect. Unlike Veronica, he chose to use the mail. He informed me that he had taken legal training while in prison and discussed the possibility of suing me for reasons that were not clear, though, they apparently had to do with my talking with Veronica.

As I later learned, there is a subculture that seems to transcend any single prison. The most notorious among the serial killers apparently share information, either directly or through women who befriend them. Veronica had been linked with more than one killer after she went to prison, though whether this was true is not known. She denied any involvement with such men, and by the time she was talking with me, she was not the same woman who had been convicted of attempting a look-alike murder to free Bianchi. Since the killers were also never stable, it is possible they believed what they were saying even if it never actually occurred.

Whatever the case, I sent him a letter telling him about my son. I told him how I had come to realize that children do break and that it is up to adults to reach out to them. The only way to assure a child a safe, healthy adult existence is to heal both the obvious and the hidden traumas.

By this time we had also adopted twins whose "gentler" history involved being crack babies born two and a half months premature, then rejected for adoption 20 times. The difference was that they were so young when we got them—just in their second year of life—they did not realize the rejections they had experienced. They went from the foster home to our home and remember nothing of life before they became our second and third sons.

Raheem was in fifth grade when he began to change in ways so subtle that no one noticed. He would begin talking, sometimes appropriately, sometimes inappropriately, such as in school or Sunday school. He would say he would stop, but he could not. His voice was properly soft so that he was obviously not trying to be disruptive or call attention to himself. But he would talk and talk, never willing or able to stop.

Within a few hours, the talk would become exaggerated. Sometimes he would be the greatest basketball player his age. Sometimes he would be spending the millions of dollars he was going to get as a professional basketball player. Always he talked about kid dreams though to a degree that was extreme. He would dominate conversations. He would give no one else a chance to talk. He had to be the center of attention, or so it seemed.

At other times the talk would turn angry. He would remember some much earlier, minor slight in school, at the playground, or elsewhere and begin talking about it. He would get angrier and angrier, talking endlessly about whatever it might be. Eventually he would be irate and out of control, sometimes verbally attacking anyone who disagreed, sometimes throwing something or pounding his bed.

The first counselor we tried assumed Raheem needed anger management counseling. We also realized that he was probably hypoglycemic, something that had concerned us earlier. We drastically reduced the sugar in his diet and carefully watched what foods he ate at home. He seemed to improve, though there were still days of what we came to call "motor mouth," followed by either manic outbursts or great anger.

The counselor decided that Raheem, now thirteen, should follow a basketball team model to control himself, since Raheem loved basketball and the counselor liked sports metaphors. When Raheem felt himself losing control, he would have a "team" of people he could call to talk about the problem—his principal, his favorite teacher, his coach, a wise friend, Leslie and me, etc. He would choose among the team members as he felt appropriate for whatever was making him angry. Raheem and the team would contain the extremes of his emotions.

It was a nice idea until Raheem attacked me with a table knife.

An afternoon of motor mouth had followed a number of problems. He had not slept well. He had not eaten at regular times because of basketball practice. Being late for dinner and other factors triggered the hypoglycemia. And, he had the serious trauma of losing a beloved portable CD player to a boy he previously thought was his friend.

The loss of the CD player was seemingly a minor problem. Raheem had saved some money and could afford one of the inexpensive CD players sold in various discount music and video stores. I promised him I would take him to get one, but it would not happen until the end of the week. I had a difficult work schedule that was too exhausting for me to take him to the store before either Thursday or Friday. However, he would definitely have the new one by the end of the week.

Everything was fine until Sunday night. I had worked late and was eating dinner late. Raheem was sitting, talking with me, when he demanded to go get the CD player. "I want it now!" he said firmly.

"I know," I said. "It's hard having your old one stolen, and it's even harder when you know the thief was a friend. I'll try to take you Thursday, but you'll have it no later than Friday."

"I want it now!" he repeated, becoming angrier.

"I understand," I said. "But even if we could go out, it's quarter to ten and all the stores that are still open will be closed before we can get there."

"I want to go to Target right now!" His body language changed, his fists clenched, his shoulders tensed.

"Target is closing right now," I said, surprised. We had never shopped there, the nearest Target at least a twenty or twenty-five minute drive. He might have seen its ads in the Sunday newspaper, but he did not know the place from personal experience.

The anger kept building, even as I reminded him that we had agreed when we would go to the store. "It's disappointing," I said. "But it's only four or five more days at the most, just like we discussed. And since it's so late on a Sunday night...."

"I want it now!" he shouted, picking up a table knife and lunging at me. The move was totally unexpected and I have no idea what would have happened if I hadn't trained in martial arts for several years. I grabbed his wrist, disarmed him, and thought I calmed him down.

Raheem went into his room, seemingly embarrassed and wanting to relax. We called a friend who is a professional counselor and headed a neighborhood mental health clinic. She explained that whatever was happening, it could not continue. If he tried to act violently again, we were to call the police and have him transported to the psychiatric department of our university hospital's excellent pediatric unit. She also told us to explain this to Raheem so he would have reason to get control of himself.

"Hopefully it's over," she said. "But you must warn him of the consequences of repeating the behavior, then do exactly as you say if he has another outburst like that."

Raheem came back in the room, his body language relaxed. I suggested he go to bed since it was late, and then we'd see how the next couple of days went for everyone's schedule. Then he attacked again.

I held Raheem on the floor, talking quietly to him. Leslie called 9-1-1 and explained the situation. They asked if he was on medication and she said he wasn't. She gave the name of the therapist, and two officers arrived in a few minutes.

While we waited, I told Raheem we loved him but we would not let him hurt himself or others. We explained that he was going to the hospital. We explained that the police would take him but I would follow. I would not leave his side.

The police were wonderful. They explained to Raheem that he was going to the hospital. They did not handcuff him. They did not hold him. So long as he was calm, everything would be fine. Fortunately he went quietly and I followed. We did not go to the university hospital, though, because the officers were under orders to go to the nearest emergency room. That was at the county hospital, an excellent facility where the staff had saved Leslie's life several years earlier when a tumor was crushing her brain. This was also where she had miscarried. I was delighted to be there, trusting the people who worked there.

The emergency room nurse took Raheem's vital signs. Blood chemistry work was done, and the staff's first concern was a hypoglycemic reaction. He was brought apple juice to drink until his blood sugar level was where it should be. Then, after being watched by security, it was explained that he would be placed in a special locked room.

The nurse said that while they evaluated all the tests and arranged for transportation he could have me in the room and the door would be left open. If he did not want me in the room, I could sit just outside, visible through a window, but the door would be locked. He would need to have me get permission to take him to the bathroom. He would also need me to get the staff to unlock the door. The security was such that the door could only be opened on both sides with a key.

Raheem was angry with me for taking him. He felt he was fine and should get some rest so he could go to school. He did not remember attacking me, though he had talked with the transporting officers about it. He ordered me out of the room and the door was locked. He lay on a special examining table, staring at the wall.

Within an hour, Raheem needed to go to the bathroom. He also wanted me near him. The door was left unlocked and I stayed by his side until a psychiatric resident, exhausted from lack of sleep, was able to talk with Raheem, talk with me, and review Raheem's body chemistry tests. Then he ordered him transported to an adolescent facility a half hour's drive away. A driver was sent, and Raheem was finally taken shortly before six A.M. The staff explained by telephone that I was not to come with him but to call later in the day. They would run a battery of medical and psychological tests to determine what was happening.

Exhausted, I drove home. Leslie met me at the door, and when she held me, I cried uncontrollably. I was part terrified, part relieved. Yet the kindness of the staffs of both facilities somehow made me certain he would be all right.

Nothing was accomplished the first two or three days. Raheem told the staff he did nothing wrong and had no problems. I had attacked him for unknown reasons. I was the problem. He was glad to be away from our home.

And then the motor mouth returned. Raheem acted out again and again over the next two days, sometimes manic, and sometimes violent. To our great relief, the diagnosis was finally possible.

Raheem officially has a condition called Rapid Recycling Bi-Polar Type 2. Despite the name, it has little to do with what is now called Bi-Polar Disorder but was previously known as manic-depressive illness. Traditional Bi-Polar takes many days for the changes to occur. Some go from normal to depressed and back. Some go from normal to manic and back. And some go from normal to manic and from normal to depressed. Always the timing covers several days.

The Rapid Recycling Bi-Polar Type 2 can happen daily or even hourly. Some psychiatrists do not feel it is a valid diagnosis, but the staff nurses and counselors who work the various mental hospitals and locked wards all are aware of it. Fortunately, it is treatable. In Raheem's case, this means that once a day he took 5 mg. of a pharmaceutical called Zyprexa. With it, he had complete control. He would be no different from anyone else. He could marry, raise a family, and hold whatever job he desired. Since he was a brilliant youth, he could become a doctor, a lawyer, an architect, or anything else. Most important, the drug simply let him have the same emotional controls that the majority of people experience. It did not dull his senses or alter his personality in any unhealthy manner, the way some medications for psychiatric disorders are prone to do.

Raheem also went into counseling. His therapist, Andrea Omerza, was a small woman with a delightful sense of humor who worked for a decade in locked juvenile wards treating boys and girls with conditions like Raheem's. She knew the extremes of the problem, frequently having had to put boys Raheem's size (just short of 6 ft. tall at age 13) and larger into restraints by herself when they acted out physically before their conditions could be treated. That fact alone caused our son to instantly respect her. More important, Andrea took great pride in helping the children who are suffering come to an understanding of what is wrong, what is not wrong, and how to handle the passage through adolescence under controllable conditions.

We have learned that Raheem's condition is genetic. His mother had it, apparently using street drugs and alcohol to self-medicate against the pressures that Raheem, too, experienced. Raheem's children will also have it, though when he is ready for marriage, he and his wife can either adopt or work with the doctors from birth so that their children get medication when appropriate and learn from their earliest years how to handle the biochemically triggered emotional problems. Without the counseling and medication, without the violent acting out being stopped quickly and safely, Raheem might have crippled or killed. The innocent victim could have been a teacher, another child, or a stranger on the street who became angry at Raheem's behavior, creating a confrontation that would end in tragedy. Or, he might have severely hurt himself, perhaps taking his own life.

For a while, things went well. What we didn't consider was that Raheem was growing. He had added several inches since he was first diagnosed. He was several pounds heavier. Adolescent hormonal rushes kicked in. And he was still taking just the 5 milligrams of Zyprexa.

There was a second forced hospitalization, though this time the violence was only in the planning stage.

"Why do you think you're here?" asked the resident physician on duty in Rainbow Babies and Children Hospital emergency room.

"I'm going to be here a couple of hours and then I'm going home," said Raheem, quite calmly. I was standing in the doorway, as he well knew. He was on an examining table. "But I'm not going to live with that bastard. I'm going to get my clothes and go live with a friend."

"And then what are you going to do?"

"I'm going to come back and kill him."

"Do you have a plan?" the doctor asked. Neither the expression on her face nor the tone of her voice indicated that anything being discussed was abnormal.

"Oh, yes, I have a plan. But I'm not going to tell you because you'll tell him and he'll tell the police…" There was a pause, then a frustrated sigh and a slightly sad, "And they'll make me stop."

The doctor smiled, walked out of the room with me, and said, "Laurelwood." Raheem was transferred to a psychiatric facility for adolescents where he had medication changes and intense counseling. The Zyprexa went to 20 mg. per day and a drug named Concerta was added to help him think more clearly. When he was released from the locked facility a week later, I had my son back. He chatted happily, went to McDonald's, was anxious to get back to school, wanted to draw and write and read, and was delighted to be home with me.

There has been a third forced hospitalization—a brief one—after an unusual outburst of violence and an effort to leave the car in the midst of rush hour traffic, because "I hate you. I've always hated you and Leslie and the twins. You just won't listen to me."

So now he takes Concerta in the morning, along with 5 mg. of Zyprexa and 300 mg. of lithium. The same doses of lithium and Zyprexa are repeated mid-afternoon, and there is a last 20 mg. of Zyprexa in the evening. At the same time, we are working to get Raheem into a special school connected with our local system. The school has staff who work with bright kids who have genetic problems controlled by medication. They are used to bipolar children like Raheem and can deal with their combination of extreme immaturity, unusually mature insights, and difficulty working with others.

Raheem walked away from therapy sessions with Andrea, much to our sadness. He is now in a community program that works to combine all facets of treatment, aiding the parents as well as the child. We take each day as it comes, the underlying stress never leaving, yet always with hope.

Certainly there was a good chance that one day Raheem would have been locked away in an institution, no one caring what was wrong, just wanting to get him off the streets. And, as his psychiatrist has warned us, should he, as an adult living on his own, choose to stop his medication, such a fate may yet be his. But from the stability he has attained and the changes being tried as his body develops into full manhood, we are hopeful that he will accept the reality of his condition, continue with the medication, and enjoy life to the fullest.

For the moment, because of both the horror of what happened and the help we have received, Raheem is active in church, in sports, and in life. He has volunteered backstage work in a community theater since he is too young for paying jobs. He is handsome, gentle, and respected. The problems we face, and they are many, are now most often the problems of trying to live with a moody adolescent. They are the same ones every teenager's parents talk about. They are normal and they are transitory. Raheem's bad decisions are because of youth, naivety, and/or immaturity, and a problem when you look several years older than you are.

The genetic condition is, we hope, controllable. And while I can't make life decisions for our son when he is an adult, I can spend the roughly four years I have left before he can legally walk out of our lives helping him understand his condition and learning to control his behavior. He may still make the wrong choice, but I will not feel I failed, if he does, I will feel only intense sadness. However, if I do not devote myself to helping him understand the choices he does have, including the ones that are critical for his future, then I will have failed.

And always in the back of my mind is the knowledge that "somebody" helped and is helping my son. There was no "somebody" intervening in the life of Ken Bianchi and too many other youths.

In some ways I see Raheem as my legacy of the Hillside Strangler. He is the victim of genetics, of course, and Ken Bianchi was not. Bianchi's traumas were the results of external triggers that could have been avoided had the medical professionals not ignored him when they recognized his needs. And, while children like Raheem can act out violently, they also can be helped to overcome the circumstances that made them victims from birth. Had we not adopted Raheem, had we not expected more from him than the paperwork claimed, perhaps he would have been another lost soul, both victim and victimizer in the manner of a Hillside Strangler.

Whatever the case, the knowledge has haunted me. I hoped my readers would understand that children break. Problems early in life can have long-term impact. The lack of bonding, being in the midst of abuse and/or neglect, family difficulties where loving parents lack the knowledge to behave appropriately towards the children they are raising, and numerous other experiences, including homelessness, all cause lasting pain. Problems must be handled when observed, and they must be handled later in life as well.

Raheem, like Ken Bianchi, was adopted. Both boys had bonding problems. Both boys were seen by social workers and medical professionals very early in life. Both boys acted out inappropriately when young. Yet "somebody" reached out to Raheem— adopting parents, medical professionals, counselors, and teachers. And each time there is a "somebody" in the life of any troubled child, there is hope.

All adopted children are likely to have rejection issues. After all, their "real" parents left them—through death, illness, breaking the law, being unfit, being unable to care for them, or for myriad other reasons adults recognize as valid.

Children cannot discern the difference between situations for which they are responsible and those that are a part of life outside their control. This is no different than children of divorce who fantasize that if they act differently, they can magically restore the family in which they were first raised. The fact that the divorce has to do solely with issues between the parents is beyond their understanding. Likewise, they do not realize that life with two parents living separate lives often in no way diminishes either of their love for the child who is now shared at a distance. Divorce can improve a child's quality of life depending upon the parents' actions towards each other and within the family before the divorce occurred.

Adoption raises both similar issues and those that are more extreme. Raheem's parents are dead, their love for drugs and the lifestyle necessary to have them was greater than their love for the life they produced. He can no more undo that reality than he could stop his mother from taking drugs while he was forming in her womb. Yet he does not remember his years in foster care, other than the residual pain of rejections, the specifics of which he no longer recalls. He has to deal with this each day in his relationships with friends, teachers, and eventually in the workplace and eventually with the woman with whom he wishes to make a lifelong commitment.

But Raheem has experienced both consistent parenting since his adoption and psychological counseling. He is learning that it is all right to work with another person in order to get through difficult times. He is learning that there is no shame in reaching out for help from others. And, he is learning that the inner demons that can cause all of us so much pain can be overcome, that life ultimately holds love and joy, peace and happiness in far greater quantity than anger and pain.

Ken Bianchi, the Hillside Strangler, taught me that "somebody" must reach out to hurting children, and my personal faith tells me that God hit me over the head a few times until I realized that I was "somebody."

Raheem taught me that I was wrong in thinking I could not love a child. He showed me that I cannot help but love, regardless of circumstances, regardless of anyone else's feelings. And he showed me not only the violence that lurks beneath the surface of even the most beloved of troubled youth, but also the ease with which healing is possible, the ability to enlist others to assist in helping a child into productive adulthood. There are frustrations, moments of anger, and times of self-doubt, yet together within the community of "somebodies," the horror stories that have occurred for others can be avoided in the future. Even in the circumstances in which Raheem finds himself, having to deal with a genetic condition, he has learned it is as controllable as a thyroid problem or mild diabetes, neither of which prevents people from achieving long life, great happiness, and success in any chosen profession.

Could Ken Bianchi, a man entering his second half century of life, been helped if others had reached out to him? Probably, though no one will ever know. And even if he had been helped, he may have chosen violence as a way to deal with misunderstood anger. There are no guarantees in life other than if we adults fail to reach out, there is no hope at all.

So what is the rest of the story? For some—the parents, children, and other loved ones of the victims—it is a life of pain, of scar tissue so thin that it can be ripped from the heart by a song, a picture, or a thought about what was and what might have been.

Ken Bianchi's son is potentially among these victims. The last time I was with the child, he was only slightly older than Raheem's age when we adopted him. He sat on my lap at the kitchen table, a plate containing a few green beans and some maple syrup placed in front of him. He made a train. He played with the sticky beans. And when he got tired for a moment, he rubbed his hair with his hand, leaving the same disgusting mess all parents know when their children decide that food can also serve as a toy.

Ken's son was deeply loved by both his parents. He also looked like his father when Ken was a little boy.

Does the boy know who his father is? I have no idea. I have not seen his mother in many years, and the last person she needs in her life is someone to remind her of the months of hell when she first loved and then came to fear a man who had repeatedly raped and murdered.

Will the young man fear himself? Hopefully not. Chief Mangan, who went on to head the Spokane, Washington, police department before retiring, offered to provide any help desired, and I know that promise was heartfelt, real, and open-ended. Did the boy need it? Did his mother seek it? Or is he unaware of the nightmare in his family?

Perhaps it does not matter so long as no one is so foolish as to think that the son will be like the father. Their backgrounds are totally different. The stresses each faced in life were not the same. Yet just the loss of his biological father, a man who truly loved him, has made him another victim of the Hillside Strangler.

The women who have sought a relationship with Ken, as well as other serial rapists and serial killers, are not going to be helped to find self-esteem unless they reach out for it. They are adults, acting in a way that leads to ridicule by others. Their situation is sad, yet they have choices. They are in the free world. They are capable of seeking help. They may have endured tragedies and/ or abuse over the years, but they are usually no longer in the circumstances that led to their own personal traumas.

Angelo Buono, Bianchi's cousin who helped with approximately a dozen murders, was first sent to Folsom Prison and later to the California State Penitentiary. He was a coward his entire adult life, never facing a threat from which he did not back away. Sometimes the threat came from employers who caught him stealing tools before Buono opened his own business. Sometimes it seemed to come from the truth.

I was called as a defense witness in Angelo Buono's trial many months after it first started. I had to tell what I knew and what Bianchi had discussed with me. I never did understand why I was a defense witness, because my testimony reinforced the idea that Buono was guilty.

I was scared when I went into the courtroom. The trial was one being covered throughout the world. There was no death penalty in California at the time because the U.S. Supreme Court had ruled unconstitutional the California law for executing prisoners, and new regulations were being written. However, I knew that Buono was facing life behind bars, and I was one of those who might help place him there. It was the right thing to do and it was a burden of conscience.

I assumed that Angelo would hate me or look to me with what little hope of a free future he might think he still had. I expected something. Instead, the entire six hours I was on the witness stand, Angelo Buono sat slumped in his seat, looking at the floor. He showed no emotion at all.

I was also surprised by my reaction to Angelo. He was a thin little man with Mediterranean features. I don't mean that he was short. I never saw him stand. He was simply small, like the Wizard of Oz was revealed to be when Dorothy and her friends pulled back the curtain and discovered that the public image was created with smoke, mirrors, and mechanical effects. Angelo looked to me like a bug on the sidewalk, oblivious to the fact that he could be squished under a shoe at any moment. It was doubtful he would have had the courage to kidnap, rape, and murder a woman without the impetus of his cousin, though it seemed obvious that once he had a partner to render false courage, he would delight in the fear of his victims.

Once convicted, Angelo stayed in his cell in the early months of captivity. He was afraid of being hurt by others for his crimes. He was the type of man other prisoners hold in disdain, though, if there were overt threats, they were not discussed with the media.

Buono met the wife of a fellow prisoner when the man was serving five months for assault with a deadly weapon in early 1983. That couple was divorced in May 1983. Then, the inmate's ex-wife, Christine Kizuka, a supervisor at the Los Angeles office of the state Employment Development Department, gradually developed a friendship with Buono. She had three children at the time.

Christine and Angelo apparently fell in love and were married in 1986. It was a safe relationship for her and did not change Buono's self-isolation, including after he was moved to the Calipatria State Prison. He had jobs at the prison, but a single cell for his protection, again because of the nature of his crimes. Then, on September 21, 2002, Buono was found dead in his cell. He died of natural causes, probably related to a long time heart condition. He was 67 years old.

There is little publicity about the cases anymore, though the investigation and ultimate understanding of the Hillside Strangler murders is still studied by students of law enforcement, criminal justice, and abnormal psychology. It is a classic story, filled with emotional illness, issues of the system for caring for unwanted children, and police efforts flawless in their execution against overwhelming odds.

When the murders and subsequent arrests occurred, the story was like a boulder that had been tossed into the center of a pond. The parting water exploded like the ocean's surf roiled by a sudden summer storm. Today the ripples continue their journey, smaller, slower, less noticeable unless you look beneath the surface. But lives continue to be influenced one generation later, and perhaps that influence will continue with generations as yet unborn. I suppose it is the nature of the beast, the legacy of the violence, the aftermath of understanding. And however life becomes when the ripples disappear and the water is again as smooth as glass will ultimately be the conclusion of the rest of the story.